Performance and Politics in Tanzania

African Expressive Cultures

Patrick McNaughton, editor

Associate editors

Catherine M. Cole

Barbara G. Hoffman

Eileen Julien

Kassim Koné

D. A. Masolo

Elisha Renne

Zoë Strother

Performance and Politics in Tanzania

THE NATION ON STAGE

Laura Edmondson

INDIANA UNIVERSITY PRESS
Bloomington and Indianapolis

This book is a publication of

Indiana University Press
601 North Morton Street
Bloomington, IN 47404-3797 USA

http://iupress.indiana.edu

Telephone orders   800-842-6796
Fax orders   812-855-7931
Orders by e-mail   iuporder@indiana.edu

Portions of chapter 3 appeared as "National Erotica: The Politics of
'Traditional' Dance in Tanzania," in _TDR_ 45 (1) (May 2001): 153–170.

Portions of chapter 4 appeared as "Tanzanian Drama and the Mapping of
Home" in _Theatre Research International_ 27 (2) (July 2002): 164–177.

The paper used in this publication meets the minimum requirements of
American National Standard for Information Sciences—Permanence of
Paper for Printed Library Materials, ANSI Z39.48-1984.

Manufactured in the United States of America

Library of Congress Cataloging-in-Publication Data

Edmondson, Laura, date
   Performance and politics in Tanzania : the nation on stage / Laura
Edmondson.
      p. cm. — (African expressive cultures)
   Includes bibliographical references and index.
   ISBN 978-0-253-34905-7 (cloth : alk. paper)—ISBN 978-0-253-21912-1
(pbk. : alk. paper)   1. Performing arts—Tanzania—Political aspects.
2. Performing arts—Tanzania—Social aspects.   I. Title.
   PN2995.4.E36 2007
      792.09678—dc22   2006037727

1 2 3 4 5 12 11 10 09 08 07

To Robert

Erokamano, jaerana

Contents

ACKNOWLEDGMENTS

Students of the Swahili language quickly learn two of the most famous proverbs—
"little by little fills the measure" (*haba na haba hujaza kibaba*) and "haste, haste
has no blessing" (*haraka, haraka haina baraka*). Given the length of time it has
taken for the publication of this book, I have apparently taken these proverbs to
heart. The blessings, though, have been abundant, as I have encountered so many
remarkable people along the way.

This book is filled with the names of performing artists in Dar es Salaam,
particularly the members of Mandela Cultural Troupe, Muungano Cultural
Troupe, and Tanzania One Theatre. A heartfelt *shukrani* to these artists, who
redefined my concept of generosity with their readiness to respond to my
countless questions with thoughtfulness and care. I hope this book does at least
some justice to the vigor and dynamism of their performances. Norbert Chenga,
Captain John Komba, and Bakari Mbelemba (Mzee Jangala) deserve special
mention for their hospitality and graciousness. I also wish to thank the students
and faculty at the Bagamoyo College of Arts, particularly those students in my
acting and playwriting classes who gave me a unique and valuable perspective
on the processes of theatre-making in Tanzania. Thanks to Rashid Masimbi for
granting me permission to examine restricted files in the National Archives, and
thanks to Joel Mkude at the Dar es Salaam cultural office for helping me to track
down information on various theatre companies. I will always be grateful to
Louis A. Mbughuni, who introduced me to Tanzanian performance during my
first experience of fieldwork in 1993, and to Augustin Hatar at the University of
Dar es Salaam, who invited me to present some of my research to his theatre
students. Thanks to Amandina Lihamba for giving me access to the university
students' undergraduate theses on theatre and performance, and to Penina
Mlama for allowing me to audit her Traditional African Theatre class.

During my fieldwork in Tanzania, I benefited greatly from the companionship of Tim Kelsall, Claire Mercer, and Kathleen Mulligan-Hansel. Their
smart and committed work on the political culture of Tanzania has shaped and
honed my thinking on citizenship and democracy. An additional thanks to Tim
for his careful and informed reading of an earlier draft of my introduction—
although, of course, all shortcomings are my own. My field research and writing
were supported by fellowships and grants from the University of Texas at
Austin, Florida State University, the National Endowment of the Humanities,
and the American Association of University Women. My gratitude to each.

This project was originally conceived during my graduate studies at the
University of Texas at Austin. Thanks to Oscar Brockett for telling me to do what I
love, to Charlotte Canning for making me laugh even as she prodded me into
becoming a better writer, and to Omi Osun Olomo/Joni L. Jones for showing me
how to integrate academia and passion. Thanks to Tom Postlewait for setting me

on the path of theatre studies in the first place, and to John Lamphear whose enthusiasm for East Africa steered this path to Tanzania.

During my years at Florida State University, I had the pleasure of associating with colleagues whom I can only describe as stellar—Stuart Baker, Mary Karen Dahl, John Degen, Anita Gonzalez, Jean Graham Jones, Carrie Sandahl, and Alan Sikes. Their dedication to their work and intellectual energy have sustained me in countless ways. Mary Karen has been an extraordinary mentor; I owe her a debt that I could not possibly repay. Jean took considerable time and energy to respond to an earlier draft of my introduction, and her commitment to a truly global understanding of theatre and performance continues to inspire me. I single out Carrie for being that rare combination of a terrific colleague and a dear friend; she was a lifeline to me and my family throughout the process. To the late John Degen: I hope that I have been half as good a writer as he. My gratitude to Shannon Walsh and Jane Duncan for dedicated research assistance. As I made the transition to my new institutional home at Dartmouth College, I am grateful to Peter Hackett for arranging my teaching schedule to facilitate the final preparation of the manuscript and to Effie Cummings, Maggie Devine-Sullivan, and Brenda C. Haynes for making this transition so painless and even enjoyable.

At Indiana University Press, I gratefully acknowledge the efforts of Dee Mortensen, whose faith in this project was crucial to its survival, and to Miki Bird for guiding it through the final stages of publication. I also wish to thank the reviewers of previous versions of the manuscript for pushing me to reconceptualize and reinvigorate the project, and Jane Curran for her skilled copyediting.

I owe my most profound debt to my family, whose emotional support has been unsurpassed. Thanks to my brother and sister-in-law, John Ben and Melissa Edmondson, for generously allowing me the use of their camera for all those months of fieldwork. Thanks to my parents, Ben and Barbara Edmondson, for giving me the freedom to imagine new worlds. Thanks to my brothers and sisters-in-law in Dar es Salaam (Johnson, Samwel, Sunday, Jane, Anna, and Evans Ajwang') for their companionship at performances, babysitting, and *pilau.* To Robert Ajwang', my husband and research associate, to whom this book is dedicated: the combined languages of Luo, Swahili, and Kuria are not enough to express my gratitude for your careful reading of every chapter, assistance with translations, steadfastness, and love. And to our sweet daughters, Johari and Amina, who made their appearances as this book was slowly coming together: you are the greatest blessing of all.

Performance and Politics in Tanzania

INTRODUCTION

Acts of Complicity

Meanings, Methods, and Maps

In Dar es Salaam on June 21, 1997, a visiting Ugandan government official watched as Tanzania One Theatre performed *lizombe,* one of the most famous traditional dances (*ngoma*) in the country.[1] In honor of the occasion, a special "high table" had been set up for the foreign guest and accompanying Tanzanian officials in the ramshackle space of Vijana Social Hall, located in Kinondoni neighborhood. In the final moments of the dance, two pairs of male and female performers, all of whom wore T-shirts bearing the face of Tanzanian president Benjamin Mkapa, simulated sexual intercourse through explicit pelvic rotations. The few hundred spectators greeted this erotic display with their usual cheers of delight, paying scant attention to the state officials within their midst.

About a month later, also in Dar es Salaam, Muungano Cultural Troupe produced a skit (*kichekesho;* pl. *vichekesho*) for an audience of police officers and their families at the Changombe police station compound.[2] In the opening scene, three thieves with heavily padded stomachs and tattered clothing broke into a home while the family was attending a wedding. As one thief passed the goods to his partners-in-crime through a window, two dignified, well-dressed police officers caught them in the act and prepared to take them to jail. As the officers congratulated each other on their skill, the thieves erupted into an argument that rapidly turned into a fistfight. The dignity of the police officers disintegrated as they became caught up in the slapstick-style brawl and started to hit the thieves' padded stomachs with sticks. As the frustrated officers began to punch each other instead of the thieves, their quarry cheerfully escaped to the sounds of appreciative audience laughter.

Two days later at T. Garden Bar in the nearby neighborhood of Buguruni, Mandela Cultural Troupe collaborated with the famous singer Remmy Ongala and his band Orchestra Super Matimila to stage a "Who Is Uglier?" contest. The evening began with Mandela's performance, which consisted of a mixture of *ngoma,* a *kichekesho* about a father who steals his daughter's underwear, acrobatics, and a full-length play (*igizo;* plural *maigizo*) about a young man suffering from AIDS. After this succession of seemingly unrelated acts, the audience swarmed onto the stage to dance with enthusiasm to the music of "Dr. Remmy" and his band. The evening concluded with the actual contest, in which several male contestants—including Ongala himself and Mandela's star actor and founder, Bakari Mbelemba—competed for the prize of a television set. At the audience's insistence, the prize was bestowed upon a local Buguruni resident against the judges' preferred choice.

Such moments skim the surface of the many delights that Tanzanian popular performance held in store in the mid-1990s.[3] Mandela, Muungano, and Tanzania One Theatre (TOT) performed in bars and social halls throughout Dar es Salaam, Tanzania's largest and arguably its most vibrant city, drawing enthusiastic audiences primarily from its masses of working poor.[4] These performances encompassed a dizzying mixture of acrobatics, *ngoma,* skits, full-length plays, the genre of Congolese dance music known as *soukous,* and *taarab,* an extremely popular form of coastal Swahili music in which indigenous, Arabic, and Indian influences coalesce. Muungano's *kichekesho* about the police officers and TOT's *ngoma* were not performed in isolation; instead, they made up just one small segment of the entire performance, which often lasted for several hours. In addition to erotic dances, slapstick comedies, and moralistic plays, one might also see pythons slithering on the stage, a contortionist smoking a cigarette with his feet, and Muslim women in sequined gowns belting out *taarab* songs of love and betrayal. This theatrical smorgasbord epitomized the creativity and innovation that serve as hallmarks of African popular culture, which freely appropriates and transforms indigenous and foreign performance traditions to produce multifaceted commentaries on contemporary mores, politics, and daily life.

Audience reactions intensified this sense of excitement. Enthusiastic spectators called out advice to the characters in the full-length plays or joined in the *ngoma* as an expression of ethnic identity. Through the process of *kutunza*—tipping performers with coins and small bills as they act, dance, or sing—spectators frequently intervened in the course of the performance. Although *kutunza* was often meant to express appreciation of the performer's skill, it could also declare a sense of solidarity with the character's plight or with the message of the song. Alternatively, the spectators openly confronted the characters, as in Mandela's AIDS play performed during the "ugliness" contest. The final scene took place at the young man's funeral, in which a coffin was prominently displayed. Several male youths in the audience responded angrily when Mbelemba, who played the father of the AIDS victim, asked the audience, "Tomorrow, who will be in the coffin?" (*Kesho nani atakuwemo ndani ya jeneza?*). These spectators challenged Mbelemba's blatant implication that they would meet a similar fate. This kind of passionate response helped to create a forum in which the voices of the *walalahoi,* the underclass, were resoundingly heard.

This description is undoubtedly familiar to scholars of African popular theatre, which is frequently championed as a site of transformation, creativity, and resistance. In *Power and Performance: Ethnographic Explorations through Proverbial Wisdom and Theater in Shaba, Zaire,* Johannes Fabian summarizes this scholarly tradition when he states that "the kind of performances we find in [African] popular culture have become for the people involved more than ever ways to preserve some self-respect in the face of constant humiliation, and to set the wealth of artistic creativity against an environment of utter poverty" (1990, 19). Sarah von Fremd more explicitly theorizes Ugandan popular theatre as a tool of resistance, belonging to "the savvy maneuvers, tricks, and diversions of urban inhabitants who consume and invade political power in unexpected ways" (1995, vii–viii). As scholars increasingly turn their attention to examples of popular culture throughout sub-Saharan Africa, a wealth of strategies is revealed in which local consumers and artists counteract official dictates through the medium of popular theatre, visual arts, fiction, and music.[5]

The snapshots of Tanzanian performance that I have provided would easily fall into these scholarly categories of resistance and resilience. The Ugandan guest who attended TOT's performance was indeed treated to a showcase of Tanzanian "traditional" culture but with an erotic twist that elides conventional ideas of official, state-sponsored theatre. The dignified police officers in Muungano's *kichekesho* devolved into slapstick-style comic figures as if to mock the apparatuses of the state. In addition to protesting the message of the play, Mandela's audiences also successfully intervened in the selection of the winner of the contest. These moments not only serve as testaments to the strength and creativity of urban poor Africans but also bear witness to the transformative potential of popular performance.

But if these moments are placed in more detailed context, the picture of resistance becomes considerably more multidimensional, even paradoxical. TOT is sponsored by the ruling political party CCM (Chama Cha Mapinduzi, the Party of Revolution), which founded the company in the early 1990s as the country began to prepare for the first multiparty elections in 1995. Through subtle and not-so-subtle references to CCM as "number one" throughout the performance, TOT worked to legitimize the party's political dominance. At the same time, TOT became notorious for its liberal sprinkling of titillating sexual references throughout the songs, dances, and plays; indeed, the *ngoma* performance described above, in which the dancers simulate sexual intercourse, was relatively tame when compared to the lyrics of TOT's more notorious *taarab* songs. Although TOT readily pushed the boundaries of stage decorum, its seeming transgression was actually complicit with CCM's bid for power among urbanites who were titillated by and attracted to the bawdy entertainment.

Although TOT served as perhaps the most vivid example of the links between political power and popular culture, Muungano also actively participated in affirming the power of the state. As if to counteract the satirical representations of police often found in *vichekesho*, Muungano's *maigizo*, or full-length plays, consistently depicted them as efficient and helpful. Indeed, the police characters in *maigizo* often provided a sense of closure reminiscent of deus ex machina through their interventions in heated domestic disputes or criminal activity. In one such play, for example, the police arrested a young man for seducing and impregnating his girlfriend as an example of their dedication to morality and order.[6] Given that mob justice, in which crowds pursue and attack suspected thieves, was the prevailing "order" in Dar es Salaam in the 1990s, this positive portrayal of the police conveyed a flattering attitude toward the state.

On its part, Mandela performed a version of patriotism through an emphasis on educational theatre. As an additional source of income, Mandela often participated in theatre-for-development projects. The AIDS play performed during the "ugliness" contest, for example, was originally commissioned by the National AIDS Control Programme, which included drama in its educational awareness campaign. Mandela frequently reproduced these developmental plays for their commercial performances in social halls and bars. This process of recycling created a bridge between popular theatre and theatre for development as if to answer the nationalist call of Tanzanian theatre intellectuals for socially relevant drama that exceeded the boundaries of "mere" entertainment.[7] The rhetoric of social relevance was not confined to plays, as indicated in the emcee's opening remarks in which he stressed that the "ugliness" contest was meant as a reminder that people should not be judged on their appearance, color, or gender.[8] This apparently incongruous statement recalled a cultural nationalist ideal that Tanzanian artists should educate as well as entertain the masses.

Mandela was not alone in these iterations of patriotism, as all three companies regularly punctuated their performances with praises of Tanzanian traditional culture, or *utamaduni,* in a rhetorical gesture that could be perceived as colluding with the cultural nationalist agenda to preserve these traditions. TOT, for example, usually opened its performances with a "modern" dance song (*muziki wa dansi*) called "Utamaduni," in which the male performers donned grass skirts over their slacks and sang lyrics such as, "Today we are all family / We are praising our culture" (*Leo sisi jamaa / Tukiusifu utamaduni wetu*). Muungano's version of *lizombe,* which was equally as erotic as TOT's version previously mentioned, included a Swahili chorus in the midst of the Ngoni lyrics: "Culture is a tool of our inheritance / even our grandfathers danced ngoma" (*Utamaduni ni chombo cha urithi wetu / hata mababu zetu walicheza ngoma*). In the midst of melodramatic plays and energetic musical acts, the performances of TOT, Muungano, and Mandela marked out a painstakingly cultivated nationalist stance.

The straddling of nationalism and popular culture itself is nothing new, as popular artists throughout sub-Saharan Africa convey an investment in national unification as an alternative to ethnic conflict. Fabian, for example, describes the way that the Zairean popular visual artist Tshibumba Kanda Matulu upholds the idea of a unified nation even though he articulates an opposition to the oppressive state (1996, 271–273).[9] Generally, however, these manifestations can be loosely categorized under the rubric of grassroots nationalism, which challenges the dominance of top-down models of nationalism through emphasizing "the continuing appeal (and ceaseless reformulation) of nationalism in public discourse, and its shaping by the actual people whose values it claims to invoke" (Herzfeld 1997, 10). Although intersections of popular culture and nationalist rhetoric provide rich terrain for the exploration of popular, "bottoms-up" nationalism in which official discourse is reshaped for alternative ends, these theoretical frameworks do not adequately explain the unique articulations of nationhood in Tanzanian popular theatre, which not only betrays an investment in national unity as an abstract ideal but also works to sustain the state and its structures of power.

An alternative approach would be to disentangle grassroots expressions of nationalism from capitulations to state power. In other words, dignified police officers and praises of Tanzanian culture could be interpreted as a kind of sugar-coating that made the performances palatable to the powers-that-be. But to adopt this line of reasoning would affirm an oppositional model of state versus society that obscures the networks of intimacy that the Tanzanian state cultivated in the postcolonial era.[10] After becoming independent from British rule in 1961, the Tanzanian government adopted a range of strategies in order to build a cohesive nation out of approximately 130 ethnic groups and affirm its legitimacy as a fledgling state. It enacted legislation to ensure that groups that usually belong to civil society, such as women's organizations and trade unions, were co-opted and transformed into organs of the ruling party (Kelsall 2002, 608)—a process that intensified in 1964 when opposition parties were formally banned. Long-established villages were uprooted and reorganized into co-operative societies, and households were reorganized into ten-house units headed by a party representative in the state's bid to infiltrate local communities. Through a range of state mandates under the leadership of President Julius K. Nyerere, party, state, and nation became inextricably linked during the first two decades of independence.

Although Tanzanian subjects responded to these coercive strategies with a variety of micro-level resistant acts (Hyden 1980; Tripp 1997), the pervasiveness of state-society links in postcolonial Tanzania also cultivated a widespread investment in the nation-state. The theatre companies serve as a touchstone for this historical legacy of complicity and interdependency. In the early years of independence, the government followed a fairly conventional path of national culture with the establishment of three state-sponsored performance companies: the National Dance, Drama, and Acrobatics Troupes. In 1967, however, a unique turn of events occurred when the Arusha Declaration, which marked the formal beginning of Tanzania's socialist era, ushered in a particularly radical era of cultural nationalism. In an attempt to mimic the rhetoric of the People's Republic of China (Askew 2002, 158), the state declared a "cultural revolution" in which European and so-called capitalist forms of artistic expression would be discarded in favor of indigenous forms with appropriately socialist content. Even when the three national troupes were disbanded in 1981, a burgeoning commercial theatre movement carried on the mission of nation-building as the companies continued to pay faithful tribute to the ideals of traditionalism and socialism. In the absence of official, state-sponsored performance troupes, commercial theatre companies served as what could be termed "surrogates" (Roach 1996) of national culture, ready to perform at state-sponsored functions and for official guests. Although TOT would seem to be the most obvious candidate for surrogation given its affiliation with the ruling political party, Muungano and, to a lesser extent, Mandela also played this role. It is noteworthy, for example, that the Ugandan government advisor visiting Dar es Salaam was escorted not only to TOT's performance but also to Muungano's show the following evening. Both companies served as a surrogate of national culture, with all of the connotations of back-scratching and reciprocity that the honor entailed. Attempts to distinguish between official and popular culture repeatedly break down in the face of these multidimensional and even contradictory events.

It also becomes virtually impossible to distinguish between moments of transgression and capitulation. For example, it is significant that I never found instances of performances that openly criticized the state or the ruling political party. This absence perhaps served as an indication of an intimidated or passive cohort of performing artists, fearful of retribution from above. Although I do not discount the presence of anxiety in these articulations of cultural nationalism, an understanding of the complicit relations between the state and the theatre companies suggests that this lack of criticism was at least partly linked to an underlying investment in the status quo.[11] The ruling political party of CCM, which is still intertwined with the state despite legislation to disentangle the two entities, continues to be conceived in the national imagination as a rock of stability that will safeguard the country from the internecine fates of Rwanda or Burundi.[12] Instead of depicting the state as the enemy to be breached and challenged, theatre performers and audiences confirm their loyalty as if in defiance of international dictates that situate "free" markets and liberalization as the panacea for Africa's political ills.[13] Although the coercive strategies of the Tanzanian state must be recognized and fully explored, a nuanced analysis of the intimate relations between state and subjects is crucial to an understanding of Tanzanian postcolonial subjectivity.

The uniqueness of Tanzanian popular theatre calls for theoretical approaches that push beyond oppositional models of resistance or capitulation.[14] What I saw in Tanzanian theatre was far more intimate and *convivial,* to borrow Achille Mbembe's term to describe the postcolonial relations of rulers and ruled. In *On the Postcolony,* Mbembe argues that frameworks of resistance should be replaced with an understanding of "the dynamics of domesticity and familiarity," in which both dominant and dominated vie for power within the same cultural space (2001, 110). This intimacy entails a dialectical relationship in which the people and the state bargain with one another for access to power. For example, in a passage that particularly resonates with my understanding of Tanzanian theatre, Mbembe dismantles the conventional demarcation between unofficial and official cultures in African contexts. While "the popular world borrows the whole ideological repertoire of officialdom," the official world returns the compliment through the mimicry of "popular vulgarity" (2001, 110). Although the forces of creativity in the popular arts are more commonly understood in the context of evading state oppression, as in the studies of Zairean and Ugandan performance previously cited, Mbembe clears the way for an understanding of how this process of borrowing and mimicking unleashes the forces of innovation and creativity on both sides of the postcolonial equation.[15] Instead of adhering to tired notions of the state "versus" the companies, or the state "versus" the audiences, Mbembe's theories serve as a model that can be applied to Tanzanian performance in which audiences, theatre companies, and the state are understood as *players* instead of oppositional forces.

Mbembe uses conviviality in association with connivance to call attention to the multiplicity of survival strategies that the populace cultivates in order to counteract or elide the dominance of the African state. The despotism of nations such as Cameroon, which serves as the backdrop for the majority of Mbembe's ideas, creates a space in which "ordinary people guide, deceive, and toy with power rather than confronting it directly" (2001, 128). In contrast to his emphasis upon working within systems of oppression, this book assumes a more optimistic tone, using the term *conviviality* to underline a sense of collaboration. Here I follow the lead of Francis B. Nyamnjoh, who uses the notion of conviviality, with its connotations of "the spirit of togetherness, interpenetration, interdependence, and intersubjectivity," to suggest a model of African agency. In place of the Western model, which stresses the empowerment of individuals who pursue their self-interests despite modes of political or cultural oppression (2002, 111–112), he puts forward the concept of *domesticated* agency, a collectivization that "emphasizes negotiation, concession and conviviality over maximization of pursuits by individuals or particular groups in contexts of plurality and diversity" (116). Nyamnjoh's work clears space for a multifaceted concept of agency that need not be defined solely in terms of resistance but also recognizes the possibility of working with the state rather than against it.[16] My observations and experiences of popular performance in the mid-1990s as well as my research into the history of popular performance in the postcolonial era indicate that state-society relations were characterized by a sense of energetic exchange in which the positive, even hopeful, connotations of "convivial" as used by Nyamnjoh do not seem amiss.

These approaches help to exceed oppositions between official culture and popular counter-culture and recognize a postcolonial context in which state and society work together on the nationalist stage in a fluid, dynamic, and interactive process. As I mapped out the contours of this vigorous practice in Tanzanian performance, I found that a single framework could not adequately capture its complexities and nuances. Instead, I employ a variety of terms throughout this book such as *collaborative nationalism, alternative nationalism, strategic nationalism,* and *cosmopolitan nationalism* in order to unpack the overlapping voices and crisscrossing agendas that characterized these cultural expressions. A "poetics of nationhood" provides an umbrella phrase for this multiplicity of practices, strategies, and processes that were marshaled in the composition of the nation on the popular stage. TOT, Muungano, and Mandela far exceeded the idea of "performing the nation" in the sense suggested by Kelly Askew (2002).[17] Rather, they were performing, transforming, and reforming the nation in a continuous cycle of collaboration, complicity, and conviviality.

Contestation also played a critical role in the historical moment of the mid-1990s, a time when debates over national identity had assumed fresh urgency. In 1996 and 1997, when I conducted sixteen months of fieldwork, Dar es Salaam was experiencing a transformative shift in which concepts of national identity were particularly fluid and ambiguous. As a result of a sustained economic crisis, Tanzania acceded to the demands of structural adjustment in the mid-1980s, which paved the way for the privatization of state-run enterprises and a market-run economy. Political liberalization and "democratization" followed in the 1990s, further diminishing the authority of the single-party state. Although CCM strategically managed to maintain power following landslide victories in the 1995, 2000, and 2005 presidential elections, these changes have radically altered the national landscape.[18] Despite the International Monetary Fund's and World Bank's imposed definition of democratization as a multiparty system of governance, marginalized groups readily appropriated the term for their own purposes: political parties, women's organizations, and privately run newspapers have used the rhetoric of democratization to agitate for social change. In the wake of this massive transition, Tanzania was transformed into what Max Mmuya calls an "expanded social and political space" in which "previously unheard voices and newly emerging forces" appeared (1998, 10–11). Although the concept of transition threatens to be overused since all formations of national identity are constantly destabilized in response to external and internal pressures, the era of the mid-1990s was a particularly rich moment for the production of new kinds of subjectivities and agendas.

In my exploration of popular performance in this atmosphere of upheaval and change, I found considerable evidence of its potential as a mode of civil society and grassroots democracy. TOT, Muungano, and Mandela could be understood as microcosms of the nation in which new configurations of gender, ethnic, and religious identity were tested and explored before a highly participatory audience. Conventional notions of morality and tradition yielded to daring narratives in which the social order was threatened and even overturned, as in the example of Muungano's *kichekesho* previously mentioned. The traditional moralizing tone of these dramatic forms in which thieves, con men, and adulterous wives received their "just" deserts yielded to narratives in which the villains could escape and even triumph in the end. Definitions of womanhood seemed particularly prone to redefinition as urban female characters, typically demonized as lustful or immoral, began to reclaim the stage with greater layers of complexity that exceeded tired stereotypes. Confronted with these instances of creativity and innovation, I was frequently inclined to interpret these performances as examples of the freewheeling exuberance of popular culture that escaped the legacy of nationalism or complicity with the state.

The trick is to excavate these moments of transformation without spinning off into romanticized ideas of autonomy or transgression. To do so would perpetuate what threatens to become a reductive meaning of resistance in cultural studies and postcolonial theory, "which seems to mushroom too easily everywhere" (Loomba 1998, 244). My point is not to deny the existence of resistant acts; indeed, this perspective is particularly understandable in countries where the state serves as a blatantly oppressive presence against which its disenfranchised subjects define themselves. To interpret Tanzanian performance in this vein, however, would obscure the ways in which these cultural expressions are fully enmeshed in social and political networks of interdependencies.

It should be noted that African and Africanist scholars have already called considerable attention to the failings of resistance as a theoretical framework in African contexts. In *Postcolonial Identities in Africa,* Richard Werbner draws upon Mbembe's work to understand the cultural politics of African postcolonial identity as a process of toying with power, thus exceeding what he calls the customary "overemphasis" on resistance (1996, 2–4). In the same volume, Filip De Boeck urges scholars to analyze cultural practices and forms not only through the framework of hegemony and resistance "but also of adaptation, accommodation and collaboration" (1996, 94). This understanding has produced a wave of scholarship that recognizes the futility of opposing moments of collusion to moments of resistance.[19] Interestingly, though, these clarion calls "to pursue... genealogies and histories that take us beyond the simple binary of resistance and capitulation, into a world of proliferating and multivectored agency" (Piot 1999, 178), are seldom answered in studies of African popular culture and arts. These cultural expressions are consistently defined as modes of autonomy, seemingly free of the anxieties and interdependencies that typically characterize postcolonial existence. Werbner refers to the "fun spaces" or "flights of imagination" in cultural forms such as African rap music, where "people indulge in the pleasures of playful self-fashioning" (2002, 3).[20] In an otherwise nuanced discussion of African civil society, Célestin Monga writes categorically that "artists from all fields may be said to fall into two basic groups; those who have the support of the government and those who do not" (1996, 95). On the one side are those who defend the established order; on the other are those artists, "championing a popular culture attuned to the times," whose themes "are the striving for a better world, criticism of the prevailing sociopolitical order, and resistance to any kind of totalitarianism" (96). Such sharp divisions ensure that popular culture continues to be theorized as immune to the dramaturgies of power that permeate the African postcolony.

The complexities of Tanzanian performance, which both defends the established order *and* strives for a better world, offer new ways of thinking about African popular culture. An exploration of these performances through the lens of the poetics of nationhood leads to a *creative* understanding of resistance, one that encompasses befuddled police officers, confrontational spectators, contortionists, and suggestive dance. The shifting allegiances among and between the theatre companies, their audiences, and the state culminated in an explosion of multi-narratives and unwieldy, often contradictory, versions of Tanzania. To return to Werbner, the "flights of imagination" and "fun spaces" in Tanzanian popular theatre should be recognized but not at the expense of understanding the hard work involved in the act of imagination and the seriousness of play.

My own intervention into this dynamic process produced another series of shifting allegiances as I sought to negotiate the rivalries among TOT, Muungano, and Mandela. Given that I am also a player in this construction of Tanzanian performance, I now expand these frameworks to include the research process itself.

On September 7, 1997, my research associate, Robert O. Ajwang', and I were watching a typically rowdy performance of Muungano in Friends Corner Bar in the Manzese neighborhood. As usual, I was writing a description of the performance in one of the tiny notebooks I favored; I liked to believe that they made me seem less conspicuous. Also as usual, Muungano included one of its most famous acts, the snake dance (*ngoma ya nyoka* or *buyeye*). The term "dance" is a slight misnomer, since it consisted mostly of allowing a python to slither around on the stage. In the majority of the bars and social halls where the companies performed, the performance area was on the same level as the audience, and the snake dance became the occasion for much shrieking and scattering of spectators since the python often came precariously close. In contrast, the stage at Friends Corner was about five feet high, and the snake dance was relatively restrained.

Norbert Chenga, the head of the company, apparently decided that the evening needed some livening up, and he announced to the audience that the *mtafiti*, the researcher, in the audience was going to assist Muungano with the snake dance. My reaction was the sense of acute discomfort that I experienced whenever the so-called objects of my research turned the tables and took charge—a fairly regular occurrence throughout my time in Tanzania.[21] My "assistance" consisted of standing on stage while the snake handler draped the python around my neck. On the high stage of Friends Corner Bar, I was transformed into a passive spectacle for Muungano's audience, who appreciatively cheered. As was so often the case in these performances, however, the seeming innocence of this moment represented another episode in the power play of complicity.

Scholars of African popular theatre commonly employ methodologies of ethnographic research, which has traditionally emphasized a sustained period of fieldwork focusing on a specific village, a bounded community, or, in this case, a theatre company. Karin Barber, for example, worked with the Oyin Adéjobi Theatre Company for several years, excavating a wealth of insights into the creation of dramatic works in the Yorùbá popular theatre (2000); similarly, Muungano served as a focal point for the research of Siri Lange (1995) and Mark Plane (1995) in their works on Tanzanian popular theatre. This approach emphasizes historicity, individual agency, and specificity, which, as Margaret Drewal argues (1991), helps to overcome the Western tendency to homogenize African ritual and performance. Immersion in the quotidian operations of the politics and aesthetics of a particular company serves as the gateway to an in-depth understanding.

Although I also immersed myself in the dynamics of Tanzanian popular performance, my own method was more diffuse. Instead of concentrating on a single troupe, I divided my time among the three major companies of Dar es

Salaam.[22] In addition to the several months I spent in Dar es Salaam, I also lived for four months in Bagamoyo at the College of Arts, a national performing arts school that offers courses in *ngoma,* music, drama, and the visual arts. I also traveled in the northeastern area of the country for a few weeks accompanying TOT and Muungano on tour. It might be argued that my understanding would have been enhanced had I narrowed the scope of my fieldwork. If I had focused on Muungano, for example, I might have developed a greater understanding of the rehearsal process, the members as individuals, and the dynamics of the group, all of which would have fleshed out my ideas. Moreover, I would have felt free to take advantage of "co-performance," in which the ethnographer dances, sings, or acts with the locals in order to ferret out embodied knowledge about the performance tradition and foster cultural rapport (Conquergood 1991, 187; see also Turner 1975, 28–29). Studies of African performance repeatedly depict the act of co-performance as the hallmark of a successful ethnographic enterprise (Askew 2002; Barber et al. 1997; Barz 2003, 24–25; Cole 2001, 10; von Fremd 1995, xvii; Plane 1995, 9). In my case, the constant moving between and among the three troupes, which included visiting individual performers and attending rehearsals and performances, precluded this particular ideal.

My choice to broaden the scope of my research reflects recent changes in ethnographic theory. Although the methodologies of single-sited ethnography and co-performance encourage a wealth of insights, they uphold a concept of self-contained culture that has become increasingly challenged in the last decade. As George E. Marcus persuasively argues (1998), theoretical concepts of intersubjectivity and historical circumstances of globalization have questioned the single-sited method of ethnography, in which the researcher concentrates exclusively on a specific fieldwork site or cultural production. This singular focus perpetuates outdated notions of culture as an isolated entity that the ethnographer must "penetrate" and understand; moreover, it tends to preclude awareness of the larger network of forces in which the site is enmeshed. In a similar vein, the methodology of co-performance is aligned with the increasingly outdated anthropological concept of cultural rapport—the notion that the researchers finally succeeded in crossing the cultural threshold and were welcomed with open arms. Marcus points out that this "ice-breaking" moment of crossing cultural boundaries treats the scene of fieldwork as a bounded culture and therefore reifies the self/other binary. Rapport converts the fieldsite "into a proper mise-en-scène of fieldwork—a physically and symbolically enclosed world, a culture for the ethnographer to live within and figure out" (1998, 109). Co-performance tends to reify this construct, as the moment in which the researcher is asked to perform is depicted as the catalytic ice-breaking moment in which the mysterious workings of performance are suddenly made familiar. In the midst of participatory rhetoric, borders and hierarchies remain intact.

As an alternative, Marcus uses the term *complicity* to suggest an anthropological positioning that emphasizes rather than elides cultural difference. He persuasively argues that "[i]t is only in an anthropologist-informant situation in which the outsideness is never elided and is indeed the basis of an affinity between ethnographer and subject that the reigning traditional ideology of fieldwork can shift to reflect the changing conditions of research" (1998, 119). This framework disrupts notions of the fieldsite as a contained location that the ethnographer has managed to enter. Instead of resorting to oversimplified claims of binary breaking between anthropologist and informant, Marcus suggests that they negotiate across the divide, which becomes an actively contested boundary rather than a theoretical construct. An emphasis on the complexities of collusion displaces sites of objectification and containment.

My multi-sited methodology meant that I was vulnerable to becoming a pawn (albeit a highly privileged one) in the power plays among TOT, Muungano, and Mandela. From Wednesday to Sunday, Ajwang' and I attended performances throughout the city, alternating among these three companies. Since a few members of TOT were my neighbors, and because I was particularly fascinated with its connection to the ruling political party, I usually attended more of TOT's performances than those of Mandela and Muungano. Since these three troupes were keenly sensitive to any indications of favoritism, however, I tried to conceal this special interest. This attempt at concealment failed when Ajwang' and I accompanied TOT on a political campaign in the Kagera region in northern Tanzania. Although this trip clarified TOT's relationship with CCM, I believe it affected my relations with Norbert Chenga, the head of Muungano. Upon my return to Dar es Salaam, he substituted distant politeness for his usual friendliness. As part of the system of negotiation and complicity that marked our relationship as (Western) researcher and (African) subject, my act of betrayal was met with silence—a particularly powerful bargaining tool at the disposal of informants.

It could be said that I withheld a bargaining chip of my own since I did not perform with any of the troupes. Among the three, Muungano is the most accustomed to incorporating European and U.S. researchers into their performances. Mark Plane, for example, played the role of a European boss in a Muungano play during his research on popular Tanzanian drama (1995), and Siri Lange, a Norwegian anthropologist who wrote her master's thesis on Tanzanian theatre (1995), performed *ngoma* with them. In their work on West African popular theatre, Barber, John Collins, and Alain Ricard point out that the ease with which foreign researchers are incorporated into popular theatre is symptomatic of the openness and novelty seeking of modern popular genres. They also stress the importance of researchers asking themselves, "Why are we being allowed, or encouraged, to participate? In what capacity? On what terms?" (1997, xi). In the instance of Muungano, a white performer would have served as a key commercial attraction that none of the other troupes would or did have. Not surprisingly, Muungano offered me the same opportunity as Lange, but I demurred, knowing that my friendly relations with TOT and Mandela would likely suffer as a result. The nature of my multi-sited research would have required me to perform on an equal basis with all three troupes. Because of the considerable drain on time and energy that this commitment would have entailed, I chose not to pursue this option.

But this refusal on my part was hardly a deterrent, as Muungano still managed to find ways of incorporating me into the performance. These moments typically happened without any forewarning, such as the time Chenga announced to the audience that I would take part in the snake dance. Although TOT and Mandela were not as overt as Muungano, they also found ways to ascertain that the spectators were aware of the *mzungu* (European or Anglo-American) in their midst. What I find interesting is that this strategy allowed the troupes to capitalize on my presence while excluding me from the epistemological privilege that co-performance usually affords. In other words, I can hardly lay claim to a more in-depth knowledge as a result of these seemingly random moments. As if to mock the conventional hierarchy of Western researcher and African subject, the companies called the shots, and a new version of complicity was produced.

The fluidity and exchange of these relationships might not be readily apparent to readers in forthcoming chapters due to the absence of lengthy excerpts from interviews. In an attempt to de-privilege the Western voice of authority in works such as this one, scholars often include passages in which the local actors explain the reasoning behind their choices, whether it be aesthetic, political, and/or cultural. Margaret Drewal alludes to the significance of interviews when she speaks of the importance of the performers' intentionality, or "what they *say* about what they do" (1991, 36). During my stay in Bagamoyo, I began doing formal listening by conducting interviews on tape with the faculty of the College of Arts. But as my research continued, I realized that the amount of information I accessed through these formal interviews was insignificant compared to the intricate details I picked up through hundreds of conversations I had with the students over meals, while watching performances, or through working with them as a director or teacher. Once I had returned to Dar es Salaam, I seldom conducted another formal interview, preferring to record the information gained through the countless informal conversations I had with performers and managers in my field notes. Tanzanian theatre artists have absorbed a great deal of official rhetoric concerning the importance of "tradition" and the role of theatre in the education of society; it seemed that once my tape recorder was brought out, I received another earful of this rhetoric. On the one hand, these experiences clarify the potential weaknesses of a multi-sited methodology. My wide-ranging approach precluded an in-depth level of familiarity and intimacy, which might have encouraged the performers to exceed the level of rhetoric in the context of a formal interview. Certainly, numerous researchers have been able to record articulate and evocative testimony from African artists and performers.[23] On the other hand, my decision to emphasize the productions and performance texts helps to unpack the multi-layered discourses of state and nation in which the performers are enmeshed. Ethnographer and performance theorist Dwight Conquergood usefully cautions against the reliance upon interviews as a primary source of information, commenting that "[much of] cultural knowledge is embodied in gesture, action, and evanescent event; it is powerfully experienced, tacitly understood, but hardly ever spelled out, and if expressed, then more often than not in highly allusive, elliptical, and indirect ways" (1992, 85). Similar to Fabian's experience, in which a Zairean theatre company created an entire play in order to adequately respond to his questions about a particular proverb, I found the performances to be eloquent and powerful articulations of the multiple and contradictory facets of Tanzanian identity.

The intricacies of Tanzania's poetics of nationhood are explored in three parts. The first part, "Imagining the Nation," outlines the concepts of collaborative and alternative nationalism. In chapter 1, I explore the processes of collaborative nationalism as they evolved throughout the post-independence era, through which the state and performing artists participated in the transformation of popular theatre companies into surrogates of national culture. In chapter 2, I use the concept of alternative nationalism to theorize the performances of the three theatre companies that are the focus for the remainder of the book—Muungano, TOT, and Mandela. Specifically, I explore the ways in which these three companies called upon the performance traditions of dance, music, plays, and acrobatics to develop alternate versions of nationhood. In order to adequately address TOT's role in the popular theatre landscape, I also introduce the idea of strategic nationalism, suggesting that nationalist rhetoric helps to conceal the company's political alliance with CCM.

The second part, "Sexing the Nation," narrows the discussion in two ways: it singles out the politics of gender as a focal point of analysis and hones in on the specific performance traditions of *ngoma* and *maigizo*. In chapter 3, I return to the framework of collaborative nationalism to explore the state's attempts to domesticate the erotic dances of southern Tanzania that urban audiences preferred. Specifically, I unpack the movement of *kukata kiuno* (to cut the waist), an erotic, hip-swaying movement of women that is especially prevalent in southern dances. In chapter 4, "Popular Drama and the Mapping of Home," I employ the concept of alternative nationalism to explore the metaphorical use of home as a microcosm of the nation in the performances of Muungano, TOT, and Mandela. I focus in particular upon Muungano's "Such Matters" ("Mambo Hayo") and TOT's "Control Yourself" ("Ushinde Moyo Wako"), two plays in which the forces of alternative nationalism worked to explode the "traditional" village as a bedrock of safety and stability, opening paths for new configurations of female citizenship.

In "Contesting the Nation," I return to the popular performance in its entirety. Chapter 5 examines how Muungano's and TOT's versions of nationhood clashed and coalesced in a formal competition held in 1997. Although this particular competition culminated in the production of new meanings and new narratives of the nation, it also foreshadowed TOT's eventual triumph as the undisputed leader of the popular theatre scene. This foreshadowing is fully realized in the concluding chapter, which summarizes my disappointing findings in 2001—disappointing because the layers of multivocality contained in the complex assortment of performance traditions had receded due to the encroaching forces of *soukous* music. The complexity and creativity of the popular theatre had dissipated, leaving a pallid reflection of its former exuberance. By 2001, in a disturbing reminder of CCM's consolidation of power since the formation of a so-called multiparty system, TOT's victory over the "opposition" of Muungano and Mandela seemed assured.

A latent theme throughout the book is that nationalism "works" in Tanzania. Although a number of the unifying forces that helped to cultivate a deep-seated loyalty and investment in the nation-state had disappeared by the end of the twentieth century, a sense of social cohesion continues to make the country stand apart.[24] Stability and cohesion are not necessarily laudable qualities since they are often built upon the erasure of difference; indeed, my research revealed a wealth of exclusions and suppressions upon which Tanzanian nationalism depends.[25] Nevertheless, I also found an abundance of creative energy and artistic labor invested in the exploration of national identity in the post-socialist era. My hope is that this book will shed light on the complex process of collaboration and contestation through which these explorations occurred.

PART ONE

Imagining the Nation

ONE

Performing, Transforming, and Reforming Tanzania

A Historical Tale

In writing a history of postcolonial Tanzanian theatre, I could tell a story of how the International Monetary Fund and the World Bank domesticated the fiercely anti-colonial, socialist, pan-Africanist government into a meek capitalist one under the rubric of democratization. I could then trace a similar tale in the history of theatre companies, in which actors and playwrights eagerly joined the struggle to build a socialist nation only to be eventually co-opted by the forces of tourism and development. For evidence, I could point to the multitude of theatre companies that flourished in Dar es Salaam during the socialist era only to crumble under the onslaught of structural adjustment policies. Seamlessness and linearity would unite in a neat package that situates oppressor and oppressed in binarized terms.

The history of postcolonial Tanzanian theatre is, however, a far more convoluted—and considerably more interesting—story of complicity and collaboration. Customary terms such as *resistance, appropriation,* and *co-option* do not do justice to the complex paths and detours that these performances carved out. Top-down or grassroots models of nationalism are incommensurate with the example of Tanzanian performance, in which the state, performing artists, and audiences interacted in a dynamic process that I term *collaborative nationalism* in order to emphasize their various roles as collaborators rather than as hegemonic or resistant forces.

This term is not without its problems since the concept of collaboration implies a sense of equality that might elide the privileged status of the state and its agents. To be sure, the state clearly sought to maintain its upper hand through the passing of a series of regulations that governed the operations of the theatre companies. Also, the companies performed a relentless patriotism through ceaseless praises of government policy, the party, and Nyerere, which indicates a certain level of fear, or at least anxiety, about overstepping these bounds. Nevertheless, the complex, even contradictory nature of these relationships between the state and the theatre companies meant that these boundaries and parameters were fluid and subject to change. In using the term *collaborative nationalism,* my intent is to emphasize the dynamic nature of Tanzanian national performance in which the state borrowed from popular culture and vice versa in an ongoing cycle of shadowing, adaptation, and, indeed, co-creation.

I also explore the forces of creativity that collaborative nationalism unleashed. Creativity and innovation are widely understood as hallmarks of African popular culture in which global and national dictates are transformed for local consumption. Although I recognize similar forces at play in Tanzanian popular theatre, I found that the networks of complicity called forth additional reserves of creativity. The processes of negotiation demanded new strategies on both sides of the postcolonial equation as they engaged in intricate choreographies of power. Instead of remaining a distant oppressive force, the state actively interacted and engaged with local producers of national performance.[1] Indeed, the state was not limited to conventional nationalist scripts but indulged in some improvisations of its own, as the discussion of *sarakasi* (acrobatics) reveals. It is not my intention to whitewash creativity as a purely positive term since agents of power can and do employ these forces of creativity to maintain or reestablish systems of dominance. My point is to open up conventional ideas of understanding creativity as a trademark of local agency and excavate the layers of complexity that the term contains.

I also draw upon Joseph Roach's concept of surrogation in order to complicate the standard tale of grassroots creativity and hegemonic coercion. In *Cities of the Dead: Circum-Atlantic Performance,* he suggests that cultural performances tell stories of "incomplete forgetting" (1996, 7) and that traces of those carefully forgotten histories survive through the medium of performance. In an oft-quoted passage, he writes: "In the life of a community, the process of surrogation does not begin or end but continues as actual or perceived vacancies occur in the network of relations that constitutes the social fabric. Into the cavities created by loss through death or other forms of departure . . . survivors attempt to fit satisfactory alternates" (2). His use of the term "survivors" is especially evocative when applied to postcolonial contexts where the social fabric was torn through colonial suppression and/or co-option of indigenous traditions and cultures. In the aftermath of colonialism's "epistemic violence" (Spivak 1985, 130),[2] the survivors include the newly independent state anxiously attempting to prove its legitimacy as well as the newly independent citizens testing the waters of postcolonial national identity. Roach repeatedly calls attention to the power plays of erasure and forgetting unleashed in the processes of surrogation, asking such "obdurate questions" as "Whose forgetting? Whose memory? Whose history?" (1996, 7). In a similar vein, one might ask, why were some productions of Tanzanian nationalism judged satisfactory and others discarded? For whom were they satisfactory? As this historical account reveals, both the state and subjects worked together to produce these alternates in a multi-layered process of collaborative nationalism. Loren Kruger glosses Roach's concept of surrogation as "imposing, transforming, reclaiming the scripts and behaviors of the past in the present" (1999, 10)—a phrase that captures the series of moves and countermoves involved in the shaping and contesting of cultural memories.

The complexities and nuances of this path were not readily evident in the state's initial forays into the production of national culture. My historical narrative begins with Nyerere's inauguration speech in 1962 as the first president of the Republic of Tanzania, a speech that foreshadowed a conventional course of Third World nationalism that depended upon the usual opposition of Western versus African culture. Upon the unveiling of the Arusha Declaration five years later, however, the state embarked upon a more experimental path. Hundreds of cultural troupes began to flourish in factories, branches of the army, and parastatal organizations throughout the country. The state readily borrowed from these local models of national culture and even appropriated some of the more successful examples as surrogate national troupes once the official versions were declared defunct in 1981. Through a complex process of economic and political liberalization in the late 1980s and early 1990s, this plethora gradually consolidated into the triad of Muungano, Mandela, and Tanzania One Theatre, which seized the helm as the vanguards of national culture.

This cyclical process of surrogation culminated in a new version of national culture, a multifaceted creation that embraced the nuances of postcolonial Tanzanian identity. The framework of collaborative nationalism helps to chart a new course that not only complicates conventional concepts of co-option, oppression, and resistance but also seeks to understand the contradictory and ambivalent impulses that pervade the nationalist project.

HESITANT BEGINNINGS

When Julius Kambarage Nyerere assumed the presidency of what was then called Tanganyika in 1962, his inauguration speech adhered to relatively conventional tropes of Third World nationalism.[3] In order to counteract the colonial legacy that defined indigenous culture as "worthless—something of which we should be ashamed, instead of a source of pride" (1967, 186), he pitted *dansi,* or Western forms of dance, against *ngoma* in a culture war between traditional Africa and modern Europe:

> When we were at school we were taught to sing the songs of the Europeans. How many of us were taught the songs of the Wanyamwezi or of the Wahehe? Many of us have learnt to dance the "rumba" or the "chachacha" to "rock'n'roll" and to "twist." . . . But how many of us can dance, or have even heard of, the *Gombe Sugu,* the *Mangala,* the *Konge, Nyang'umumi, Kiduo* or *Lele Mama*? . . . And even though we dance and play the piano, how often does that dancing . . . really give us the sort of thrill we get from dancing the *mganda* or the *gombe sugu*— even though the music may be no more than the shaking of pebbles in a tin? It is hard for any man to get much real excitement from dances and music which are not in his own blood. (1967, 186)

This speech is hardly remarkable from the standpoint of postcolonial studies given that newly independent Third World countries often articulated a desire to "reclaim" a glorious precolonial culture.[4] The ubiquity of this rhetoric might explain why Terence O. Ranger dismissed Nyerere's erasure of the complexities of dance traditions such as *mganda,* which exemplified postcolonial notions of hybridity through its integration of colonial military formations and indigenous musical rhythms, as an "obvious, but superficial, irony" (1975, 122).[5] Much less superficial are the cultural anxieties and ideological agendas that Nyerere's speech contained. Out of the plethora of performance traditions that existed at the time of the speech, which included *ngoma, muziki wa dansi, taarab, kwaya, vichekesho,* and *maigizo.*[6] Nyerere singled out *ngoma* and *muziki wa dansi* as the sole examples of the entire performance pantheon in a move that bore witness to the controlling tendencies of the newly independent state.

The speech positions colonialism as a monolithic force that inexorably suppresses precolonial traditions. In defining an opposition between the dominant colonizer and the submissive colonized, Nyerere set the stage for a reversal of power in which the state could appropriate that agency and mark out its legitimacy on the world stage. It is noteworthy, for example, that Nyerere's speech thoroughly diminishes the potency of *ngoma*. In portraying *ngoma* as a vanished phenomenon, he renders it a passive victim of the colonial onslaught. Granted, his audience consisted of the newly elected Members of Parliament, many of whom represented the educated elite, or "Black Europeans" (*wazungu weusi*) and therefore were more likely to internalize those colonial attitudes that categorized *ngoma* as "primitive" or, at best, "precious" (Ranger 1975, 130). Nevertheless, the sweeping terms of his speech erases the thriving popularity of local *ngoma* among the majority of the Tanzanian population. It is particularly telling that this speech eliminates the role that *ngoma* played in the nationalist movement that brought him to power. For example, Susan Geiger (1987, 1997) found that coastal Muslim women used the performance networks of *ngoma* to promote the nationalist movement in the 1950s.[7] Of the four women's musical groups that became directly involved in TANU (Tanzania National Union) politics, one practiced *lelemama,* which, interestingly enough, is included in Nyerere's list of "forgotten" traditions.[8] Work such as Geiger's raises questions concerning the degree of coincidence that Nyerere's omissions contained.[9]

It also seems significant that the speech excludes the unique role of *dansi* as a tool in the national struggle by depicting it purely as a sign of colonial oppression. In Ranger's description of the popularity of ballroom dance traditions among the nationalist elite, he remarks, "it was sometimes hard to distinguish between a branch of the African Association [a nationalist organization] and an elite dance club" (Ranger 1975, 96). Although *dansi* tended to be associated with Christianity on the mainland (126), Laura Fair found that Muslims in Zanzibar not only embraced *dansi* but also used it as a means of actively promoting the nationalist cause. They played upon the popularity of *dansi* among the youth in order to lure them to political meetings: "Dancing to foxtrots and wearing fancy gowns provided them with a cover for political education and organizing and a very effective means for attracting younger and less politically minded individuals into their organizations" (1994, 519). This local appropriation and transformation of this emblem of European modernity serves as yet another example of how indigenous and so-called European practices alike were marshaled to serve the nationalist cause. In Nyerere's speech, however, *dansi* is uniformly portrayed as a tool of the colonialists, a practice that needs to be suppressed in order to allow its weaker opponent of *ngoma* to survive.

The state, of course, would serve as *ngoma*'s benign protector. In order to counteract the colonial legacy of shame, Nyerere announced the formation of the Ministry of National Culture and Youth: "I have set up this new Ministry to help us regain our pride in our own culture. I want it to seek the best of the traditions and customs of all our tribes and make them part of our national culture" (Nyerere 1967, 187). Nyerere's statement claims a sense of agency for the postcolonial state, one that would single-handedly counteract the psychic violence of colonialism. This institutional agency is readily repeated in narratives of Tanzanian theatre history, which situates his speech as a turning point in the development of Tanzanian national culture.[10] In other words, the speech launched a linear path of nationalist culture in which the newly formed ministry founded a National Dance Troupe in order to fulfill its charge to resuscitate indigenous culture.

The story of this "revival," however, is perhaps more accurately told as one of hesitance and distaste. More in an attempt to imitate the example of the famous Ballet Africaines of Guinea than as a direct result of Nyerere's speech, in 1963, the ministry hired nine local dancers to form a troupe that would provide entertainment at official occasions (Office of Culture 1964d).[11] Three of these dancers were sent to Guinea to study with the Ballet Africaines for six months in an attempt to improve the Tanzanian troupe; however, the lackluster quality of these performances are painfully evident in a ministry official's scrawl in response to a request to have the troupe perform abroad: "I do not consider our group good advertisement for the Republic overseas. Why can't he contact some of the local *ngoma* troupes?" (Office of Culture 1964b). Although *ngoma* contained significant potential as a popular national symbol since it was accessible to all Tanzanians regardless of their level of formal education or religion, this thriving tradition was reduced to an object of scorn. Not only were the dancers paid minimal wages, but the ministry's attitude toward them also reeked with condescension.[12]

This attitude stemmed at least partly from a sense of disdain for *ngoma* itself. In 1969, Minister of Agriculture D. N. M. Bryceson gave a speech in which he denounced those villagers who danced *ngoma* at the expense of contributing to the building of the country (*Uhuru* 1969a). The editors of *Uhuru* endorsed his speech, noting with disapproval the continued tendency for villagers and rural migrants in Dar es Salaam to indulge in weeklong *ngoma* performances (*Uhuru* 1969b). Despite the "thrill" to be had in rattling pebbles in a tin, as described in Nyerere's speech, one was apparently not to get carried away and forget to plant his maize. Thirty years later, *ngoma* continues to invoke scorn from members of the middle and the upper classes, who tended to see these dances as *chafu* (dirty). Like the colonial state itself, which sought both to suppress these forms as "uncivilized" and to resuscitate them as safe expressions of traditional culture,[13] the founding and development of the National Dance Troupe was riddled with contradictions.

In a study of European national theatre, Loren Kruger identifies a pattern in which "the tastes and habits of the dominant minority, author-ized as (universal) art, reproduce the prestige of that minority while those of subordinate classes or groups are denied this legitimation and marginalized as entertainment or social disruption" (1992, 17). Until the late 1960s, Tanzania seemed determined to adhere to this European model in which the tastes of the few were imposed upon the masses. The national elite sought to marginalize *ngoma*, a thriving performance tradition of the subaltern classes, as an embarrassment to the national cause and instead promoted drama as the preferred national symbol. In these early years following independence, the state seemed surprisingly unconcerned with drama's troubled history as a tool of colonial submission. In the British colonial education system, drama provided lessons in Christian morality and English instruction, instilled through conventions of proscenium-style staging and careful adherence to written scripts.[14] The stilted school productions discouraged experimentation and innovation, leading Jane Plastow to categorize drama as "the form over which the colonialists maintained tightest control" (1996, 70). In a seemingly blithe erasure of this history, as early as 1963, plans were made up for the construction of a national theatre for the production of plays (Office of Culture 1963; 1964a). The plans were shelved not because of anxiety over its association with the colonial agenda of creating a submissive Christian male elite and its theoretical lack of suitability as a national symbol; instead, the ministry simply lacked the economic resources to fulfill its vision of a fully equipped theatre building (Office of Culture 1964c). To return to Kruger's paradigm, drama was not only a taste of the dominant minority but a privilege; as such, it required the Eurocentric trappings of a "picture frame proscenium arch and fancy footlights" (Mollel 1985, 21) to solidify its connotations as an elite form.

Thus far, these half-hearted attempts to establish a national culture give little indication of the dynamic process ahead. The advent of the socialist era cleared the way for a fresh path, one that would challenge the elite/popular divide and redefine the precolonial past as a source of power instead of as an object of disdain. In 1967, Tanzania launched a determined plan to build a radical socialist state as outlined in the Arusha Declaration. The declaration provided a practical blueprint for the realization of Nyerere's philosophy of *ujamaa* (socialism, literally "familyhood"), which he explored in his booklet *Ujamaa: The Basis of African Socialism*. This treatise locates his vision for an egalitarian, democratic, socialist society in the precolonial past, which he described as based in the three fundamental principles of mutual respect, communal living, and hard work (1968b, 107–108).[15] In keeping with the demands of Janus-faced national discourse, in which the postcolonial state must simultaneously straddle the (traditional) past and the (modern) future (Nairn 1977; see also Lange 1995, 36), Nyerere's concept of *ujamaa* fused modern concepts of socialism with notions of precolonial egalitarianism. Although the rhetoric of *ujamaa* was clearly commensurate with his agenda to reclaim traditional culture as articulated in his inauguration speech, the concept of *ujamaa* adopted a more radical approach to history with its intent "to achieve a radical delinking in the present while laying the foundation for a more egalitarian and self-reliant society in the future" (Joseph 1999, 40). No longer a passive reification of nostalgia that calls for the state's protection, tradition here assumes a vigorous, more muscular role in the formation of the nation-state itself.

Although the declaration was primarily concerned with prosaic, practical issues of socialist policy and excluded any discussion of artistic endeavors, theatre artists and intellectuals responded to the idea of a "cultural revolution" with zeal.[16] As described by Penina Mlama, "[a]ll of a sudden" European plays were removed from school libraries and no longer performed: "Since the schools were the main exponents of European theatre this meant almost the total disappearance of European theatre practice from the Tanzanian theatre scene" (1991, 99). The faculty at the theatre department at the University of Dar es Salaam, which was founded the same year that the declaration was announced, launched a concerted effort to revolutionize the colonial model of drama and reclaim it as part of an indigenous heritage through the production of plays that intermingled dance, music, and drama and also contained educational or socially relevant content (Plastow 1996, 134–141). In the wake of these efforts, the ministry founded the National Drama Troupe in 1974. Whereas the previous attempt to found a drama company was based on elitist tastes, the National Drama Troupe brimmed with promise as a form that assuaged the modern leanings of the elite and also drew upon the country's precolonial heritage, at least in a rhetorical sense.

Even more promising was the formation of the National Acrobatics Troupe. Nyerere himself played a key role in the creation of this unique socialist-styled performance tradition.[17] An admirer of Mao Zedong, Nyerere forged friendly relations with the People's Republic of China that included a series of visits and cultural exchanges. May Joseph links Nyerere's passion for Leninist/Maoist theories with the idea of a nation forged and sustained by youth: "The establishment of organizations such as the Tanzanian National Service and policies such as 'Education for Self-Reliance' cohere with Marxist principles of producing the state through the training of young people as citizen-workers" (1999, 58–59). In 1965, six girls and fourteen boys between the ages of nine and fifteen were sent to China for a training program in acrobatics; ten additional boys joined them in 1968 to study Chinese music. These thirty young citizen-workers would return home in 1969 to offer a new kind of nationalist symbol that overturned tired notions of Western/African divides.

Their homecoming launched a vogue for acrobatics—or *sarakasi* (from "circus acts" as it would be called in Swahili)—that made it both fashionable and nationalist. They began touring as the National Acrobatics Troupe, which introduced this novel expression of nationalism throughout the country. In 1974, the ministry sent several *sarakasi* members to various regional cultural offices with the charge of establishing regional groups (Jumbe 2001). These directives facilitated a wave of local troupes in regions, schools, and villages; within a few years, *sarakasi* had become a defining element in Tanzanian performance, as indicated by the aspiring acrobats who wrote to the Dar es Salaam cultural office in the mid-1970s to request a position with the National Troupe (Office of Culture 1974; 1976a; 1976b). Although *sarakasi* was duly brought into the nationalist fold when the Chinese-trained musicians began integrating patriotic lyrics with indigenous melodies, *sarakasi* retained the global connotations that lent it international prestige. The youth's embrace of *sarakasi* signifies one of the many "informal ways in which youth imbibed and made local forms of socialist desire, whether in antagonism or consent" (Joseph 1999, 68). In this instance, these youths physically embodied their consent through their acrobatic feats.

The formation of the *sarakasi* troupe marked the completion of this first phase of national performance. After a conventional stab at cultural nationalism through the formation of a traditional dance troupe, the state expressed its discontent through subsequent creations of a drama troupe and a Chinese-trained acrobatics troupe. This tripartite model of nationalist performance invoked Tanzania's precolonial heritage through dance, its colonial history through drama, and its socialist future through acrobatics. The radicalization of the Tanzanian state through *ujamaa* unleashed an innovative interpretation of the performing arts.

Despite the potential of this tripartite model to more fully realize the complexities of Tanzania's past, present, and future, the drama and dance troupes continued to occupy a marginalized status. In an ironic tribute to the success of Tanzania's cultural revolution, the National Drama Troupe's emphasis on Swahili plays meant that it became incoherent in foreign contexts. Since *ngoma* was commensurate with foreign tastes accustomed to the exoticism of African dance, the National Dance Troupe received numerous invitations abroad and garnered more material and moral support as a result (Lihamba 1985, 382). While the National Dance Troupe traveled to West Germany, Algeria, Guinea, Romania, and Italy, the drama troupe had to content itself with a single overseas trip to work with Friteatern theatre in Sweden. A lack of cultural capital prevented the drama troupe from flourishing and left it mired in postcolonial ambivalence. In a similar fashion, *ngoma* continued to languish despite its greater command of international attention. Rather than allowing the diversity of ethnicities to clash against each other in a plethora of languages and styles, the dances were painted over with a veneer of repetitive movements and a general lack of skill.

Although Tanzanian theatre scholars increasingly called for the integration of the performing arts in order to counteract the colonial legacy of separation and isolation, the three national troupes remained stubbornly divided with separate performances, tours, and musicians (Bernard 2001). Even though the members lived together in the same hostel, this arrangement fostered tension instead of unity; the greater food allowances given to the *sarakasi* performers, for example, was a typical bone of contention (Office of Culture 1970; 1971b). This separation persisted when the College of Theatre Arts was established in Dar es Salaam in 1975 in order to provide training for new members of the groups. Students studied only one of these three forms; overlapping was apparently not an option. Theatre scholar Amandina Lihamba comments dryly, "This was a peculiar approach in a country which did not only have complex traditional performances but had promised to try and reclaim them" (1985, 381). In the domain of official culture, the "shreds and patches" of national culture (Gellner 1983, 56) were not yet stitched together, and the colonial legacy of separation and isolation endured.[18]

A brief discussion of the gender politics in the national troupes helps to clarify the layers of anxiety contained in these halting attempts to create national culture. In performances of nationalism, a marginal figure—usually a representative of a sexual, religious, or ethnic minority—often serves as a focal point for anxiety (Bhabha 1994, 144). My research suggests that the female figure served as this role in the context of Tanzanian nationalism. The dance and drama troupes in particular upheld the predictable, almost clichéd axiom of postcolonial nationalism that women are excluded from the building of the state. As Gayatri Spivak puts it: "[O]ne is obliged to suggest that, even if, in the crisis of the armed or peaceful struggle, women seem to emerge as comrades, with the return of the everyday . . . the old codings of the gendered body . . . seem to fall into place" (1992, 102). Although her use of the word "obliged" implies a certain amount of reluctance to adhere to this dominant feminist narrative, she goes on to confirm that nationalism cannot, in the end, serve as a means of female liberation. To return to Geiger's findings as an example, coastal women used *taarab* and *ngoma* to collaborate in the nationalist movement, but "with the return of the everyday," they were allowed on the nationalist stage only in a subservient role.

The National Dance Troupe particularly illustrates the troubling intersection of gender politics and nationhood. Although the troupe was plagued with a high turnover rate among all members, female dancers were particularly difficult to retain, since they frequently took leaves of absence to care for ill parents or to bear children (Office of Culture 1969a; 1969b). Indeed, the main subject of a 1972 meeting concerned the "discipline" of those female dancers who disrupted the continuity of the group with frequent maternity leaves (Office of Culture 1972). A more dramatic incident occurred in 1966 when a husband demanded that his wife quit employment since the work was making her "thick-headed" (Office of Culture 1966). The conflicting demands of nationalism and gender codes created a web of ambivalence in which female dancers seemed to be unduly caught.

In 1965, the search for female dancers prompted the first of many recruitment trips to rural Tanzania (Office of Culture 1965). These trips were not generalized missions in search of the "best" dancers; instead, the officials operated from specific plans to recruit female representatives from select tribes, such as a Digo woman or a Makonde girl (Office of Culture 1967). In a move that recalls Michael Herzfeld's description of traditionalism as a device that relegates "their subjects as ancestral or prototypical, closer to nature, and constrained from speaking with their own voices" (1997, 160), the ministry imported these prototypes of indigenous womanhood to fill up preordained slots in the national troupe. Once in Dar es Salaam, this raw material was fashioned into a domesticized version of nationalism, in which the female dancers were consigned to repetitive "waist wriggling" (*kukata kiuno*) despite the variety and complexity of movements that indigenous dance affords.

The drama troupe followed suit in its limited range of female representation. When the troupe was founded, it contained only one female member—a move that resonated with the form's origins as an elite missionary school form from which girls would have been largely excluded. Despite the ministry's usual steps to rectify this imbalance through the recruitment of additional female members in 1975 (Bernard 2001), male characters continued to dominate most of the plays. Although its first production, *Afande,* struck a surprisingly feminist note through its story of the harassment that a female soldier in a male-dominated military camp endures (Bernard 2001), the plays performed for the rest of the 1970s devolved into a series of nationalist plays in which women played a consistently submissive role.[19] For example, *Kinjeketile,* an anti-colonial play about the Maji-Maji revolt against the Germans, circumscribes women in their roles as obedient wives, daughters, and/or victims of rape (Hussein 1970). In a similar vein, its 1978 production of *Tendehogo,* which addresses East African slavery, included only one female character among a cast of six; her role is confined to watching the male slaves revolt against and murder their Arab captor (Semzaba 1980). The drama troupe confronted the oppression of the colonial era but largely avoided the exploration of oppression within the nation itself.

In contrast to these rather predictable patterns, the National Acrobatics Troupe provided an occasional glimpse into an alternative version of womanhood. These glimpses complicate the prevailing tendency in postcolonial feminist theory to depict the African state or the forces of nationalism as monolithic forces that suppress female agency.[20] In this unwieldy tale of surrogate nationhood that strove to be "satisfactory" for all constituencies concerned, anxiety and imagination coalesced to provide new codings of the female body that exceeded the usual postcolonial mold of female quiescence.

When the six girls and fourteen boys were sent abroad to study Chinese acrobatics, they endured considerable hardship as a result of the racist attitudes of the local population; Bahati Shabani Jumbe, one of the six girls, recalled that people on the street referred to them as "baboons" (2001). The racial discrimination, however, did not extend to sexual discrimination, as the girls were treated equally from the start. Each student was encouraged to specialize in a particular area, and the girls freely chose the same daredevil stunts as the boys, such as gymnastics and tumbling, rather than what would later be considered the more "ladylike" stunts of juggling and balancing on a bicycle (Jumbe 2001). Although separation from their families was another hardship to endure, this distance provided the girls with freedom from the family demands that constrained their female counterparts at home. The young children were united as *ndugu,* "comrades," a gender-neutral term that Nyerere advocated to erase class and gender differences among the citizenry.

The *sarakasi* troupe, in which the girls trained alongside boys in acts of physical prowess, achieved the most radical vision of female strength. The athleticism of balancing, contortionism, and somersaulting stands in sharp contrast to the silent rape victim in *Kinjeketile* or the smiling women dancers in *ngoma*. The ministry's continued investment in maintaining a mixed-sex troupe led to a well-organized series of auditions in 1971 to recruit six more girls for the acrobatics troupe.[21] Two of these girls, Mary Materego and Ada Mfungo, would go on to become two of the most famous acrobats in Tanzania due to their skill in contortionism and, in Mfungo's case, balancing furniture in the air with her legs. Only *taarab* would be comparable as a performance tradition in which individual women could reach this level of fame.

In the end, however, the potential of this radical vision was contained. The girls, who had become young women during their years abroad, returned to a home that castigated them for refusing to adhere to the traditionalist, domesticated role. They faced accusations of witchcraft from awestruck audience members, which suggested that the physical acts of prowess could only be explained by supernatural means. The girls were also told that they would be unable to bear children—a widespread belief that caused parents to prevent their daughters from practicing acrobatics and carrying on the tradition (Jumbe 2001). Alternatively, their existence was simply ignored: photographs of the troupe in *Uhuru* depicted only the male members of the group, and its articles and captions did not mention the girls' existence (*Uhuru* 1970; 1972b; 1978a). *Sarakasi* might have temporarily opened doors for women, but society took steps to contain this bold interpretation of female citizenship.

This brief detour into the gender dynamics of the national troupes helps to illuminate the complex beginnings of Tanzania's initial experiments with national culture. As the next section explores, the potential of the Arusha Declaration and the boldness of *ujamaa* were more fully realized in the formation of the cultural troupes, an alternative branch of nationalist performance that existed alongside the national troupes throughout the 1970s. For a few heady years, until their rapid decline in the late 1980s, these alternative versions of national culture multiplied and flourished in tribute to the "chaotic pluralism" of the postcolony (Mbembe 2001, 108), providing an array of options that captured the complexity and nuances of postcolonial life. At the same time, however, the cultural troupes cannot be theorized as autonomous expressions of grassroots nationalism. The state's coercive bent as hinted at in Nyerere's inauguration speech raise the distinct possibility that the cultural troupes' vociferous expressions of patriotism were at least partly motivated by fear.

SOCIALIST IMPROVISATIONS

The Arusha Declaration provoked a wildly enthusiastic response. In marches and parades throughout the country, citizens rushed to display what could be interpreted as a domestic version of "Tanzaphilia," a term coined by Ali Mazrui (1967) to describe the outpouring of praise for the declaration from socialists across the globe. Issa G. Shivji, a political scientist at the University of Dar es Salaam who seldom hesitates to criticize the government, concedes that "[m]any African regimes have experimented with socialism . . . but few can claim that their ideologies have had the consensus of the popular classes that the Tanzanian state enjoyed during [the decade following the declaration]" (1992, 44). On a similar note, Joseph, who was living in Tanzania during this transition, writes that "during those electrifying early years, as policies were still unfolding, the air was thick with the promise of change" (1999, 52). Such statements suggest that these expressions of loyalty stemmed from grassroots nationalist fervor. To that end, an explosion of performing arts troupes between 1967 and 1974 that formed in parastatals, factories, and army branches throughout the country could also be explained as a manifestation of these "electrifying" years. This interpretation would emphasize the ways in which these groups exceeded the tripartite model of drama, dance, and acrobatics to call upon additional performance traditions such as *kwaya* in order to express support of socialist policy, Nyerere, and the party. In the "glamourous, exciting, and even insouciantly hopeful" post-Arusha period (Stren 1981, 592), state and citizens seemed to actively collaborate in the formation of an anti-colonial, socialist African state.

Other findings suggest, however, that these celebrations of the declaration were at least partly motivated by fear. In her research on the post-Arusha era, Aili Tripp found that "[d]isaffection with the declaration was not voiced at the time because any open criticism would have been severely muted" (1997, 174). The state's investment in shaping compliant subjects, as reflected in the state's formal establishment of a one-party state in 1965, complicates the notion of a popular nationalist consciousness.[22] Jonathon Glassman notes in his discussion of *ujamaa,* Nyerere's "rhapsodic descriptions of bucolic communalism" downplayed the potential of contestation and innovation in African public rituals (1995, 269). He calls attention to Nyerere's statement that "although [the tenets of *ujamaa*] were not always honored by every individual [in the precolonial era], *they were not challenged*" (1995, 269, citing Nyerere 1968b, 338). This authoritarian ideology was not confined to theoretical musings; as early as 1964, Nyerere sought to repress artistic expression through imprisoning the popular singer Kalikali for his songs satirizing and criticizing the government (Songoyi 1990). This context provides a pointed reminder of the external forces that permeated local expressions of support.

The expressions of praise among the cultural troupes should also be contextualized in the vulnerable status of the performing artists employed by these organizations.[23] Calls for dancers were answered by hundreds of applicants desperate for work. Rather than conducting auditions, some parastatals reportedly hired these dancers on the basis of their ethnic group alone (Mbelemba 2001); Makonde people, for example, were widely believed to possess "natural" talent in dance. These newly employed dancers balanced precariously on the bottom rungs of society since dancing *ngoma* was not considered a rare skill. As such, it seems unlikely that they would have risked losing their jobs, let alone landing in detention as in the case of Kalikali, through the performance of critical works. The state also took steps to integrate the groups into the machinery of the state. For example, the party secretary for each parastatal served as the supervisor of these troupes; also, in 1976, the government decreed that these performing artists had to be employed as workers in the factory rather than exist as autonomous artists within the institution (Mkoloma 2001). These policies could be summarized as classic gestures to contain the potential of artistic transgression.

These gestures apparently worked. Even when the country slipped into an ever-escalating economic crisis in the late 1970s, causing national morale to plummet and what Tripp (1997) calls a "culture of noncompliance" to take hold, the cultural troupes faithfully continued to pay tribute to the state.[24] In order to transform *ngoma* into an effective vehicle of praise, the troupes discarded traditional lyrics in favor of Swahili praises of Tanzania, Nyerere, and government policy. *Kwaya* (from the English word "choir"), a form linked to hymns that German missionaries translated into Swahili or ethnic languages, played a particularly prominent role in the promotion of the state. In his analysis of the colonial versions of *kwaya,* Gregory Barz classifies hymns as "one of the most highly developed tools used in the colonization and domination of land and people, body and spirit" (2003, 20). On the one hand, the reclamation of this tool in the post-independence era could be interpreted as a powerful inversion in which this colonial tool is transformed to serve the interests of building an anticolonial, socialist state. On the other hand, the troupes' interpretation suggested that the form retained a quiescent tone since the lyrics did not deviate from their promotions of national unity and socialism.[25] A form of recitative poetry in dialogue form called *ngonjera* also took hold among the cultural troupes; like *kwaya, ngonjera* adhered to a single line of unadulterated praise and support.[26] The potential for complexity within the lyrics and poetry of these forms was carefully contained in the interests of state promotion, which, in its very blatancy, suggests an anxiety to assure the state of their loyalty and usefulness. The insistency and repetitiveness of these patriotic praises caused Mlama to dismiss the cultural troupes as mere "parrots" of official rhetoric (Mlama 1991, 103)—an interpretation that the examples of *kwaya* and *ngonjera* easily uphold.

These fervent expressions of loyalty raise the possibility of what Mbembe has termed "intimate tyranny," in which subjects have "internalized authoritarian epistemology to the point where they reproduce it themselves in all the minor circumstances of daily life" (2001, 128). When applied to the specific context of Tanzania, however, I believe Mbembe's formulation of power and control is only of limited use since he implies that the public performances of loyalty serve as camouflage for the "real" acts of transgression that are occurring underneath. Geiger's research on the role of women in TANU raises an alternative possibility—that the widespread devotion to the charismatic Nyerere reflected a deep-seated loyalty. Geiger found that former female TANU activists were invariably supportive of Nyerere and the Tanzanian state regardless of subsequent economic and social declines, a pattern that she attributes to the persistence of a popular nationalist consciousness (1997, 204). In making a connection between TANU activists and the cultural troupes, I am suggesting that the troupes were at least partly motivated by this kind of consciousness. Although *ngoma,* drama, and *sarakasi* were regularly included in these versions of national culture, the groups exceeded this tripartite model of nationalism and rehabilitated additional performance traditions by putting them to a socialist use, demonstrating a sense of agency and *investment* in the production of socialist and/or nationalist scripts.

In particular, the role of slapstick comedy, or *vichekesho,* complicates the idea of timid and anxious theatre artists. *Vichekesho* developed during the colonial era independently of the stilted British drama practiced in mission schools, possibly out of imitations of the Charlie Chaplin films that were widely popular.[27] Colonial records indicate that local performers used *vichekesho* to portray ignorant Africans unable to comprehend European technologies and therefore were permeated with racist ideology that idealized whites (Lihamba 1985, 43). In a transformative twist, the cultural troupes appropriated the form in order to ridicule those Tanzanians who refused to accept the enlightened path of socialism. The cultural troupes moved beyond the scripted forms of *ngonjera* and *kwaya* into the realm of improvisation in their display of allegiance for the Arusha Declaration and Nyerere.

In order to reach a more nuanced understanding of these troupes, the cultural influence of *mashindano,* a collective term that refers to East African traditions of competitive performance, must also be addressed. *Mashindano* (from *kushindana,* "to compete") denotes a performance event in which groups compete in a display of musical and/or dramatic skills (Gunderson 2000, 7). The term refers to extraordinarily complex networks organized around villages, kinships, ethnic groups, regions, districts, churches, businesses, or independent companies. This deeply rooted tradition encouraged the groups to exceed the socialist mandate and carve out a space of play. Instead of participating in the ad hoc hiring process previously described in which performers could be hired on the basis of ethnic identity alone, four organizations (Tanganyika Packers, Tanita, the National Housing Corporation, and the Magereza army branch of Temeke) turned to a thriving system of *mashindano* among local Makonde groups in Dar es Salaam, which competed against each other through performances of *sindimba,* one of the most famous dances in the country (Mkoloma 2001). These local *ngoma* groups, offered the opportunity to earn wages for what had previously served as a pastime activity, agreed to be hired as the new cultural troupes for these organizations. Although this turn of events could be interpreted as a classic example of co-option in which a thriving indigenous network was appropriated for the purposes of state glorification, the cultural troupes indulged in some appropriative moves of their own. Instead of being suppressed, the networks of rivalry and competition expanded throughout the cultural troupes of Dar es Salaam. In a move that hints at the dynamic process of appropriation and counter-appropriation that was beginning to gain momentum, official performances in the national stadium on holidays served as a forum where these rivalries could play out. The cultural troupes used these displays of patriotism and goodwill toward the state as a way to play out an alternative culture of competition and rivalry (Mkoloma 2001; Akili 2001).[28]

These groups created their own criteria for winning the game. Rather than trying to out-do each other in terms of patriotism, they began expanding their repertory of performance traditions as a means of "besting" the other groups. Bora Cultural Troupe, for example, which started out as a *sindimba* group, added drama and *vichekesho* to their performances in 1977 and *kwaya* in 1978 (Mkoloma 2001). Urafiki, which originated as a *kwaya* group, added *sarakasi* in 1973, *mazingaombwe* (magic tricks) in 1974, and finally drama in 1975–1976 (Akili 2001). My attempts to ferret out specific justifications for the inclusion of these forms met with puzzled looks during interviews with former members of these groups; they would patiently explain that the group learned the form when an expert (*mtaalam*) was available to teach it (Mkoloma 2001, Akili 2001). The rhetorical justifications that plagued the selection of forms for the national troupes faded in the context of *mashindano,* which produced a space of imagination and creativity rather than one of anxiety and ambivalence. This sense of play intruded into the content of *vichekesho* in the latter part of the 1970s, as comic stories of marital discord in *vichekesho* began edging out stories of the smart socialist and stupid capitalist (Mkoloma 2001). Although blatant criticism continued to be avoided, the groups found alternative ways of recasting official culture and rhetoric.

Clearly, the cultural troupes elide definition as either manifestations of anxiety or as expressions of deep-seated patriotism. The elasticity of the performance traditions upon which they drew created an expansive framework in which loyalty, fear, and play could commingle in what was shaping up to be a highly unique production of national culture. In an acknowledgment of their growing significance in the national landscape, the state-run newspaper *Uhuru* in 1978 enthusiastically endorsed a number of these cultural troupes for their skilled performances at national celebrations and government meetings (1978b). This unique phenomenon was gaining legitimacy as well as momentum.

JKT, JWTZ, and Magereza, which refer to branches of the military, deserve particular attention as examples of the state's increased readiness to borrow from the cultural troupes to produce new models of nationalist performance.[29] Unlike the parastatals and factories, the army troupes could offer their performers a degree of prestige and security with relatively decent wages and benefits.[30] Moreover, the state required that all soldiers and officers belong to the political party of CCM. These army troupes were not only "under" the aegis of the state, as in the case of the National Dance Troupe and the cultural troupes—they *were* the state, and their high subsidies and social status earned them a legitimacy that would surpass that of the National Troupes. State legitimacy was not, however, the only factor in the army troupes' success. They also actively participated in the networks of *mashindano,* which ensured that the energies of competition galvanized their efforts. In addition to holding contests among themselves (*Uhuru* 1991c), the army troupes also successfully competed against cultural troupes and independently owned troupes once the commercial theatre was underway (*Uhuru* 1985). The vectors of legitimacy and popular appeal exemplify the unique contours of Tanzanian collaborative nationalism, in which the state freely borrowed from the cultural forms to come up with a popular *and* powerful mode of national performance.

Apparently, the national troupes were neither. After singling out cultural troupes such as JKT and JWTZ for particular praise, the writer of the 1978 editorial includes the National Dance Troupe almost as an afterthought, remarking simply that the troupe is "not behind."[31] The troupe was at a particular disadvantage when compared to the army troupes, which could lure away performers with the promise of higher pay, free housing, and benefits. For example, in November 1968, JKT persuaded four of the National Dance Troupe's members to join its own group (Office of Culture 1968); a year later, two more dancers left to join JWTZ (Office of Culture 1969c). In what was becoming an increasingly tangled world of national performance, the official troupes failed to secure legitimacy despite the rubric of state sponsorship and began to languish near the bottom of the performance hierarchy. Former members of the National Dance Troupe claim that JKT existed primarily for entertainment in contrast to the nationalist mission of the National Dance Troupe to preserve indigenous culture (Masiaga 2001; Chibwana 2001). The government, however, cared little about this distinction and regularly sent the army troupes overseas as ambassadors of Tanzanian culture (Masiaga 2001).

In 1981, the national troupes disintegrated. The Ministry of National Culture and Youth (renamed the Ministry of Information and Culture) decided to focus its financial and administrative energies on the College of Arts and disbanded the three national troupes (Lihamba 1985, 382). The College of Arts was moved to Bagamoyo, a coastal town north of Dar es Salaam, where it remains at the time of this writing. Several members of the now-defunct troupes became teachers at the college; others received a basic secretarial course and were installed at the ministry or at regional cultural offices. Such was the case of Bahati Jumbe, whose

years of training in the People's Republic of China were summarily dismissed–
she was assigned to a desk job in the ministry, never to perform *sarakasi* again
(Jumbe 2001). The elaborate equipment of the *sarakasi* troupe was locked in a
room (Chenga 2001), forgotten as a relic of the heady days of the early post-
independence period.

Or, as Roach puts it, "forgotten but not gone" (1996, 2). The role of the
national troupes had already been filled by the proliferation of cultural arts troupes
that built upon and improvised on the tripartite model of *ngoma,* drama, and
sarakasi. They called upon a variety of performance traditions that had been
ignored by the state, demonstrating a sense of inclusion and eagerness. As the
individual performance traditions began to coalesce into a single performance,
the troupes embarked on a bold experiment with the place of the past in the present, one in which the isolation and containment of the early post-independence
period yielded to productions of plurality.

RADICAL MOVES

A severe economic crisis began to engulf Tanzania in 1979, marked by sharp
declines in real wages and a "staggering" scarcity of consumer goods (Mulligan-
Hansel 1999, 60). Theories of this decline range from a wholehearted condemnation of Nyerere's socialist policies to more complex discussions that point to a
variety of factors unrelated to socialism: the 1979 war with Uganda, drought,
insect infestations, the rise in oil prices, world recession, and worsening terms of
trade with other countries (McHenry 1994, 5). In defense of Nyerere's *ujamaa*
policy, Basil Davidson notes that his "'experiments' on behalf of a general good
were an object of 'outside' scorn while the actual workings of the terms of trade,
worldwide, ensured that none of these experiments could do more than limp, or
even work at all" (1992, 222). This scorn became so virulent in the international
press that Dean McHenry termed it the descent into "Tanzaphobia" (1994, 2).
Although the crisis "drove a wedge between state and society" (Mulligan-Hansel
1999, 40), resentment and anger were channeled into the development of new
survival strategies rather than political protest.

This crisis produced a rupture in the dynamics of collaborative nationalism as
the cultural troupes turned to the commercial sphere. In the late 1970s, new bars
opened throughout the city when investors realized that the sale of beer remained
steady despite the steep drop in people's real incomes. Faced with steep declines in
state subsidies, cultural troupes turned to these bars and social halls as forums for
theatre performance (Lihamba 1985, 289). This transition sparked an explosion of
commercial theatre in which the forces of *mashindano* and simple desperation
pushed the forces of innovation to full throttle. As the trend caught on throughout
the city, the cracks and crevices of Dar were increasingly filled with theatre
companies. During the 1970s, the entertainment pages of *Uhuru* contained only
the names of jazz bands; performance was relegated to the occasional photograph
of schoolchildren performing *ngoma* or a photograph of the National Acrobatics
Troupe. By 1985, the jazz bands competed for advertisement space with an as-
tonishing number of performance troupes. Old-timers such as JWTZ, JKT, Bora,
Urafiki, and DDC Kibisa competed against Nuwa Dancing Troupe, Bima, Buguruni Theatre Troupe, Utamaduni Mapinduzi, Super Mwongozo, Super Mapinduzi, Mzizima, Mvita, Blankets Dancing Troupe, Trim Theatre, Tanzania
Culture Troupe, Pilsner Dancing Troupe, and Simba Dansing [*sic*] Troupe.[32] Upon

a foundation of economic scarcity, a celebration of heterogeneity was taking hold.

Many of these newcomers included privately owned companies. Unlike the troupes sponsored by statal and parastatal institutions, these companies would supposedly be freer to carve out an autonomous cultural space unencumbered by the state. In the maelstrom of urban popular theatre, however, these distinctions meant little as all of the troupes not only rushed to secure a fan base but also continued to pay obeisance to the nation, the state, and/or the party. The army troupes alone commanded a higher level of prestige as a result of their access to state funds; otherwise, privately owned and parastatal troupes competed as equals in the social halls of Dar. Seemingly heedless of these distinctions, networks of *mashindano* continued to thrive as the troupes boasted of their expertise in a dizzying array of forms including steel band, snake dances, and magic tricks in attempts to assert their superiority.

The economic crisis also facilitated the development of what would become a trademark of Tanzanian popular performance—the composite performance in which singular acts were assembled into a vaudeville-style show. In order to compensate for diminishing subsidies, the cultural troupes began competing for opportunities to perform at private functions as well as in local bars. Although specific acts would occasionally be requested (for example, the organizers might request *ngoma* and *kwaya* only), the groups were often simply told to fill a time slot of three to four hours, for which they would draw upon all of their various acts (Mkoloma 2001). As the complex lineage of precolonial, colonial, and postcolonial performance traditions were assembled into a single performance, the troupes produced new versions of Tanzanian history that exceeded essentialist and homogenized notions of precolonial Africa to create an improvisational space where "memory reveals itself as imagination" (Roach 1996, 29). Elitist traditions such as *kwaya* and drama, "traditional" forms such as *ngoma,* and uniquely socialist traditions such as *sarakasi* were assembled in increasingly sprawling productions that marked a critical intervention into a colonial mindset that had isolated the forms as if to contain their multivocality.

In the midst of these acts of imagination and innovation, however, the links of complicity were carefully maintained. Despite their sense of playfulness, the troupes carefully avoided incorporating new performance traditions until the state gave an affirmative nod. The example of *taarab,* a wildly popular form dominated by coastal Muslim women since the interwar period, is especially revealing of this collective sense of caution.[33] Although *taarab* is a thoroughly global form of music that culls together Egyptian, Indian, and African musical traditions, it is widely perceived as "quintessentially Zanzibari" (Fair 2001, 174) in the national imagination. A fraught and ambivalent relationship between Zanzibar and the mainland meant that *taarab* would be marginalized in the early post-independence era and "largely excluded from dominant renderings of the nation" (Askew 2000, 37). Whereas drama and *kwaya,* both of which originated as European forms, would be cheerfully recuperated in the nationalist cause, the more suspect form of *taarab* was pointedly ignored.[34]

CCM, the ruling political party, initiated *taarab*'s recuperation in the mid-1980s. In 1984, party officials requested that the army troupe JWTZ perform *taarab* as part of its performance at the celebration of CCM's twenty-year anniversary as the sole legitimate party (Komba 2001). Within a year, *taarab* had become standard fare in the performances. This revival coincided with the presidency of Ali Hassan Mwinyi, a Zanzibari whose fondness for *taarab* solidified its popularity in both official and popular spheres (Askew 2000, 37). As cultural troupes responded to these official cues through the inclusion of *taarab,* a more inclusive union that paid tribute to both Tanganyika and Zanzibar began taking shape in the expanding "nation-space" (Bhabha 1990, 4) of popular theatre.

Dansi followed a strikingly similar pattern to that of *taarab;* again, the companies waited for the state's sanction before folding this particular musical tradition into the theatrical mix. In the 1960s, an influx of Zairean musicians to Dar es Salaam fleeing political instability transformed *muziki wa dansi* into a form that increasingly seemed more Zairean than European. Throughout Tanzania's postcolonial history, *muziki wa dansi* had proven resistant to socialist recuperation and had escaped nationalization through the use of patriotic lyrics. Possibly issues of decorum played a role in its suspect status since Zairean forms such as *soukous* and *ndombolo* were notorious for their spectacularization of erotic female dancing. In 1987, however, CCM invited a *soukous* group from Zaire, led by the famous Tabu Ley, to perform.[35] As was customary in Zaire, the performance included the erotic dancing of young women in scant clothing. In response to the party's sanctioning gesture, bands and theatre troupes throughout Dar es Salaam began to include "stage shows," which consisted primarily of young women dancing suggestively to *soukous* music (*Uhuru* 1990). These developments clarify the ways in which popular and official culture were increasingly dissolving in the fluidity of Tanzanian performance.

Upon the inclusion of the stage show, the number of performance traditions had reached its peak. At the historical moment of the mid-1980s, the building blocks of popular performance included *ngoma, sarakasi, vichekesho, maigizo, kwaya, muziki,* and *taarab.* Although a few groups attempted to specialize in one or two forms, they invariably collapsed or were incorporated into a larger group.[36] The colonial legacy of separation and isolation gave way to smorgasbords of performance that included Muslim women singers dressed in long, glittering gowns, mini-skirted young women writhing to a *soukous* beat, and solemn praises of CCM. This atmosphere of heterogeneity and multivocality was, however, built upon a decaying foundation of *ujamaa.* From its ashes would emerge the three performance troupes that dominate the remainder of this book—Muungano Cultural Troupe, Mandela Cultural Troupe, and Tanzania One Theatre.

CONSOLIDATIONS AND CULMINATIONS

Since the early 1980s, Nyerere had waged a losing battle against the International Monetary Fund. As Tanzania's crisis continued to worsen, Nyerere stepped down from the presidency in 1985, leaving it to Mwinyi to negotiate an agreement with the IMF in 1986. This agreement required the abandonment of many policies that were at the heart of *ujamaa* in favor of a market-driven economy. Nyerere described this moment of capitulation in bitter terms with a reference to *The Merchant of Venice,* which he had translated into Swahili in the 1960s as *The Capitalist of Venice:* "When Tanzania went to the Washington-based institution after years of resisting, the [IMF] said like Shylock to Antonio 'Ah, at last you have come.' As it turned out, Antonio could not repay the loan. Shylock then demanded his pound of flesh" (in Tripp 1997, 79). The pound of flesh was largely taken from the masses of poor due to the sharp cuts in health and education budgets. The parastatals, which had been heavily subsidized through the state system, were also pared away as socialist excess. Bora, for example, became bankrupt and dismissed almost half of its work force; in the process, one of the most successful cultural troupes came to an ignominious end (Mkoloma 2001). The homogenizing force of international creditors began to empty Dar es Salaam of its wealth of cultural troupes.

In the wake of structural adjustment, the plethora of private and public performance troupes gradually contracted into the three companies that assumed the mantle of national performance—TOT, Muungano, and Mandela. Although most of these formerly thriving troupes collapsed during the late 1980s and early 1990s, the exact demise of these groups is difficult to discern since the performers seldom received an official dismissal.[37] For example, although DDC Kibisa has not performed since the early 1990s, the corporation still lists the performers as (unpaid) employees in order to avoid paying their pensions.[38] Like *ujamaa* itself, which continues to haunt Tanzanian politics, the cultural troupes cannot be categorically defined as "gone."[39]

The complexities of this past resonate in the formation of Muungano, TOT, and Mandela. An understanding of these three companies should begin with the life histories of Norbert Chenga, John Komba, and Bakari Mbelemba—three remarkable individuals who became the driving forces behind the three companies. Their biographies call forth the Janus-faced image of nationalism through an integration of a traditional background in *ngoma* and a modern education in which they learned *kwaya* and drama. All three men were born in the southern regions during the early 1950s on the cusp of independence: Norbert Joseph Chenga of the Mwera ethnic group and Bakari Kassim Mohamed Mbelemba of the Ngindo group were born in the Lindi region, whereas John Damian Komba of the Ngoni people came from Ruvuma (Chenga 2001, Mbelemba 2001, Komba 2001).[40] Ruvuma and Lindi, like most of southern Tanzania, are less developed than the regions of central and northern Tanzania and therefore are considered culturally "backward" and even "uncivilized." For these three men, this southern ethnicity might have provided the necessary touch of the exoticized African of the precolonial age, albeit sanitized and refined through the Christian school system. The presence of Mbelemba, a Muslim, in the system of colonial education was particularly atypical; indeed, his father's insistence that Mbelemba receive an education in the missionary school system led to a schism in his family (Mbelemba 2001). His religious background might also explain Mbelemba's preference for the relatively neutral form of drama, whereas his Christian counterparts focused on the church-derived tradition of *kwaya*.

Kwaya and drama served as the catalysts for introducing all three men to national performance. In 1974, Mbelemba successfully auditioned for the National Drama Troupe and became one of its original members; he remained with the group until its demise in 1981. Both Chenga and Komba, who had become teachers, caught the attention of government officials through their skill in teaching *kwaya*. In 1977, Chenga staged an elaborate performance for a national celebration in which his students spelled out "CCM" in their closing number; incidentally, this year marks the union of TANU with the Afro-Shirazi Party of Zanzibar to create the new party of Chama Cha Mapinduzi (the Party of the Revolution). This choreographed piece of patriotism earned him a ministry post as the supervisor of the national troupes in Dar es Salaam (Chenga 2001). A year later, Komba entered his students into a national competition for *kwaya,* where he

Figure 1. Norbert Chenga performing *masewe,* a dance of southern Tanzania, with Muungano in 1997.

Figure 2. Captain John Komba (*left*) performing *kwaya* with TOT in 1997.

Figure 3. Bakari Mbelemba, also known as
Mzee Jangala, in 2004.

impressed government officials to the extent that he was invited to join the army branch JWTZ in order to lead its cultural troupe (Komba 2001). At the time, JWTZ lagged behind its rival JKT, and Komba was charged with the mission to improve the troupe's national prominence. In the course of four years, all three men had transferred to Dar es Salaam in official cultural posts: two with the national troupes and one with the army. Although skills in colonial performance traditions paved their way into the realm of national culture, their southern ethnicity undoubtedly provided reassuring "evidence" of their knowledge of indigenous forms as well.

Mbelemba occupied a relatively marginalized status when compared to Komba and Chenga—a position of disempowerment that would translate into a more convoluted career in popular theatre. Mbelemba moved into a teaching position at the College of Arts in Bagamoyo upon the breakup of the National Drama Troupe. In 1983, he attempted to participate in the burgeoning commercial theatre of Dar es Salaam through the formation of Baragumu Cultural Troupe, which consisted of faculty members who traveled to Dar on weekends to produce shows of *ngoma, maigizo,* and magic tricks (*mazingaombwe*) (Mbelemba 2001). Like himself, the majority of the performers were former members of the national troupes; as such, Baragumu might be perceived as an attempt to integrate the old-style nationalist performance of the 1970s with the economic realities of the 1980s. Given the state's usual readiness to follow the lead of such experiments, it is significant that Mbelemba's venture did not succeed. A year later, Mbelemba left the college as a result of disagreement with the administration of the troupe, and Baragumu came to an end. Although Mbelemba did not elaborate upon the reasons for his departure, it seems likely that the faculty and the administration were clashing over the issue of the profits that Baragumu was earning. Particularly in an era of diminishing state subsidies, these profits could easily have become a source of contention.

Upon leaving the College of Arts, Mbelemba spent five years performing with various cultural troupes such as DDC Kibisa—a time he refers to as "conducting research" in preparation for forming another troupe of his own. In 1989, Mbelemba became the head of Mandela Cultural Troupe, which paid tribute to the spirit of *ujamaa* by becoming a collectively owned group (*Uhuru* 1989; Mbelemba 2001). Although Mandela was formed independently of any state institution, the members perpetuated a careful articulation of nationalism in the midst of Tanzania's massive transition to a post-socialist society. Even Mandela's name recalled Nyerere's efforts to foster a pan-African nationalism through his support of the liberation of Nelson Mandela. Mbelemba's skill as a performer and his considerable experience in the popular theatre scene undoubtedly played a role in Mandela's ability to survive the high mortality rate of theatre companies. In comparison to its more prosperous rivals of TOT and Muungano, however, Mandela occupies a precarious existence that tempers the company's investment in the ideals of cultural nationalism.

Chenga's relatively powerful position as the head of the three national troupes played a critical role in Muungano's commercial success. As the end of the national troupes drew near, Chenga displayed an uncanny awareness of the need for surrogate models of nationalism when he founded Muungano in 1980. From the beginning, he envisioned the troupe as a model group that would take the place of the defunct cultural troupes (Chenga 2001). Even the name of the troupe resonated with nationalist aspirations, since its meaning, "union," invokes the unification of Tanganyika and Zanzibar as the Republic of Tanzania. Drawing upon the legitimacy and expertise that his government position bestowed, Chenga proceeded to recruit top performers from Urafiki, Reli, Sunguratex, DDC Kibisa, and the Tanganyika Packers to create a company that emphasized *ngoma,* intermingled with the occasional *kichekesho* to allow dancers to change costumes and rest (Chenga 2001). Chenga then persuaded the female *sarakasi* performers Ada Mfungo and Mary Materego to leave the College of Arts to join Muungano (Chenga 2001). In the process, Chenga began to articulate a unique model of nationalism that expanded upon the isolationist model of the nationalist troupes that separated *ngoma, sarakasi,* and *maigizo.* Moreover, his ability to improvise upon standard nationalist scripts allowed him to recuperate female acrobats in the interests of commercial innovation instead of erasing them in the name of national decorum. His ability to anticipate both official needs and popular tastes has allowed Muungano to retain its reputation as the oldest surviving performing arts troupe in the country.

Of the three men, Komba's career most vividly demonstrates the impossibility of disentangling state power and commercial success. After fighting in the Ugandan War and fulfilling his duty as a soldier, Komba returned to Dar es Salaam in 1980 to carry out his artistic charge of improving JWTZ (Komba 2001). He used his skill in *kwaya* as a cornerstone for the group, which also performed *ngoma,* drama, and *sarakasi.* Unlike the constant shifting of performers that characterized other troupes, JWTZ performers were contracted to the army for seven years, which created a relatively stable company that continued to enjoy subsidies despite the continued weakening of the state. Komba himself exemplified the close connection between the party and the army, as his reputation continued to rely upon his compositions of patriotic and partisan *kwaya,* such as "CCM Ni Nambari Wani" (CCM Is #1)." To reward his loyalty and talent, the party selected him to become a member of the prestigious National Executive Committee in 1987 and sent him to East Germany to study music the following year. Upon this foundation of state support and party power, JWTZ began touring nationally and thus brought the composite performance tradition to the far-flung regions of Tanzania as the new cultural ambassador from the urban center of Dar. Komba's access to the upper echelons of the CCM cadre helped to shore up JWTZ's superior position in the popular theatre scene.

Throughout this historical narrative, the forces and processes of collaborative nationhood have been presented as relatively benign. Relations between the state and the theatre companies can be characterized as an intricate dance of borrowings, appropriations, and play. In the early 1990s, however, the stakes for power rose sharply as the country readied itself for multiparty elections in response to the IMF's stipulations for the dismantlement of the one party state.[41] Although this process helped to usher in a greater awareness of democratization, Max Mmuya and Amon Chaligha have pointed out that the formation of the multiparty system was carefully controlled by CCM, which "had to show to the public that it was still the champion of acrobatic politics in Tanzania" (1992, 117). On the one hand, CCM busied itself with formal severing of ties between the state and the party; for example, *kwaya* and *ngoma* lyrics in praise of CCM in commercial and state-sponsored performance were banned outright. On the other hand, as an example of its savvy ability to maintain its stronghold on the political sphere, CCM strategically employed popular performance as a powerful tool.

On July 17, 1992, Tanzania One Theatre premiered in a heavily publicized opening in Dar es Salaam (*Uhuru* 1992a; 1992b). The party released Captain Komba from JWTZ in order to form this new troupe—one that supposedly would not draw upon state funds and therefore would be exempted from the nonpartisan mandate. Its acrobats, dancers, actors, musicians, and singers were drawn from the College of Arts, DDC Kibisa, JKT, JWTZ, and Muungano, lured through the combination of CCM's financial backing and Komba's artistic and management talents. One of Komba's boldest moves was the hiring of Khadija Kopa from Zanzibar Cultural Troupe, who had been hailed as a rising star (*Uhuru* 1991b). The loss of top performers was the final death knell to groups such as DDC Kibisa; even the defense forces ceased as major players in the wake of TOT's formation. As multiple *watani* succumbed to the forces of economic ruin, CCM managed to produce a single powerful antagonist in the popular theatre landscape.

Only Muungano held its own. Chenga strategically lured Kopa away from TOT in 1993; then, a year later, Komba hired Nasma Khamis, another of Muungano's top *taarab* singers (*Uhuru* 1995). This skirmish unleashed a fierce *utani* between the two troupes that consumed the attention of theatre fans, stealing even more audiences from the few troupes that remained.[42] The forces of commodification replaced the spirit of play that characterized earlier versions of *mashindano* since the companies began to depend upon this rivalry to attract audiences. The proliferating surrogates of nationhood consolidated into a duality between Muungano and TOT, a development that implied the demise of the "chaotic pluralism" (Mbembe 2001, 108) that characterized popular performance throughout the 1980s.

This argument would, however, discount the sociopolitical climate in which Muungano and TOT performed. During the 1990s, cherished hierarchies were questioned and challenged as social, political, and economic spheres experienced the upheaval of national transition. Although CCM retained the presidency and the majority of parliamentary seats in the 1995 election, the opposition parties of the National Convention for Construction and Reform-Change (NCCR-Mageuzi) and Civic United Front (CUF) made impressive showings—no small achievement given the ruling party's lead of over thirty years. The shift to multipartyism created shock waves throughout urban society as it began to open up in response to the party's relinquishing hold (Tripp 1997, 195–196). Although some scholars have pointed out that multiparty politics and increased press freedoms brought ethnic, racial, and religious tensions to light (Campbell et al. 1995, 225), the opening of society also encouraged "religious, media, legal, women's, and other such associations . . . to push to expand the scope of the reforms beyond multipartyism to include greater freedom of speech and association" (Tripp 1997, 197). Women's associations in particular seized the moment to push for social change, leading to a vibrant Tanzanian women's movement in the 1990s (Tripp 1996, 294). This movement strategically used the rhetoric of democratization to link democracy in the home, or the "miniature nation" (qtd. in Tripp 1996, 298), to democracy on a national level. Although the number of theatre companies was greatly reduced, this atmosphere of uncertainty and change ensured that the popular stage continued to serve as a forum for debate and dialogue.[43]

An emphasis on TOT and Muungano would also ignore the persistence of Mandela, which struggled on as the third component that challenged the duality of their rivalry. All three troupes became household names as a result of TOT's and Muungano's frequent national tours, the broadcasting of their *taarab* music, and Mandela's radio plays. At the same time, they each carved out a niche as "miniature nations": Muungano and TOT often provided entertainment for official functions and the entertainment of foreign guests, and Mandela was often chosen for state-sponsored education and health campaigns. Instead of turning to the College of Arts, which carried on the cultural nationalist mission of preserving traditional arts, the cultural office of Dar es Salaam freely called upon these three troupes as convenient surrogates of national culture. In a sense, the state returned to a tripartite model of national culture: Muungano, TOT, and Mandela effectively filled the "cavities," to borrow Roach's term, of the defunct national and cultural troupes.

The Muungano/TOT/Mandela model of national culture, however, contrasted sharply with the old. Although each company continued to perform *ngoma,* drama, and *sarakasi* in tribute to the state's early efforts at forging a national culture, they ignored the careful isolation of these forms that characterized the official national troupes. Instead, their performances were built around *ngoma, vichekesho, sarakasi, maigizo, muziki wa dansi,* and *taarab,* each of which can be categorized as a fragment of Tanzania's history. As this variety of independent performance traditions was assembled into a single show, the performance troupes produced a new version of Tanzania's past and present, one that broke away from master narratives of colonial domination to celebrate simultaneously the socialist past through *sarakasi,* romanticized notions of tradition through *ngoma,* Christian colonialism through *kwaya,* and a cosmopolitan pan-Africanism through the strains of *soukous.* The dizzying mixture of micro-narratives and juxtapositions culminated in a mise-en-scène where contradictory stories and images intersected and overlapped. New histories that defied oppositions, binaries, and dichotomies of all species coalesced through the realm of performance and were celebrated upon the popular stage.

TWO

Alternative Nations

Locating Tradition, Morality, and Power

In 1993, the year of my first visit to Tanzania, Dar es Salaam betrayed few signs of the social upheaval on the horizon. Although the transition to a market-driven economy and multiparty democracy had officially begun, the city continued to display a systematic infiltration of the state.[1] Newspaper stands contained few options besides *Uhuru* and *Daily News,* Radio Tanzania dominated the airwaves, and the lone television station was TTV. All of these media outlets were organs of the state as befitting an ideological apparatus that sought to suppress difference in the name of unification and egalitarianism. When I returned in 1996, the change was startling. The honey-voiced deejays of the privately run Radio One could be heard throughout the city, newspaper stands overflowed with Swahili tabloids that delighted in reporting romantic shenanigans of local entertainers, and new television channels teemed with melodramas and domestic comedies.[2] On Radio One, I constantly heard the refrain of *kwenda na wakati* (to move with the times) as the jingle for the new Swahili newspaper *Nipashe.* The entire city seemed to embrace the phrase in the eagerness to leave behind the dustiness of *ujamaa.*

A mood of excitement and uncertainty pervaded Dar es Salaam in the years following the first multiparty elections of 1995. As the state withdrew from its formerly invasive role in shaping social and economic landscapes, a celebration of plurality transformed the urban sphere. The proliferation of independent newspapers and political parties, as well as the privatization of state-run enterprises, created a space in which urban Tanzania could redefine itself in the "new" post-socialist era (Mmuya 1998; Moore 1996; Tripp 1997). Although concepts of national identity are always in flux as they respond to the shifting demands of the sociopolitical moment, the process of definition and redefinition took on particular urgency during the mid-1990s, when Tanzanians were experimenting with shedding or expanding ordained notions of morality in response to political and economic change on a massive scale. The years 1996 and 1997, when the bulk of my fieldwork occurred, marked a historical moment when formations of post-socialist identity were considered, debated, and contested.

The popular stage provided rich terrain for this explosion of ideas. A complex pantheon of dramatic, musical, and acrobatic acts ensured that the popular theatre was well equipped for exploring alternative modes of citizenship.[3] Following Amy Stambach's interpretation of the Tanzanian popular press as a mode of civil society, "a vital forum in which people are grappling with distinctions between private and public" (1999, 256), these performances could be interpreted as microcosms of democratization in which ideas of morality, gender, and tradition were fiercely debated. Although the companies drew upon a shared repertory that included *ngoma, vichekesho, sarakasi, maigizo,* and *taarab,* each one constructed and performed its own interpretation of what it meant to "be" Tanzanian in the post-socialist era through unique formats and distinctive content. These versions included Muungano's old-fashioned veneration of traditional culture, Tanzania One Theatre's preference for trend setting and modernization, and Mandela's cynicism and alignment with the working poor. Although the companies exerted primary control in shaping these distinctions, the audiences readily seized opportunities to intervene and cast their own opinion in the proliferation and contestation of ideas, ideologies, and identities. Their participation created an exchange of social commentary that transformed the stage into a testing ground for national identity.

To follow Stambach's example and interpret popular theatre as a mode of civil society would, however, elide the companies' carefully wrought links with the state.[4] A democratized theatre would, theoretically, be a politicized one that confronts governmental errors and excesses. Not only did the three companies carry on a decades-long tradition of avoiding such critiques, but they often deliberately affirmed the status quo. These networks of complicity lead me to conceptualize these productions of nationhood as examples of *alternative nationalism* in order to emphasize the array of options that Tanzania One Theatre (TOT), Muungano, and Mandela provided but also to call attention to their investment in the nation-state. Whereas the *legitimacy* of the state and the nation was never challenged, I did observe performances—and moments in performances—in which national boundaries were pushed, questioned, and extended, in what could be termed nation transformation rather than political protest. Although nationalism is usually understood as an attempt to suppress difference through homogenization, in this context it served as a springboard for diversity and multivocality.

The framework of alternative nationalism is not, however, completely adequate to the task of understanding the complexities of these performances since "alternative" implies a sense of existing *outside* the mainstream if not agitating against it. TOT's affiliation with the ruling political party calls this term into question. Although the complexity of the medium and the talent and commitment of the performers ensured that TOT's performances contained provocative interpretations of Tanzanian identity, its political and economic privilege served as a reminder that the three companies did not engage in a national debate as equals. In order to more fully excavate the company's political agenda, I also employ the term *strategic nationalism* to emphasize the ways in which nationalism served as a kind of facade.

This chapter provides a panoramic perspective of the performances. This perspective reveals that what seemed to be a random arrangement of the various performance traditions was, in fact, reflective of the individual company's economic status and/or political agenda. Margaret Drewal describes performance as "forming a web of multiple and simultaneous discursive practices" (Drewal 1991, 16), an evocative phrase that resonates with the performances of TOT,

Muungano, and Mandela, whose individual performance practices coalesced in ideological webs.[5] An understanding of their access to power and economic standing paves the way for the disentanglement of specific strands—the performance of tradition, morality, and power.

ARRANGING THE NATION

Generalizations among the performances of TOT, Muungano, and Mandela were not difficult to make. All of the theatre companies performed in relatively obscure open-air bars throughout the city, outside of which were hung painted cloth banners that proclaimed Muungano as "Madaktari wa Sanaa" (The Doctors of Art) or TOT as "Jogoo wa Afrika" (The Rooster of Africa).[6] Performances usually occurred on Wednesdays through Sundays, beginning around 4:30 or 5 PM and lasting until approximately 9 or 10 PM. Each company relied upon an emcee to welcome the audience with an opening patter, remind them of the varieties of beer, soda, and snacks available, and reiterate the evening's program between each of the numerous acts. Spectators, who averaged about a few hundred per performance, were invariably lively. Children freely wandered onto the stage, and spectators intruded into the action to express their dismay or their approval of the narratives, characters, or messages of the songs. In order to be heard above the audiences' socializing, actors in the *vichekesho* and *maigizo* carried microphones. This convention means that the stage is strewn with wires as well as the few battered metal chairs that typically serve as the set. A collection of band equipment (microphones, an electronic keyboard, a drum set, guitars, and amplifiers) served as the backdrop, providing a constant visual reminder of the dominant role of music in the popular theatre repertory.

These general characteristics existed alongside critical differences. Each company used the building blocks of Tanzanian performance to construct unique performance texts in which each dance, play, or musical form was contextualized by the preceding act. Although the schedules could be altered due to special circumstances, each company generally followed a particular format over the four- to five-hour performance, as indicated in the table. The streamlined format of TOT, the sprawling one of Mandela, and Muungano's in-between approach coalesced in ideological webs in which economic and political privilege were intertwined.

The youngest of the three companies, TOT, exploded on the scene in 1992 as CCM's "secret weapon" in the war against opposition parties (Askew 2002, 247). Officially, the troupe was self-supporting—a rhetorical statement used to counteract charges from opposition political parties that CCM enjoyed an unfair advantage through TOT's popularity. Official statements notwithstanding, it was widely believed that admission fees alone did not pay for the $65,000 Bose sound system imported from the U.S. in 1997 or for the shiny red minibus emblazoned with "Tanzania One Theatre" used for the troupe's transportation. It was also believed that Captain John Komba, the head of TOT, used CCM funds to lure performers away from Muungano and other cultural troupes with offers of higher salaries. TOT's economic advantage established the main ingredients in its flashy performances—costly equipment, elaborate costumes, and talented performers—which contributed to an unprecedented rise to fame throughout the country.

I believe that this "flashiness" was linked to the troupe's political agenda. In order to promote CCM as modern and "hip" to Tanzanian urbanites, TOT embraced a modernizing ideology reflected throughout its performances. The

Table 1. Performance Format of Three Companies

TOT	Muungano	Mandela
muziki wa dansi	*muziki wa dansi*	*muziki wa dansi*
kichekesho	*ngoma*	*ngoma*
ngoma	*kichekesho*	*muziki wa dansi*
ngoma	*sarakasi*	*sarakasi*
igizo	*ngoma*	*muziki wa dansi*
kwaya	*sarakasi*	*ngoma*
taarab	*igizo*	*muziki wa dansi*
	buyeye (snake dance)	*kichekesho*
	taarab	*muziki wa dansi*
		kwaya
		muziki wa dansi
		sarakasi
		muziki wa dansi
		igizo
		stage show
		taarab

company replaced the unwieldy performances of Muungano and Mandela with a streamlined, slick production from which *sarakasi* and *vichekesho* were jettisoned. Whereas *ngoma* were sprinkled throughout the programs of Muungano and Mandela, TOT limited itself to two *ngoma* performed in succession and therefore compartmentalized this symbol of tradition instead of integrating it into the entire performance. The company also ignored old-fashioned demands for the authenticity of tradition through adapting *ngoma* rhythms to electronic music. Although this refusal to remain confined to conventional standards could be heralded as an example of TOT's willingness to chart new paths of national identity, the veneer of innovation and modernization colludes with the ruling party's agenda to shape the terms of post-socialist national identity through the guise of popular culture. TOT's image as a trend-setting, hip alternative to Muungano resonated with CCM's anxiety to shed its image as the old guard, unable to "move with the times."

While TOT enjoyed its expensive "American sound system," as the emcee proudly referred to it in English throughout the performance, Mandela struggled to make do with ramshackle equipment. Although Mandela secured a national reputation through Bakari Mbelemba's radio character Mzee Jangala, who made frequent appearances in Mandela's *maigizo,* the company was unable to compete on the same level as TOT and Muungano. Mandela usually performed in smaller, run-down bars and charged an admission price of 500 shillings (70 cents) for adults, half the price of TOT and Muungano. Although Mandela boasted a stereo sound system and electric guitars, its equipment was shabby, and ear-splitting feedback frequently accompanied the music. Its poverty pervaded the format of the performance itself, which was particularly unwieldy in comparison with its rivals. Since the troupe could not afford to employ specialists in each form, the performers were called upon to fulfill a variety of skills: to dance, act, perform *sarakasi,* sing, and play instruments. As a result, they required interludes of *muziki wa dansi* between each act so they could change costumes and rest. Whereas TOT's performances bore the taint of CCM politics, Mandela's were marked with the rough edges of impoverishment.[7]

Muungano's layout marked a compromise between the unwieldiness of Mandela and the slickness of TOT. It was perhaps not coincidental that Muungano occupied a middle-class status of sorts between the wealthy TOT and the impoverished Mandela. On the one hand, Muungano was not sponsored by a political party and therefore lacked TOT's considerable access to economic and political resources. Muungano's costumes and equipment could not compare to those of TOT, which spared no expense in creating the flashiest performances. On the other hand, Muungano occupied a distinctly higher rung on the popular theatre hierarchy than the impoverished Mandela—for example, it boasted newer equipment, charged twice the admission price, and often served as entertainment for official visitors of the state. This middle-class status translated into performances that conveyed a sympathetic stance for disenfranchised citizens but also shored up the company's connections with the state.

Muungano's performance text delineated this careful compromise. Of the three companies, Muungano could be categorized as the most old-fashioned and loyal. The company retained *ngoma, sarakasi,* and *maigizo* as the foundation stones of Tanzanian national performance but avoided the trendier, more controversial options such as the notorious stage show that featured gyrating female dancers in revealing clothing. This sense of loyalty could perhaps be traced to Muungano's genesis in 1980 as a substitute for the defunct national troupes and its continued relationship with the state. But given the current climate of international demands for neoliberal economic reforms and democratic modernity, this stubborn adherence to the cultural nationalist era of the 1960s and 1970s might also be interpreted as a challenge against the pell-mell changes in Tanzania's political and economic spheres. John L. and Jean Comaroff call attention to the "robust debate" concerning neoliberal reform and multiparty government taking place in contemporary Africa, noting that "[f]rom across the continent come accounts of a widespread suspicion that formal democracy is not always all that is it cracked up to be" (1999, 20). Muungano's careful articulation of socialist-era nationalism marked a unique contribution to this continental debate.

The dynamics of audience participation in all three companies were also pervaded with ideological nuances. Although it is a truism of African theatre that audiences are highly participatory, this generalization should not obscure the material factor of class. Middle and upper classes generally disdained the rowdiness of the popular performances and classified them as "uncivilized" (*ya ushenzi*). As an example of this distaste, a neighbor of mine in Kijitonyama, the aspiring middle-class neighborhood where I lived for five months, expressed shock when I told him the nature of my research and informed me that he would "feel shame" (*kuona aibu*) to take his girlfriend to those performances. Interestingly, he added somewhat eagerly that perhaps they could accompany me to a show of TOT or Muungano, implying that the performance itself was appealing but that they needed to be associated with a *mzungu* to deflect its lower-class taint.[8] The intensity of audience participation was a mark of this lower-class status from which Tanzanians such as my neighbor preferred to distance themselves.[9] These performances could be understood as a mode of civil society that was particularly well suited for the masses of the urban working poor.

The broad category of the urban working poor, however, is stratified in itself. The 1,000-shilling ($1.40) admission price of TOT and Muungano ensured that their audiences represented the "upper crust" of Dar's underclass, signified as such by their carefully pressed secondhand clothes and cheerful generosity in

Figure 4. *Sarakasi* is a trademark of Muungano's performances.

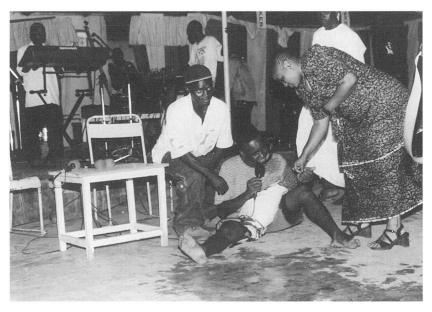

Figure 5. A female spectator *anatunza* (tips) a weeping male character in a Muungano *igizo.*

tipping the performers with small coins. Mandela, however, charged 500 shillings, which meant that its audiences were more impoverished than those who attended the performances of TOT and Muungano. Whereas TOT and Muungano were more likely to claim the larger, prestigious social halls such as T. Garden in Buguruni or Vijana Social Hall in Kinondoni, Mandela usually performed in smaller bars where spectators surround them closely on three sides. In such venues, spectators were considerably more focused and participatory than in the larger bars where the audiences tended to be preoccupied with socializing. For example, in Tukutane Bar in the Buguruni, which served as the company's rehearsal hall and Wednesday night venue, the intimacy of the space and the boisterousness of its spectators ensured that Mandela's performances were especially exciting and intense.

At the other end of the spectrum, TOT's audiences were perhaps the least participatory due to the company's staging preferences. In most of the bars that served as theatres, a small, roofed stage was located at one end, upon which the band equipment remained throughout the performance. Although Muungano and Mandela usually performed their dances, plays, and acrobatics in front of the stage on the same level as the audience, TOT's performers often remained on the raised stage with the musicians. The physical barrier of the raised stage meant that its spectators were less inclined to intervene in the performance. Upon receiving its new musical equipment and sound system, TOT effectively barricaded the stage with a line of tall microphone stands that subdued participation to an even greater extent. Although this practice was meant to show off the expensive equipment, the suppression of audience intervention was highly commensurate with TOT's ideological stance of preserving the status quo.

This collection of ideologies in the performances of TOT, Muungano, and Mandela resonates with Achille Mbembe's discussion of multiple identities as a strategic device of postcolonial subjectivity. He argues that "the postcolony is made up not of one 'public space' but of several . . . the postcolonial subject has to learn to bargain in this conceptual marketplace" (2001, 104). The term "marketplace" is a provocative one; on the one hand it denotes a field of potentiality, but on the other it contains traces of neoliberal philosophy that conflates freedom and democracy with capitalism. It is a concept that seems particularly appropriate in a fledgling capitalist economy, in which options and choices theoretically open up for the consumption of audiences only to conceal the absence of genuine political alternatives. The nuances of this term continue to resonate throughout this chapter as I explore the ways in which TOT, Muungano, and Mandela have each carved out a unique cultural space in which ideologies of tradition, morality and power play out.

ALTERNATIVE PASTS

In the late 1960s and 1970s, state and subjects colluded in the cultural nationalist agenda to "reclaim" precolonial traditions, galvanized by President Julius K. Nyerere's philosophy that socialism heralded a reclamation of Africa's communal and harmonious past (1968b). Postcolonial theorists have thoroughly deconstructed and critiqued this characteristic pattern of postcolonial nationalism for its essentialist underpinnings (Bhabha 1984; Said 1993, 228–230, 275–276; Spivak 1988, 135–136, 246), particularly in relation to the national elite's investment in the shaping of these romanticized myths. However, the role of ordinary citizens in *perpetuating* "the official fictions that underwrite the apparatus of domination" (Mbembe 2001, 111) must also be considered, given the incessant tributes that Tanzanian performing artists continue to pay to *utamaduni.* One might argue that these companies were complicit in state agendas through upholding the fiction of a coherent traditional/national culture.

Instead of empty posturing, however, the performances contain creative interpretations of traditionalism that imply a sense of ownership and a deep-seated investment. For example, the ubiquitous presence of *ngoma* in the performances of all three companies might be perceived as a vestigial link to the cultural nationalist agenda of reclaiming traditional Tanzanian culture from the former German and British colonizers. But to classify the valorization of tradition simply as a manifestation of obeisance to the state would dismiss the companies' investment in interpreting the place of the past in the present. The unique ways in which tradition and traditionalism circulated among the three troupes demonstrated their collective ability to revise or improvise nationalist histories. Popular performance transformed staid discourses of traditionalism into actions and practices that expanded the parameters of citizenship.

Before launching into a discussion of these transformations, the theoretical minefields involved in writing about tradition should be addressed. Although the term itself implies that it can be separated from modernization with all of its connotations of Western ideas, practices, and urban spaces, the concept is, in fact, a modernist invention that defined the colonial subject as a coherent other to the European self (Strathern 1995). In *Remotely Global* (1999), Charles Piot persuasively argues that "traditional" aspects of postcolonial African life are in fact modernities because they intensified in response to the vagaries of the colonial and postcolonial eras. He invokes theories of hybridity to emphasize the creative process in which indigenous and foreign practices are integrated to produce new cultural expressions. In the field of African popular culture, the concept of hybridity has allowed scholars to evade some of the pitfalls associated with the well-worn oppositions of local/global, traditional/modern, and indigenous/foreign since they can focus on the processes of artistic innovation instead of trying to extrapolate modern or traditional elements.[10] Hybridity, the watchword of postcolonial theory, calls for a destabilization of polarities between "the West and the rest" in order to emphasize this process of creolization (Hannerz 1987), or what Bogumil Jewsiewicki (1997) has provocatively called the "cannibalization" of Western practices and ideas. The history of Tanzanian performance abounds with traditions that confound neat classifications; *beni,* a competitive dance tradition that intermingled indigenous rhythms with the movements of German military formations (Ranger 1975) readily comes to mind as one of the more well-known examples. Even dances such as the foxtrot and the waltz were transformed from attempts to "ape European styles of dancing and dressing" (in Ranger 1975, 96) to an explosion of jazz bands that drew upon an eclectic mix of Latin American, Congolese, indigenous, and European styles. Each tradition in the popular theatre pantheon, ranging from *vichekesho* to *taarab,* can be understood as a product of hybridization, creolization, or cannibalization.[11]

The rhetoric of hybridization should not, however, gloss over the specific connotations of these various forms. Despite the complex histories of each individual act, the performances contained a self-conscious use of traditionalist rhetoric that the framework of hybridization does not fully explain. Muungano, TOT, and Mandela regularly invoked tradition in an essentialist, even simplistic fashion that belied the complex ways that it played out in performance. This traditionalist rhetoric conflicts with the celebratory attitude of hybridization, which is often presented in a positive light in opposition to the "tired nationalist claim" of nativism (Spivak 1988, 136).[12] A celebration of cultural creativity in Tanzanian performance cannot ignore the fraught and ambivalent ways that essentialist discourses continued to circulate. Whether celebrated or condemned, tradition was carefully marked off in ways that suggest its powerful status in the national imagination. Although this sense of anxiety often translated into attempts at suppression and control, it could also serve as a springboard for creative interpretations of Tanzania's multiple pasts and potential futures.

At first glance, Muungano's performances exemplified this essentialist stance. At the risk of appearing old-fashioned, Muungano stubbornly upheld the socialist-era mandates of the Ministry of Culture through its valorization of traditional African culture. Through newspaper and radio advertisements, promotional banners, and the emcee's introductory speeches, Muungano consistently marketed itself as a producer of *sanaa za asili,* the traditional arts. For example, the emcee frequently reminded the audience of the *utafiti* (research) that the company carried out in the villages, which helped to shore up the company's rhetorical authenticity of tradition. Muungano's purist stance was also displayed in its *maigizo,* which consistently depicted traditional practices with a sense of respect, in contrast to the mocking attitude that the other companies assumed. In the midst of so-called modern trappings—electronic keyboards, microphones, and bass guitars—Muungano peered backward into the past, carving out an identity as a bastion of the traditional arts.

Because cultural nationalism relies upon rather rigid concepts of authenticity and tradition in order to define itself against colonial culture, it would theoretically suppress creativity and innovation. Accordingly, Muungano's performances contained considerable evidence of traditionalism as a homogenizing force. Muungano's romanticization of tradition meant that it was *always* depicted in a positive light, particularly in the *maigizo* in which it served as a marker of a character's honesty and morality. Traditional women were, for example, consistently represented as moral and upstanding wives and mothers in contrast to their urban counterparts, who served as seductresses and adulterers. Likewise, traditional healers (*waganga wa kienyeji*) were portrayed as upright members of society who took their profession seriously in contrast to the comic "witch doctor" stereotypes that appeared in the *maigizo* of Mandela and TOT. These essentialist underpinnings culminated in a moral universe in which tradition was equated with goodness in contrast to the evils of modernity. The predictability of this pattern worked to sanitize and control the vibrancy of traditional practices and rural spaces into a domesticated seamlessness that undermined Muungano's resourcefulness and ability to take imaginative leaps.

Beneath the predictability of stereotypes, however, Muungano's plays and performances brimmed with a sense of optimism that I found to be highly compelling. Muungano's performances conveyed a sense of hope, or what Loren Kruger calls "a subjunctive enactment of a desirable future . . . through the embodiment of ideas and ideologies in the performance of citizen-subjects" (1999, 10). Throughout my research, Muungano's performances often pushed the boundaries of the nation-state to include marginalized populations such as the working poor, southern ethnicities, and women. This expansiveness might seem at odds with the rigidity of its purist stance, but I believe that the two were connected. Despite state rhetoric that seeks to privilege tradition as a marker of national pride, tradition occupies a questionable status in the national imagination, seen as an embarrassing marker of cultural backwardness rather than as a touchstone of national pride. A traditionalist stance declared a sense of allegiance with disenfranchised Tanzanians for whom tradition served as a source of power. Tradition could be relied upon in ways that the state could not, the party could not, and neoliberal ideology could not. Traditionalist rhetoric provided a foundation upon which Muungano could find its footing and forge an alternative nation in which *walalahoi* could, at least occasionally, triumph.

Although Muungano churned out an array of traditionalist stereotypes, the company also *inhabited* indigenous practices and rural spaces in ways that did not domesticate tradition as a remnant of a fictional past. Muungano's version of the *bugobogobo* dance, which incorporated images of the Ugandan War and contemporary societal issues, helps to clarify this interpretation. The first part of the dance acknowledged its perceived origins as a Sukuma harvesting dance through the swinging of the hoes through the air and around the dancers' bodies. Then, the dancers replaced the hoes with wooden rifles. While they marched in place, they took aim over the heads of the spectators—a moment that paid tribute to the 1979 Ugandan War in which Tanzanian forces overthrew Idi Amin. After setting down the guns, the women and men divided into sides and began fighting each other in mimed hand-to-hand combat, enacting a stylized war between the sexes. This final segment was meant to acknowledge the burgeoning women's movement and thus incorporate contemporary societal issues into the dance. After demonstrating female virtuosity in work and in war, the dance ended with a reminder that despite their abilities, Tanzanian women were still struggling for their rights. This interpretation illustrates Muungano's use of traditionalist discourse as a *resource* rather than a limitation in which nostalgia gave way to action.

Whereas Muungano embraced tradition, TOT scorned it. TOT's flashy performances, dominated by its expensive Bose sound system, seemed to shrug off the shackles of authenticity. Even the characters in *maigizo* mocked traditional practices as old-fashioned and backward, turning instead to wealth and urban sophistication as the keys to success. In conversations with students and faculty at the College of Arts in Bagamoyo, which considers itself the "savior" of the traditional arts (Vestin 1993, 16), TOT was regularly condemned for its lack of respect for *utamaduni*. Muungano, however, was praised for its attempts to maintain a degree of authenticity. A clear-cut demarcation between the two companies could be discerned in the performances as well as through their respective tactics of self-promotion.

Upon closer examination, however, TOT's attitude toward tradition cannot be so easily summarized. Despite its overriding agenda to cultivate a hip and modern image, the company faithfully included *ngoma* in its repertory. This peon to cultural nationalism endured despite its primitivist connotations for urban Tanzanians that are linked to a colonial history in which the forms were suppressed as "uncivilized" or resuscitated as safe expressions of traditional culture. Siri Lange tells of a family of Chagga, considered one of the most educated and modernized ethnic groups,[13] who scorned *ngoma* as "a dirty thing of the uncivilized tribes of the south, from people who they claimed were unhygienic and who engaged in witchcraft and sorcery" (1995, 59). Similarly, students at the College of Arts admitted to me that they would "feel shame" (*kuona aibu*) if their friends in Dar es Salaam or Arusha saw them perform *ngoma,* using the words *dirty* (*chafu*) and *uncivilized* (*ushenzi*) to explain the perception of *ngoma* in urban settings. These connotations of *ngoma* seemed to clash with TOT's carefully cultivated image as modern and hip.

TOT resolved this contradiction through a process of rehabilitation. In 1997, TOT gradually eliminated the southern dances and instead filled the *ngoma* "slot" with dances from the northern ethnic groups of the Kuria and the Sukuma, the pastoralist Maasai, the southwestern Nyakyusa, and the coastal Zaramo.[14] The significance of this move is contextualized in the dominance of *ngoma* from the southern region of Mtwara, which is populated by ethnicities, particularly the Makonde, who are widely perceived as "backward" due to their observances of certain indigenous practices such as scarification rites and initiation ceremonies. TOT prided itself on this newfound ethnic diversity that extended beyond the Makonde; for example, TOT's members enjoyed pointing out to me that Muungano and Mandela did not possess this degree of variety. Clearly, TOT was developing a new version of tradition that encompassed a greater number of ethnicities in its scope—a seemingly radical move that would recast tradition as a sign of inclusivity.

It was also recast as a sign of modernity. By the time I completed my fieldwork in 1997, each one of TOT's *ngoma,* with the interesting exception of *lizombe,* was consistently performed to an electronic beat. On the one hand, this integration of Western technology and traditional musical genres falls under the rubric of hybridity and thus serves as an example of a collective refusal to adhere to rigid categories. On the other hand, the integration of *ngoma* with the incessant use of electronic music—which is *perceived* as a sign of modernization—must be contextualized in TOT's anxiety to market itself as a hip alternative to the "old-timers" of Muungano and Mandela. In contrast to these two companies, which used only drums and other non-Western instruments during *ngoma,* TOT's *ngoma* selections were sandwiched together and painted over with a veneer of electronic music. In this particular context, I find Homi K. Bhabha's consideration of cultural difference to have more resonance than hybridity. He theorizes cultural difference as "the separation of totalized cultures that live unsullied by the intertextuality of their historical locations, safe in the Utopianism of a mythic memory of a unique collective identity" (1994, 34).[15] This strategy domesticates diversity and multiplicity through the process of pigeonholing them as uncontaminated acts. Through the totalizing effect of electronic music, TOT polished the rough edges of *ngoma* with connotations of modernization and flattened Tanzania's wealth of ethnicities into a homogenized nation.

In contrast to TOT's sense of polish and seamlessness, rough edges proliferated in the performances of Mandela. Its productions conveyed a cynical attitude in which the balm of tradition and the lure of modernity served as traps instead of assets. Its ideological stance was perhaps best captured in Filip De Boeck's description of "the space of tradition" as "only a poor image and faint reminder of a past long gone," whereas "the space of modernity . . . presents an illusion of development while remaining beyond the reach of most citizens" (1998, 28). In the process of performing what De Boeck calls a "catch-22 situation," Mandela produced a succession of ruptures that exploded binaristic notions of tradition and modernity in a radical critique of the post-socialist era.

Like Muungano, Mandela paid careful tribute to its cultural nationalist past, shunning the use of electronic music during *ngoma* and filling its lyrics with praises of *utamaduni.* Mandela's highly ambivalent conception of tradition, however, meant that tradition was simultaneously respected, feared, and mocked—an attitude that captured its complexity in postcolonial urban life. In the *maigizo,* for example, characters frequently consulted traditional healers (*waganga*), who were invariably depicted as buffoons. As the *mganga* enacted the spells, he rubbed his buttocks on the ground, uttered nonsensical chants, and rolled his eyes in an exaggerated manner to depict possession. Then, in an abrupt change of tone, these comic scenes concluded on a serious note, as in the example of a play about AIDS in which the *mganga* shed his exaggerated persona and informed the HIV-infected protagonist that the illness was too powerful for his charms.[16] These reminders of the role of tradition as a living, breathing entity in everyday life were perhaps best illustrated the day when one of Mandela's performers was possessed by a spirit in the midst of the performance and carried out of the social hall.[17] In the world of Mandela, tradition was a source of both comedy and fear.

Mandela's representations of modernization also struck an ambivalent note as the performances pushed against and expanded the rhetoric of development. In order to raise money, Mandela often participated in development projects, such as educating the public on malaria in collaboration with the Tanzanian chapter of the World Health Organization and promoting condoms with the National AIDS Control Programme. For these projects, they created an entire performance around an educational message, marshalling *ngoma* lyrics, *kwaya* songs, and *maigizo* for the cause. These development projects were recycled for Mandela's nightly performances in the bars; for example, songs about birth control, HIV, or malaria were often performed during *kwaya,* and audiences occasionally observed *maigizo* about characters suffering from AIDS. Although these moments responded to the cultural nationalist call for educational theatre that contributes to the building of the nation, Mandela complicated this rhetoric through its refusal to adhere to a simplistic notion of modernization in which development serves as a euphemism for Westernization. Even when Mandela created plays that were funded by development organizations, which could have easily derailed into condescending accounts of recalcitrant traditionalists learning the error of their ways, Mandela produced nuanced works that charted unique narratives and open-ended conclusions. In a play about malaria that was sponsored by the World Health Organization, Mzee Jangala's attempt to follow the advice of development "experts" led to chaos: in his zeal to clear the area of mosquitoes, he cut down the crops of his neighbors and sparked outrage throughout the village. Meanwhile, his wife followed the experts' advice and spent their meager savings on a mosquito net, which meant that no money remained to buy medicine to treat their daughter once she became infected.[18] The play suggested that solutions to deeply embedded problems such as malaria exceeded blind adherence to developmental slogans. Mandela was also capable of recasting these slogans in ironic contexts: for *ngoma,* the dancers often wore the same message-laden T-shirts used for the development campaign, which meant that a performance of erotic southern *ngoma* could simultaneously exhort the audience to wear condoms. Even when singing the developmental messages in *kwaya,* the troupe sang listlessly, and the women, who were supposed to be moving their arms in sync with the music, were frequently offbeat. This awkwardness was emblematic of Mandela's hesitancy toward embracing the message of modernization that the songs contained.

Figure 6. This play by Mandela, "Hali Hii" ("This Condition"), was originally created for an AIDS prevention program. Bakari Mbelemba (Mzee Jangala), who played the father of the young man who died of AIDS, can be seen at the rear of the coffin.

This section only scratches the surface of the multiple ways in which tradition, traditionalism, and traditionalization were deployed in popular performance. Its pervasive force throughout formations of morality, democracy, and power bore witness to its vigor and muscularity that defied notions of a rigid ideological stance that the term usually conveys. As the next section suggests, the traditionalism of Muungano and Mandela could not be disentangled from their articulations of democracy.

MORAL STANDARDS

The intersection between tradition and morality pervades Nyerere's philosophy of *ujamaa* since he believed that precolonial African society operated within an ethical system in which the basic needs of all of its members were fulfilled. Although he acknowledged the inequalities existed, "they were tempered by comparable family or social responsibilities, and they could never become gross and offensive to the social equality which was at the basis of the communal life" (1968b, 108). This conception of African socialism has been duly commented upon and critiqued for its fictionalizing and essentializing of the diversity of traditional cultures (Lofchie 1976). Others have recognized that Nyerere's homogenized version of traditional Africa concealed an investment in the suppression of dissent (Glassman 1995; Tripp 1997). Although an awareness of the reactionary and coercive qualities of his philosophy helps to counteract tendencies to lionize Nyerere and romanticize *ujamaa*, here I wish to emphasize the significance of *ujamaa* as the basis of Tanzanian morality and ethics.[19] As

Cranford Pratt has noted (1976; see also Metz 1982, 383), the guidelines and principles of *ujamaa* were meant to revive an egalitarian ethos that had been suppressed through the trauma of colonization. Nyerere's philosophy is based on the idea of the inherent goodness of humanity in which collective interests are put ahead of individual gain, a philosophy that manages to be both reactionary in its essentialism but also radical in its promise.

If, as newspaper headlines in the mid-1990s declared, *ujamaa* was effectively defunct as a political system, what kind of ethos was taking its place? Nyerere implied that the spirit of *ujamaa* survived the travails of colonialism, which suggests that the belief in the inherent goodness of humanity would perhaps persist despite the changing political structures. A less idealistic position would point out that privatization and a market-run economy encourage expressions of greed and avarice to efface conventional notions of morality. At the very least, the dismantlement of *ujamaa* would open up a new cultural space in which a greater diversity of social norms and mores could be tested and explored.

My research suggested that concepts of morality and justice were fluctuating. Accounts of popular performance in the 1980s and early 1990s indicate that the dramatic narratives of *maigizo* and *vichekesho* relied upon rigid concepts of poetic justice that called for the punishment of thieves, con men, and adulterers. In 1996 and 1997, however, these characters operated within an unpredictable social system, the laws of which could not be easily defined. Through a unique combination of despair, cynicism, and hope, *vichekesho* and *maigizo* provided provocative glimpses into these changing moral standards. In the process of exploring these narratives, I find that the contours of morality, tradition, and democratization were thoroughly intertwined.

An example of these moral codes was contained in the guise of slapstick comedy. *Vichekesho,* improvisational skits of about ten to fifteen minutes in length, have appeared in the popular theatre repertory from its earliest incarnations in the cultural troupes of the 1970s. These earlier versions of *vichekesho* invariably ended with the restoration of the social order and the affirmation of moral codes in which the culprits were punished. Even though the *vichekesho* of the 1980s were concerned primarily with relating humorous stories of daily Tanzanian life, these versions sought to moralize rather than ridicule: "The culprits or the quick-witted are usually engaged in anti-social behaviour and they are *always* caught, unmasked or brought to justice" (Lihamba 1985, 284, emphasis added). Mark Plane's exposure to *vichekesho* in the early 1990s revealed the use of slapstick, ridicule, and an exaggerated sense of reality "to point out the absurd, the vicissitudes of urban life, and to allow people to laugh at themselves" (1995, 78); still, he notes that the social order invariably triumphed in the end, which indicates that the emphasis upon conventional codes of morality remained relatively intact.

By the time I began my research in 1996, the *vichekesho* consistently concluded on a note of chaos.[20] The plots usually involved a domestic conflict concerning a love affair, an insult, or theft. As the conflict escalated, the social order intruded through the figures of policemen, fathers, and local representatives of the government (*wajumbe*).[21] Instead of restoring order, however, the authority figures became caught up in the struggle, and all of the characters began physically fighting each other, even if they were supposedly on the same side of the conflict. Although the violence was comically depicted, the fights were vivid in their lack of restraint. For example, a standard male character in *vichekesho* was the "pregnant guy," as I called him in my field notes because of the stuffing under his shirt. This stuffing was meant to provide padding for being hit multiple times in the stomach with a stick during the concluding fight. This unrestrained violence was meted out indiscriminately, regardless of the circumstances of the conflict and who was originally at fault. Through the medium of *vichekesho,* Muungano and Mandela gleefully overturned the social order through the mockery of traditional figures of authority.

Muungano and Mandela relied upon cross-gender play as another mode of ridicule, as both companies delighted in plots that centered on a father's curious penchant for wearing women's underwear.[22] In a typical scenario, a daughter of the household searches frantically for a missing article of clothing such as a slip, and she blames her sister for stealing it. Eventually, suspicion turns to the well-padded father, and the article of clothing would be discovered under his *kikoi* (pl. *vikoi*), a rectangular piece of cloth wrapped around the waist worn by coastal Muslim men. In one of Muungano's versions of this plot, the ubiquitous *mjumbe,* the local representative of CCM, was also recruited to look for the article of clothing. Interestingly, in the concluding brawl, both the father and the *mjumbe* were exposed in women's undergarments, meaning that the final moments revealed the seamy underside of state and patriarchal authority. It is noteworthy that Muslim men were the ones who were feminized and ridiculed, since their custom of wearing *vikoi* allowed their outer clothing to be easily ripped off to reveal lingerie underneath. Although certain norms were affirmed through gender and religious stereotypes, the form's sense of exuberance and mockery cannot be denied.

The *vichekesho* of Mandela also struck a political note through a critique of class privilege. Although conflicts between neighbors over money or material goods were a common feature of both Muungano's and Mandela's *vichekesho,*

Figure 7. In this *kichekesho* of Mandela, a young girl attacks her sister in the mistaken belief that she had stolen her slip. It is finally revealed that her father is wearing the slip under his *kikoi.*

Muungano's plots usually concerned a fairly substantial material object such as a radio or 100,000 shillings ($140). In Mandela's versions, conflicts erupted over much smaller items, such as a lost cigarette or 200 shillings (30 cents), but the actual fights were equally intense in a reflection of the economic desperation of its characters.[23] In an especially vivid *kichekesho,* a poor man demanded 1,000 shillings ($1.40) from his poorer neighbor to contribute to the emptying of his pit latrine, which the neighbor used since he did not have access to his own. When he failed to extract the money, the man planted feces by his neighbor's house to cause him trouble with the police, and the feces were smeared on the policeman's face in the ensuing brawl.[24] Such moments were characteristic of the harsh, cynical world of Mandela and undoubtedly resonated with the many spectators in the audience excluded from the supposed advantages of a liberalized economy.[25]

A comparison of Muungano's and Mandela's freewheeling *vichekesho* with TOT's domesticated versions helps to clarify their sense of originality. While Muungano and Mandela sought out innovative subject matter, TOT repeatedly used the same plot of a married woman luring a male passerby into her home.[26] Despite her repeated assurances that her husband was in Mwanza, his unexpected arrival interrupted their tryst, and the composed wife attempted to pass off her panicked lover as a brother. Instead of exuberant brawls in which hierarchies were overturned, the fight consisted of a relatively contained struggle between the returning husband and the panicked lover. Although the wordplay and humorous facial expressions of the actors ensured that the audiences enjoyed this particular *kichekesho,* the lack of physical action and unoriginal plot worked to tame one of the most unruly forms of popular performance.

As the schedule of the performance moved from the relatively simple plots of *vichekesho* to the convoluted tales of *maigizo,* tropes of transformation and morality became increasingly entangled and complex. Like *vichekesho, maigizo* previously upheld conventional moral codes. Plane and Lange both note that the plots of *maigizo* in the early 1990s consistently contained moral lessons (Lange 1995, 119, 121–136; Plane 1995, 135–136), which meant that good characters were rewarded and evil ones punished.[27] By the mid-1990s, changing rules culminated in an unstable, even nihilistic world.

TOT's plays epitomized this shift as the company delighted in presenting *maigizo* in which unethical characters triumph over the honest ones. In an especially popular play, the parents urged their daughter to desert her hardworking, honest husband for a rich, highly educated African who spoke only Arabic and English. As the deserted husband exited weeping—collecting several coins from sympathetic female spectators along the way—the rich man carried off his new wife in his arms to Europe, with the gleeful parents close behind.[28] On the one hand, the punishment of the honest husband and reward of the scheming parents suggested a kind of insouciance toward established social norms and therefore could be linked to new formations of identity in a post-socialist era. On the other hand, the ultimately triumphant characters in TOT's plays were consistently members of the upper class, and the poor, honest *walalahoi* were caught in a narrative of inevitable defeat. In the end, these plays reaffirmed the superiority of the privileged class and the stability of the status quo.

Although a cynical tone also pervaded the *maigizo* of Mandela, it intermingled with a sense of despair. Rarely would an upper-class character appear in its plays; instead, as in Mandela's *vichekesho,* all of the characters were united in their quest for economic survival. Instead of encouraging a sense of collaboration, this desperation often meant that the characters turned on each other. In its plays, none of the characters enjoyed a happy ending; instead, closure usually consisted of unresolved conflict and an atmosphere of mutual hostility. Although this lack of closure is reminiscent of *vichekesho,* Mandela's plays lacked the form's characteristic playful tone but instead conveyed a tone of desperation. In this world, hierarchies of class remained firmly in place.

In contrast to TOT's cynicism and Mandela's pessimism, Muungano alone conveyed a sense of optimism as its disenfranchised characters could occasionally triumph. This triumph usually occurred through the medium of romantic love—a narrative device that TOT's and Mandela's plays distinctly lacked. Although weddings, affairs, and unplanned pregnancies were plentiful in the plays of all three companies, these events usually served as motivations or strategies to achieve economic gain in the plays of TOT and Mandela. For example, a marriage might have served as a means for a poor woman to gain access to the bridegroom's wealth or as a way for parents to free themselves from the economic burden of a daughter. But in the case of Muungano, marriage created a utopic realm in which hierarchies of ethnicity, urban/rural divides, or class at least temporarily dissolved in its characteristic happy endings. In Muungano's world, a more hopeful nation began to emerge in which the disempowered could escape the quagmires of poverty and defeat.

A comparison of father figures helps to clarify the differences between Muungano and Mandela. In the *maigizo* of both companies, the father's authority seemed precarious given his children's penchant for disobedience and even ridicule. Mzee Jangala, a recurring character in Mandela's plays, frequently came to blows with his children, who refused his country lifestyle and ran off to the city against his wishes; in Muungano, the fathers watched in dismay as their daughters insisted upon marrying husbands of their choice. In Mandela's plays, however, the rebelling child was usually punished, as in "He Who Does Not Listen" ("Asiyesikia la Mkuu"), in which a disrespectful son who mistreated his father became insane and therefore received his "just" reward.[29] In contrast, the children in Muungano escaped censure through the appeal of true love. In "Loving Each Other Shouldn't Be Trouble" ("Kujuana Isiwe Taabu") a tough, cigarette-smoking young daughter refuses to accept her father's choice of husband in favor of her lover, another rebellious and angry youth.[30] Typically, the daughter would have served as a symbol of the ills of urban society and subsequently be punished. In a similar *igizo* that Muungano performed in the late 1980s, the young girl became pregnant and died as the result of a surreptitious abortion (Lange 1995, 130–132). In "Loving Each Other," however, the street-wise girl was sympathetically portrayed, and her father finally capitulated to her will. The headstrong daughter, who could be perceived as a symbol of the perceived ills of urban society in her refusal of gender and age norms, triumphs in the end.

I believe that these domestic rebellions contained political overtones. Of those few plays I found that explicitly addressed multipartyism or CCM, all relied upon an allegorical use of the family to express either criticism or praise. The symbolic use of the family is, of course, typical in state discourse as it helps to legitimize its authority, "offer[ing] a 'natural' figure for sanctioning national *hierarchy* within a putative organic *unity* of interests" (McClintock 1995, 357). In his speeches, Nyerere regularly invoked the inherent generosity and economic egalitarianism of the "traditional" African family to shore up the seeming naturalness of a socialist system; even *ujamaa* itself translates to "familyhood."

Playwrights and theatre companies who aimed to criticize CCM's dominance strategically appropriated the trope of family to confront national hierarchies. For example, two plays that explicitly criticized multipartyism—neither of which were performed by the three companies being discussed—used a tyrannical father to represent CCM. His wives and children, who symbolized the opposition parties, banded together to challenge his dominance.[31] On a more subtle level, the destabilizations of patriarchal authority found in the plays of Muungano and Mandela suggested a reworking of the "miniature nation" (in Tripp 1996, 298) within the household to reclaim and rehabilitate the process of democratization of which CCM professed its support.

Again, a comparison with TOT clarifies this political bent. Whereas the plays of Mandela and Muungano frequently revolved around the conflict between parents and children, this conflict simply did not exist in the world of TOT. Like the daughter who agreed to her parents' get-rich-quick scheme in the play about the honest husband who was deserted for a rich one, the children never challenged their parents' wishes. This seamlessness of parental authority extended to *vichekesho* as well, for only Muungano and Mandela ridiculed father figures through feminizing them. This avoidance of one of the most popular topics of *maigizo* was suggestive of TOT's investment in maintaining authority. The father might be corrupt, but he remained firmly in control.

I believe that Muungano and Mandela enacted what Awam Amkpa terms "postcolonial desire," which he glosses as "the act of imagining, living, and negotiating a social reality based on democracy, cultural pluralism and social justice" (2004, 10). Unlike TOT, neither troupe was sponsored by a political party and therefore lacked the economic and political resources that their rival enjoyed. From these positions of disenfranchisement, their methods of questioning and testing the status quo positioned them as opposition parties against the conservative stronghold of TOT. As an alternative to the global mandates of multipartyism and a market-driven economy, Muungano and Mandela broadened the scope of the debate to include the urban and rural poor.

Stuart Hall astutely notes that "[h]egemonizing is hard work" (in Denning 1990, 14). Throughout this chapter, I have repeatedly referred to TOT's veiled discourses of power as manifested through its interpretations of tradition and morality. Muungano and Mandela might have actively engaged in a nationalist debate, but TOT constantly intervened to shape its terms. In the final section, I explore the more explicit ways in which TOT's "hard work" was conducted on behalf of CCM.

POWER PLAYS

In contrast to Muungano and Mandela, TOT's affiliation with the ruling party entailed a commitment to preserving the status quo despite the changing political climate. In critical theory, the term "negotiation" is typically associated with peripheral communities seeking to evade the grasp of the dominant order. In a discussion of the tendency to valorize this concept, Spivak cautions that "[i]f we think of negotiation only as a positive term, then I think we are sort of laundering it in some ways" (1990, 148). In a similar fashion, I suspect that the idea of creativity is "sort of" laundered, particularly in the context of African popular culture. Political theorist Célestin Monga has called attention to "the remarkable creativity of African leaders," who have appropriated the rhetoric of democracy to serve their despotic purposes and thus "have brought their discourse and repressive techniques up to date" (1996, 47). Mbembe echoes Monga when he writes that the era of democratization and weakened states have ushered in "new forms of legitimate domination" and "formulas of authority built on other foundations" (2001, 76). Although the Tanzanian state is less repressive than the examples Monga and Mbembe use—most notably Cameroon—their warnings resonate throughout this discussion of TOT, whose creative appropriation of the techniques of negotiation serves as a reminder that new forms of domination exist alongside new formations of national identity.

When TOT was first founded in 1992, John Komba was straightforward about TOT's links to CCM (Askew 2002, 247). By the time I began my fieldwork, this affiliation with the party had become more covert, perhaps in response to the protests of opposition parties that identified TOT as an unfair advantage (264). Komba had begun to disavow TOT's political affiliation through his insistence that TOT simply works for peace and national unity (*Guardian* 1996; 1997b). As if to prove this apolitical stance, TOT adopted a fervent cultural nationalist rhetoric that surpassed even Muungano's. Although all of the troupes sang praises of Tanzanian *utamaduni* in *ngoma*, TOT went a step further and also included such lyrics in *muziki wa dansi* and *kwaya*. Identical rhetoric was thus repeated through a variety of musical genres, leaving the innocuous word of *utamaduni* ringing in the audience's ears after a performance. This tactic of strategic nationalism helped to disguise TOT's aim to support and promote the ruling political party.

Alternatively, as I discovered, Komba resorted to denial. In an interview with Askew in 1993, Komba stated outright that TOT was created for the promotion of CCM in response to the introduction of the multiparty system (2002, 252). Interestingly, his open acknowledgment with Askew was not repeated in my presence. During a performance in the Dar es Salaam neighborhood of Temeke, a stronghold of the opposition party NCCR-Mageuzi, the TOT members wore T-shirts with President Benjamin Mkapa's face printed on the front and "CCM #1" emblazoned on the back throughout the performance.[32] I had previously seen the performers occasionally wear these shirts for an *ngoma*, but never had I seen them worn so insistently throughout the performance. Even characters in the dramatic sketches wore the shirts, with other costume pieces such as *khanga* (patterned cloths) draped over them in such a way that Mkapa's face still peered out. I asked Komba about the shirts in a fairly indirect way, mentioning I was curious about the costume choices for the evening. Komba knew at once to what I was referring and said firmly that the T-shirts were merely "decoration" (*urembo*). I alluded to the Temeke setting; Komba simply repeated himself. Typically, in postcolonial Africa, such subterfuge and denials are attributed to subordinate groups attempting to avoid censure from above; here, the pattern was reversed.

A closer examination of TOT's musical acts illustrates the infiltration of CCM politics into the performance itself. TOT prided itself on its musical genres; as readers might recall from the previous chapter, its initial success was at least partly due to Komba's national fame as a composer and singer of *kwaya* music, which had earned him the nickname "Dr. Komba." To reward his popular compositions in praise of CCM such as "CCM Ni Nambari Wani" (CCM Is #1), the party elected him to the prestigious National Executive Committee, which exerts considerable power over the selection of political candidates. During my fieldwork, Komba never performed these praise songs except in the context of political rallies or private CCM functions because of regulations that allowed political campaigning to take place only in the daytime in open areas. In other words, to sing "CCM Is #1" in a bar at night would have been illegal. Although TOT technically adhered to these regulations, its investment in reaffirming structures of power was still forcefully present. For example, in the popular song "Mambo Sasa" (Matters Now), Komba laments the violence in Rwanda, Burundi, Somalia, and Mozambique. In the concluding lyrics, TOT suddenly praises "the Party" for keeping the peace in Tanzania. This brief reference was meant to remind the audience of CCM's main selling point in the multiparty era—its perceived success in creating a relatively stable and peaceful country. Although every spectator would have known to which party he was referring, the vagueness of the phrase apparently allowed TOT to adhere to campaign laws. These not-so-subtle reminders of CCM's supremacy served as ideological underpinnings for the company's rhetorical claims of preserving *utamaduni* and national peace.

Taarab has also fallen prey to TOT's political agenda. A brief note of historical context will help to clarify the significance of this particular appropriation. Although *kwaya* has served as a tool to promote various political agendas since independence, *taarab* has generally been consigned to the realm of "pure" entertainment.[33] This wildly popular form is dominated by women, both as performers and as fans. During one of Muungano's performances, when an *igizo* was becoming tedious, some of the women in the audience began calling out for the *igizo* to end so that the *taarab* music could start. When the musicians finally began arranging the stage for *taarab,* the women loudly expressed their approval, pointing out that they had been waiting for it throughout the show.[34] These women were characteristic of the outspoken and passionate *taarab* fans in the audience, who responded to the singers by swarming onto the stage to dance while belting out the words to their favorite songs. It was also noteworthy that the singers themselves were invariably women. Although each company included male *taarab* singers, their dignified and restrained tones were usually overshadowed by the passion and intensity of the charismatic Muslim female performers.

In a display of its creative powers of appropriation, TOT harnessed this passion and intensity for political gain. In November 1997, my associate, Robert Ajwang', and I accompanied TOT on a CCM campaign in the Kagera region located in northwestern Tanzania.[35] I had expected TOT to follow the usual custom of singing political praises of the candidate through *ngoma* and *kwaya;* instead, aside from a few choir songs such as the inevitable "CCM Is #1," TOT almost exclusively performed *taarab.* They chose *taarab* songs with open metaphors that could easily be interpreted to fit the campaign; for example, they sang a popular song cautioning the listeners that they are deceiving themselves by "jumping around," as well as a song about being careful what they put in their mouth.[36] Although these compositions would typically be heard as cautions against marital infidelity, in this context they warned the observers against being "unfaithful" to CCM. The performers held green CCM flags as they sang, apparently to ensure that the connection would not be missed. Although individual spectators undoubtedly interpreted these songs to suit their own personal histories and agendas regardless of TOT's attempts to influence their reception, these examples of the "erotics of politics" (Sommer 1990, 76) suggest that shades of CCM also emerged in the sexual innuendo of *taarab.* This strategy is especially noteworthy given that NCCR-Mageuzi, CCM's most significant rival, was popular among women due to the outspoken support for women's rights of the 1995 NCCR presidential candidate, Augustine Mrema (Maliyamkono 1995, 48). Perhaps, through its daring *taarab* music, TOT intended to cultivate a wide following among female fans who could conceivably tip the scales at the ballot box in favor of CCM.

Although this political use of *taarab* could be categorized as a relatively straightforward example of cultural appropriation, TOT's interpretation of *muziki wa dansi* proves more ambiguous. On October 2, 1997, TOT introduced a new *muziki* style called *achimenengule* that asserted TOT's cultural power on the one hand while working to conceal its political agenda on the other. The "inauguration" of *achimenengule* occurred during its first performance after receiving the new sound system.[37] After procuring the equipment in August, the company spent a month in the nearby town of Morogoro to learn new *ngoma* and practice with the instruments. Meanwhile, they dropped tantalizing hints to reporters about a special type of music they were secretly developing. This publicity strategy guaranteed the presence of numerous journalists at the inauguration at the Kilimanjaro Hotel, which at the time was one of the most elite hotels in Dar es Salaam. The journalists described the event in glittering detail to TOT's most devoted fans—the underclass of Dar es Salaam excluded from the event itself. To mark the significance of the occasion, several prominent CCM officials attended, including former prime minister Rashid Kawawa and the current minister for internal affairs. The presence of power helped to sanction a surprising interpretation of national culture.

This highly publicized event was the showcase for the long-awaited debut of *achimenengule*. Three male singers, dressed in flashy black-and-white patterned suits, performed two songs that (to my untrained ears) sounded like a livelier version of popular Swahili music with strong Congolese overtones.[38] One of these two songs was frequently punctuated with the chorus "*achimenengule, wa wa!*" At one point in both songs, three of the younger female performers, dressed in gaudy halter tops and miniskirts, entered to dance in the highly sexual Congolese style of *ndombolo,* a version of the wildly popular *soukous.* Through their movements, the Congolese connotations of the new Tanzanian style became even more pronounced. When they re-entered for the second song, the female dancers lined up in front of the three male singers, who acted out their sexual arousal by thrusting their hips into the women's buttocks. The three women then entered into the audience and selected a male spectator for whom they gyrated their hips. In the Kilimanjaro show, the CCM officials were the selected audience members for these "private" performances. This pattern remained basically the same for the remaining performances of TOT that I saw until my departure two months later, as *achimenengule* had become a permanent part of its repertory.

Once the final notes of *achimenengule* had faded, Komba made a formal speech to the Kilimanjaro audience, requesting other Tanzanian musicians to use the *achimenengule* style in order to develop a national style of dance. Although the press warmly received this announcement (*Spoti* 1997; *Lete Raha* 1997a), one reporter ventured the opinion that *achimenengule* was more Congolese than Tanzanian (*Lete Raha* 1997b). In response, Komba claimed that *achimenengule* was inspired by Ngoni *ngoma* moves, and he pointed out that its name means "let's dance" in the Ngoni language. He admitted that the dance might resemble *ndombolo* but insisted that *achimenengule* is based upon Tanzanian *ngoma* and is

Figure 8. TOT's inaugural version of *achimenengule* in 1997.

uniquely designed to appeal to Tanzanian tastes (*Lete Raha* 1997b). My point here is not to determine the "authenticity" of *achimenengule* as a Tanzanian dance but to emphasize Komba's forcefulness in describing the dance as an expression of national culture. Again, this nationalist rhetoric would theoretically affirm the company's professed aim to promote Tanzanian culture and detract attention from its political agenda. In this instance, however, Komba's decision to label *achimenengule* as national music also demonstrates his sense of confidence and power. Of all the forms that made up the popular performance, *muziki wa dansi* proved especially resistant to nationalization. Even this early version of *achimenengule* mostly exhorted the audience members to dance; the lyrics did not include a single reference to *utamaduni* or Tanzania to shore up Komba's nationalist claims. With a rhetorical flourish, Komba confidently brought it into the nationalist fold, accompanied by eroticized young women who produced "private" performances for officials of the state.

It is axiomatic that the exertion of power provokes acts of resistance. Although "resistance" might be too strong a word in this particular instance, it is noteworthy that individual spectators enjoyed calling attention to TOT's political affiliation as if in mockery of its barrage of musical and spoken refrains of *utamaduni* that supposedly concealed these links. In November 1996, TOT organized a "Miss TOT" beauty contest, a lavish affair in which TOT's performance preceded the actual contest.[39] CCM was not mentioned once throughout the event, nor did the Mkapa T-shirts make an appearance. The audiences were quick to fill in TOT's silence on their own terms when Komba announced the guest of honor, an official from the Ministry of Finance. In response, one young man called out mockingly that he wanted the guest of honor to be Mrema, who, ever since his defeat in the 1995 elections, has persisted as a thorn in CCM's side. The young man's comment, which caused the audience to erupt into laughter, marked the shadowy presence of CCM despite Komba's attempts at concealment.

By naming CCM's presence, the young man's comment gestured to the potential of spectators to make this affiliation visible and therefore defuse its power. A similar moment occurred during the Kagera political rally in Muleba district previously described. A young man hissed "*fi-si*-M" during Komba's singing of "CCM #1."[40] (*Fisi,* pronounced "fee-see," is the Swahili word for hyena.) His witticism undercut the mindless slogan repeated endlessly throughout the song.

But unlike the appreciative laughter that characterized the "Miss TOT" contest, this young man in Muleba stood alone, surrounded by cheering crowds singing enthusiastically along with Komba.[41] This discussion of TOT provides a vivid warning against celebrating the multivocality that characterizes the "new" Tanzania. To do so would overlook the ways in which Western models of democracy have inadvertently allowed CCM to shore up its support. In a nuanced reading of the impact of economic and political liberalization on Tanzania, Kathleen Mulligan-Hansel acknowledges that "relaxed controls on freedom of speech and freedom of association, as well as new opportunities for the accumulation of wealth, do provide some Tanzanians with increased room for maneuver in the liberalizing political economy" (1999, 80). She cautions, however, that "liberalization should not be seen as completely transformative" given the pervasive manner in which CCM has strategically maintained its dominance. Outward appearances of plurality and heterogeneity work to conceal "significant continuity between the one-party and multi-party periods" (37).

In view of Mulligan-Hansel's remarks, Tanzanian popular performance in the mid-1990s cannot be understood simply as a manifestation of nascent democratization. A historical perspective of Tanzanian performance helps to clarify further the problems of this approach. During the 1970s and early 1980s, Dar es Salaam boasted a staggering number of cultural troupes and commercial theatre troupes that faced off in the city's social halls and bars in a fierce display of multivocality that predated the advent of multiparty democracy in the mid-1980s. Under the gaze of a single-party system, a dizzying variety of cultural troupes, independently owned companies, and army troupes vied for audiences in the social halls of bars in a display of heterogeneity par excellence. In contrast, the triad of Muungano, TOT, and Mandela could be interpreted as a collapse of diversity rather than a celebration of democracy. Under the system of socialism, the government might have dominated the media, but the performance networks thrived and proliferated in a testament of local agency and strength.[42]

I defer these questions and interpretations to the chapters that follow. The remainder of this book continues its exploration of alternative, collaborative, or strategic nationalisms that TOT, Muungano, and Mandela produced. In closing, I only wish to note that consolidation cannot be equated with silence. Though a diminished sense of plurality might have characterized the popular theatre scene of the 1990s, the three companies articulated agendas, identities, and ideologies with a vigorousness that cannot be denied.

PART TWO

Sexing the Nation

THREE

National Erotica

The Politics of Ngoma

My first exposure to *ngoma* on the Tanzanian popular stage was Mandela's version of *sindimba,* the most famous—and notorious—dance throughout the country. As a newly arrived researcher on constructions of gender and national identity in popular theatre, I tried to suppress my unease as I watched the women dance in a circle, swaying their hips in a sexually inviting way. Meanwhile, the men of the troupe approached them from behind and "tried out" each in turn. A male dancer with an especially youthful appearance approached one of the older female dancers and ground his hips into hers, eliciting shouts of laughter from the audience: "She can be your mother! Mind your manners!" (*Anaweza kuwa mama yako! Shika adabu yako!*).[1] The women steadfastly danced in their circle, smiling all the while. I dutifully watched as Western stereotypes of the "bestial sexual license of the African" (Bhabha 1994, 66) and the passive African woman played out before my discomfited gaze.

In the course of my fieldwork, I saw *sindimba* frequently performed by all three of the popular troupes in my study, in addition to several other *ngoma* that accentuated the women's erotic movements of the hips and pelvis. In contrast, the male dancers vigorously stamped their feet, turned cartwheels, and improvised comic routines around their pursuit of the ever-smiling, hip-swaying women. I learned that this hip-swaying movement, called *kukata kiuno* (to cut the waist), had become virtually synonymous with the concept of *ngoma* in the cultural imagination. The ubiquity of this image could be explained as an inevitable result of urban commodification in which African traditional dances are appropriated in order to "entertain the urban elite and reassure the developing nation that it has not ignored its national culture" (Desai 1990, 68). From this perspective, one might argue that the process of appropriation and commodification domesticated a thriving performance tradition into a cultural stereotype of African tradition. In the process, the female body was contained through this repetitive, rotating motion.

This containment, however, occurred through a complex process of inventing, counterinventing, and reinventing tradition. In this chapter, I examine the state's appropriation of *ngoma* as a national symbol and the transformation of this symbol in the domain of popular culture. Using *kukata kiuno* as a springboard for this analysis, I find that traditional narratives of top-down and grassroots nationalism are overturned in favor of a dynamic process of collaboration and contestation. Tanzania One Theatre (TOT), Muungano, and Mandela produced gleeful narratives of vigor and sexuality in which boundaries of official and popular culture were repeatedly dissolved.

In the midst of these testimonies of creativity, however, the passivity of the hip-swaying, ever-smiling female dancer persisted—as did my sense of unease that this image provoked. On the one hand, to criticize the suppression of female subjectivity in *ngoma* would simply adhere to a hegemonic brand of Western feminism that seeks to judge rather than to understand.[2] On the other hand, to ignore the persistence of this image would overlook the ways in which technologies of power permeate popular culture. In order to negotiate this conundrum, I emphasize the cultural anxiety that sustains this image of the eroticized, passive Tanzanian woman. *Ngoma* served as a cultural "sore zone" (Herzfeld 1997, 27) between colonial administrators and their Tanganyikan subjects, between the postcolonial state and theatre artists, and, more recently, between the College of Arts and popular troupes. This chapter reveals that the dancing female body provided the terrain upon which these tensions played out.

The final section of this chapter employs the concept of agency as a means of counteracting the narrative of subjugation and commodification. In an exploration of two provocative examples of female dancers who seized the "'right' to signify from the periphery of authorized power and privilege" (Bhabha 1994, 2), I demonstrate how individual performers use *ngoma* to script alternative narratives of resilience and creativity. The tried-and-true concept of agency has traditionally allowed Western scholars of African performance scholars to sidestep the academic pitfall of overdetermining neocolonial modes of power through emphasizing the actions of ordinary Tanzanians. In a provocative article, however, Francis B. Nyamnjoh complicates theories of agency in African contexts. He warns that "[t]oo much of the theory of agency merely asks about the empowerment of the individual and the extent to which individuals are creators or creatures of the social structures wherein they operate" and thus negates complicated networks of interdependency that often characterize African relationships and interactions (2002, 111). In a similar vein, I find that those moments of female agency depend upon the isolated actions of an individual and thus clarify the limited function of *ngoma* as a forum for female expression in urban popular culture.

INVENTIONS OF TRADITION

In the popular theatre performances that I observed, the emcees consistently announced the ethnic "origins" of *ngoma:* "And now we will have *kitoto* of the Ngoni! Following the acrobatics will be *bugobogobo* of the Sukuma!" The troupe would then launch into a ten-to-fifteen minute version of an *ngoma* that was undoubtedly a far more simplified version than what would be found in local contexts where Sukuma or Ngoni people predominated. Even in these condensed, perhaps rudimentary versions, however, *ngoma* contained a host of contradictions.

The uncomplicated use of words such as *Ngoni* and *Sukuma* belie a complicated history of the construction of ethnicity. As John Iliffe has pointed out, the British policy of indirect rule—governance through local administrations—created an agenda of "finding the chief," which led to the categorization of loosely associated groups into bounded tribal units. Since these efforts coincided with similar trends occurring among the Tanganyikans themselves, they appropriated the concept of ethnic identity instead of opposing it. "Europeans believed Africans belonged to tribes," Iliffe remarks in an oft-quoted phrase, "Africans built tribes to belong to" (1979, 324). *Ngoma* became a handy marker of ethnic affiliation, as demonstrated in the zeal of colonial administrators and missionaries to promote supposedly safe dances in place of "Bolshevistic," multi-ethnic ones like *beni* (Ranger 1975, 129).[3]

In a postcolonial context, the emcees' faithful iterations of ethnic origins might seem inconsistent with the state's agenda to construct a unified society. Once independence was officially secured in 1961, the state replaced the colonial agenda of "finding the chief" with the postcolonial one of *losing* the chief in order to substitute traditional authority for that of the state. Long-established villages were uprooted in the name of *ujamaa,* and secondary school students, teachers, and government officials were frequently transferred to distant regions in order to facilitate the intermingling of ethnic groups. Perhaps most importantly, the Swahili language became the language of instruction in all primary schools and the official language in state institutions, unifying the approximately 130 ethnic groups through a common Bantu language. Despite murmurings of resentment against all of these policies (Tripp 1997, 34), the state resolutely pursued what has been termed "arguably the most serious nation-building program in sub-Saharan Africa" (Miguel 2004, 360).

In the case of *ngoma,* however, this program took a series of detours. Despite rhetorical calls for "the development of our tribal cultures into one national culture" (Mbughuni 1974, 18), a process of legislation harking back to colonial management continued to designate *ngoma* as a marker of ethnic identity. In addition to founding the National Dance Troupe, the newly created Ministry of Culture took steps to ensure that its influence trickled down to the local level, building what Kelly Askew calls "a cultural administrative hierarchy" (1997, 287) through the formation of regional and district cultural committees and the appointment of cultural officers, who were charged with guiding the development of national culture. This hierarchy created an intricate network of bureaucratic procedures through which dynamic and ephemeral performance traditions were carefully contained. For example, any group organized around the purpose of "culture" must be registered and a series of permits obtained from the appropriate officer. A simple performance outside the home region requires an additional flurry of permits for leaving the home region and entering the other region for the performance. A culture tax must also be paid, and certain percentages of the proceeds of the performance must be given to both the district and regional cultural offices, as well as used to pay various taxes (Askew 2002, 194). This complex system would theoretically ensure the penetration of homogeneous national culture in all levels of Tanzanian society by means of enabling cultural officers to substitute officially sanctioned *ngoma* in place of "tribal" ones. Instead, these procedures encouraged the formalizing and legislating of grassroots performance as the property of specific ethnic groups. *Ngoma* that had moved freely within and among regions were caught in the process of bureaucratic registration and categorized as belonging to a single group.

James G. Ellison (2000) recounts this process of legislating *ngoma* in his study of *ing'oma,* a thriving *ngoma* tradition of the Nyakyusa people in southwestern Tanzania that, like *beni,* is based on German military formations.

Ellison suggests that this registering and formalizing of *ing'oma* through bureaucratic procedures leads to its definition as a Nyakyusa tradition despite its past of spreading among a variety of ethnic groups and even reaching into neighboring Malawi. Ellison tells of a dance association from the neighboring region of Iringa that created a dance that resembled *ing'oma*. The group was denied permission to perform this particular dance at an official celebration because the government wanted "*ngoma za jadi*"—those dances that were originally from the area (2000, 231). Such implicit disapproval of cross-ethnic cultural exchange would further solidify ethnic divisions.

My own research also revealed authoritative tendencies among cultural officers. In a village in Mwanza region, I saw a Sukuma theatre troupe perform *bugobogobo,* a famous Sukuma *ngoma* that transforms the actions of harvesting into a powerful dance in which the dancers swing hoes around their bodies.[4] Like other Sukuma *ngoma* groups, they had previously experimented with incorporating imagery of the Ugandan War by exchanging their hoes for wooden rifles midway through the dance. Since this particular troupe was frequently called upon for official occasions, a cultural officer told them to discard the rifles in keeping with the "tradition" of the dance—a suggestion to which they complied. These efforts of cultural officers to contain *ngoma* within the bounded limits of ethnicity and tradition seemed more aligned with colonial agendas of divide and conquer than a nationalist intent to reclaim Tanzania's cultural heritage.

In an allusion to the fundamental illogic of nationalist discourse, Ernest Gellner writes: "Nationalism is not what it seems, and above all it is not what it seems to itself" (1983, 56). Perhaps this contradiction between the rhetoric of nationalization and the practice of tribalization could simply be chalked up to the fissures and ambivalence in national policy to which Gellner refers. But I believe a more substantive explanation is located in an understanding of the margins of society as sources of anxiety. In the process of homogenization, *ngoma* legislation and rhetoric consistently revolved around issues of female sexuality and rural, primitivist Tanzania. In a discussion of English nationalism, Bhabha draws attention to "how the demand for a holistic, representative vision of society could only be represented in a discourse that was [. . .] obsessively fixed upon, and uncertain of, the boundaries of society and the margins of the text" (1994, 144). This concept suggests that the rural and the female body, both located on the margins of the Tanzanian state, serve as objects of obsession and uncertainty. As such, these bodies are subjected to state control in the effort to maintain a holistic vision of the unified nation, producing an oscillating tension between ethnicity and gender in contemporary *ngoma* performance.

This framework helps to illuminate the restricted choreography that defined female movement in *ngoma*. The College of Arts, itself a bastion of cultural nationalism, provides a useful starting point for this analysis. The College of Arts was founded in 1975 in Dar es Salaam as a training center for the national performance troupes in dance, drama, and acrobatics. Upon the dismantlement of the troupes in 1981, the government transferred the College of Arts to Bagamoyo, a coastal town of approximately 30,000 inhabitants located seventy-five kilometers from the city. Until the road was paved in 2002, the journey to Bagamoyo consumed at least three hours, making frequent journeys to and from the city difficult. As a result of its relative isolation from the bustling urban center of Dar, the College of Arts was an inconvenient surrogate of national culture despite its mission to uphold the preservation of Tanzanian performance traditions and its official status as a branch of the Ministry of Education and Culture.[5] Neverthe-less, as a state-sponsored institution, the college's performances bore the seal of official culture and therefore provided a fascinating case study of national per-formance.[6]

In accordance with the official policy of nationalization, the college taught its multi-ethnic student body a variety of *ngoma* from across the country, which supposedly reflected the diversity of Tanzania's ethnic groups. A closer exami-nation reveals that this apparent diversity could be distilled into a group of eight *ngoma*, all of which have been taught to successive generations of students for years.[7] Like a canon of literature, these dances have been distilled into a repre-sentative group of Tanzanian *ngoma* that was sanctioned by the authority of the state. These *ngoma* have been disseminated throughout the country in ways similar to those of literary canons, which are locked into a cycle of self-perpetuation through their repetitive use in education. Students usually graduated knowing only this canon of *ngoma*, which they subsequently used in their own work as teachers in various far-flung regions of the country. The extent of this reach became apparent at the 1997 Bagamoyo Arts Festival when two children's groups from the regions of Mbeya and Tanga performed *ngoma* that matched those taught at the college.[8] Even during the performance of the Sukuma dance troupe in Mwanza region described above, I found myself watching the college's versions of the *ukala* of the coastal Zigua and the *ngokwa* of the Makonde. Instead of learning these dances through localized interactions with neighboring ethnic groups, these *ngoma* were picked up through exposure to former students or faculty of the College of Arts.

An exploration of gender codes in this representative sample of the tradi-tional arts helps to clarify the ways in which the female body serves as a touchstone for nationalist anxieties. Although the erotic movement of *kukata kiuno* was excluded, or at least subdued, in this canon of *ngoma*, the women were still marked as subordinate through restrained movements that contrasted sharply with the male students' expressions of vigor and strength. Moreover, the women almost always exited before the men, leaving the men to dominate the stage in the final moments of the *ngoma*. With the stage cleared of women, the male dancers were free to indulge in gymnastic or comic antics in a final reminder of their vigorous physicality.

Two dances in particular provided vivid examples of female subservience. The popular *ukala*, a dance of the coastal Zigua people, could be perceived as a celebration of male strength. The men mimed the use of a bow and arrow in the course of the hunt, stamping their feet in a vigorous rhythm. Once the men have mimed the successful kill, the women entered for a brief interlude during which they gathered the meat and celebrated the men's bravery through song. Their presence seemed superfluous in the narrative of the dance aside from accentu-ating the men's performance of masculinity. Even when the *ngoma* was inclusive of a greater variety of female movements, the narrative of restraint intruded. In the athletic harvest dance of *bugobogobo* described above, the teachers saw fit to add an introductory skit in which the female dancers greeted the men in true "traditional" fashion by kneeling before them. Of the many versions of *bugo-bogobo* that I observed, the college alone adopted this particular introduction that situated the women's energetic and powerful movements within a framework of submission.

Students invariably responded to my questions about this pattern with the rhetoric of traditionalism. They insisted that men were permitted greater freedom of movement because it was "true" (*ni kweli*) to the way ngoma is danced "in the village" (*kijijini*)—the usual barometer of a dance's authenticity. In an ironic example of the vast difference between the codified "invention of tradition" (Hobsbawm 1983) at the college and its fluid existence at the local level, a faculty member, Stumai Halili, conducted research on *ukala* among the Zigua people. She found that one of the lines in the song, in which the men order the female dancers to prepare the meat, was removed because it was disrespectful to women.[9] The faculty subsequently resolved to discard the offending line in order to conform to the "authentic" tradition. The teachers and students had become so accustomed to singing this line, however, that they usually neglected to exclude it. Although this forgetfulness was more indicative of the force of a codified habit than a reactionary agenda, the commensurability of this particular habit with the pattern of female oppression in the *ngoma* canon was strikingly coincidental.

In the concluding section of this chapter I address an example of *ngoma* in which the students challenged this narrative of subjugation. For the most part, however, the creativity and imagination that the students and faculty displayed in other performance traditions at the college were curtailed in *ngoma*. In contrast, the theatre companies in Dar es Salaam developed a more imaginative approach toward the state's agenda of cultural nationalism. Through a counterinvention of tradition, official ideals of decorum were playfully defied.

COUNTERINVENTIONS

Muungano, TOT, and Mandela provided a vivid point of contrast to the College of Arts. Instead of the restrained and decorous renditions of *ngoma* just described, these companies freely improvised their own versions of national culture through the creation of a "counter-canon." In an intriguing discussion of nationalism, anthropologist Michael Herzfeld suggests the "possibility of the subtle recastings of official discourses that we might call *counter*inventions of tradition, in which local and minority groups variously (and often discordantly) propose a host of alternative pasts" (1997, 12; emphasis added). The official version of the precolonial past, as adopted by the College of Arts, excluded the erotic dances of the south such as the *sindimba* described above. In contrast, the popular troupes proposed an alternative past through their "subtle recastings" of the *ngoma* canon in which the sexuality of southern *ngoma* prevailed.

This counter-canon was based upon suggestive choreography. Although the popular troupes have historically used *ngoma* lyrics to praise the government and CCM, the physical movements flouted state directives that called for subdued sexuality. This juxtaposition produced a pattern in which sexual movements were danced to the tune of official praise. Theatre scholars at the University of Dar es Salaam reacted uneasily to these spectacles, as demonstrated in Elias Songoyi's study of the commercialization of *ngoma*. After relating his experience of watching a cultural troupe perform the erotic *lizombe* while singing "The chairman of Tanzania, Nyerere / Live for ever," he rails:

> [A]s one watched he could clearly see that there was no correspondence between the vigorous [. . .] waist wriggling and stamping on the one hand and the song on the other hand. What was all the violent waist wriggling [. . .] expressing? Happiness? Not at all. (1983, 34)

Leaving it to the reader to answer the question of what the dance *was* expressing, Songoyi proceeds to lament that in urban versions of *ngoma,* "movement is all that matters," as opposed to rural versions in which the lyrics provide a vehicle for responding to immediate local concerns. The movement "that matters" was, and continues to be, *kukata kiuno. Lizombe,* a *ngoma* of the southern Ngoni ethnic group, is second only to *sindimba* in notoriety for its overt simulations of sexual intercourse within the choreography.

Although the popular troupes were commonly blamed for the supposed degradation of *ngoma,* this particular recasting of tradition predated the formation of the popular urban troupes in the 1970s. In the early 1960s, shortly after independence, the government banned *sindimba* in public performances (Lange 1995, 56), indicating that authorities were already trying to establish a suitably tasteful "canon" of *ngoma.* The inevitable failure of these attempts can be traced to the 1970s, when several major parastatals in Dar es Salaam incorporated local *sindimba* groups in the formation of their own cultural troupes.[10] This process of appropriation shored up the tentative links of *sindimba* with cultural nationalism and patriotism. Louis A. Mbughuni and Gabriel Ruhumbika refer to *sindimba*'s enduring popularity in their critique of Tanzania's cultural policy:

> If you ask a primary school boy what *utamaduni,* culture, means the answer will most certainly be: *Sindimba*—a traditional dance which apparently is the favourite of school-masters, even though when performed out of context, as it is at the schools, it borders on obscenity. (1974, 276)

Schools and parastatals were encouraged to promote traditional dance in the interests of fostering national culture. Both institutions, however, cast tradition as they saw fit and participated in the eroticization of official rhetoric.

The conflation of *sindimba* with national culture endured, despite the Ministry of Culture's efforts to separate the two. Amandina Lihamba cites a ministry

Figure 9. One of the more notorious moments of TOT's *lizombe.*

directive from the 1980s that reiterates its stand on sexually explicit performances: "It is clearly understood that the guidelines for Tanzania emphasize national integrity and respect. Therefore, the nation forbids all acts which are hooliganistic in nature and corrupt values for the good upbringing of children" (in Lihamba 1985, 480). The directive then mentions nudity, vigorous hip movements "without cause," and fornication as examples of actions that were unsuitable for the stage. The positioning of *kukata kiuno* in the same category as the sexual act itself implies the magnitude of the officials' distress. More recently, an article in the English-language newspaper the *Guardian* bemoaned "the continuing waist wriggling culture," calling it the "African version [. . .] of the worldwide provocative music [referring to singers such as Madonna and Michael Jackson] which has for years been accepted as the hallmark of Western decadence" (1997e). Instead of nation formation, *ngoma* served as a symbol of nation decay.

A contextualization of *kukata kiuno* clarifies this controversy. According to popular belief, this movement is taught to girls of certain southern and coastal ethnic groups during initiation rites (*unyago*) as part of their sexual education. Although these rites are shrouded in secrecy, they have assumed an apocryphal, titillating status among urban Tanzanians. Men especially delight in sharing stories of what "really happens" during *unyago,* particularly in the rites of the southern Makonde, whose women are considered to possess special sexual skills in comparison to women of other ethnic groups. Concealed from the public eye, *kukata kiuno* is symbolic of the private space: the "inside" identified by Partha Chatterjee as the domain of the female and spiritual in postcolonial cultural nationalism (1993, 119–21). The transformation of *kukata kiuno* into public spectacle exemplifies the concept of grassroots nationalism, in which audience tastes altered the trajectory of official directives.

This counterinvention, however, largely catered to male spectators. Herzfeld points out that intimate aspects of cultural identity that "provide insiders with their assurance of common sociality" are transformed into a source of embarrassment when externally placed (1997, 3). As a result of the external placement of *kukata kiuno*—a source of "common sociality" within the confines of female initiation—female spectators shunned *ngoma* out of embarrassment and shame. In all of the performances I watched, male spectators occasionally participated in dancing *ngoma,* but only once did I see a woman do so.[11] Her participation immediately prompted comments from other spectators that she must be intoxicated, with the subtext that only chemical influence could have loosened her sense of propriety. In a discussion of her own experience as a dancer in Muungano, Lange tells of being asked if she was married and if her parents were still alive by a spectator who had seen her dance the *msewe* (a fairly sedate coastal dance) with Muungano—as if only a woman without proper guidance would indulge in such unseemly behavior (1995, 94). The postcolonial vogue of *kukata kiuno* has culminated in a collective rejection of *ngoma* among female spectators.

The extent of this rejection was clarified in a Muungano performance I observed in 1997.[12] Muungano performed *masewe,* a Makonde dance that weaves a narrated storyline into the segments of song and dance. Chenga, the storyteller, related a tale of an insolvent Dar es Salaam resident who decided to return to his home village. In the course of his various adventures on the way home, the traveler came across a dance contest among women of different ethnic groups. At this point in the narrative, Chenga selected one of the female servers (often referred to as barmaids) to come onto the stage and enact a contest between herself and a Muungano female dancer. I suspect that Chenga singled out one of the "barmaids" since they are perceived as promiscuous, and perhaps he thought she would be more inclined to participate in a display of eroticism than a random female spectator. Yet this woman reluctantly got on the stage and simply started laughing when the Muungano woman began rotating her pelvis in the movement of *kukata kiuno*. It is likely that this same woman would not hesitate to participate in *taarab* or even Mandela's erotic stage show; the context of *ngoma,* however, was too "embarrassing" for this urban woman.

Students and faculty at the College of Arts also seemed "embarrassed" over the blatant sexuality of the popular troupes' *ngoma,* and they often expressed concern that I would interpret those versions as authentic examples. Although the college's *ngoma* canon included various sensual movements for female dancers, such as slow shoulder rotations and a gentle swaying of the hips, the absence of explicit *kukata kiuno* marked the college's alignment with official cultural rhetoric. Students and faculty also disparaged the troupes' *ngoma* with the assertion that the eroticism made the entertainment unsuitable for the many children in the audience. In turn, the troupes claimed that the college's dances are uninteresting and dull. Issues of ethnicity and sexuality overlapped in this point of contention, for the intermingling of primitivism and sexuality in the southern erotic female body flaunted the cultural mission that the college supposedly upholds.

A closer examination of the college's *ngoma* reveals, however, that faculty and students also participated in this process of recasting, counterinventing, and eroticizing. Although *lizombe* was excluded from the canon, the 1997 dance majors sought to learn it on their own in response to the dance's popularity with local Bagamoyo audiences. The college's version was relatively tame when

Figure 10. Muungano's dancing contest between a female performer and waitress. The waitress is too hesitant to compete as the Muungano dancer executes *kukata kiuno.*

compared to that of the popular troupes; still, the choreography remained undeniably sexual. Instead of male and female couples simulating intercourse, a
female dancer performed a solo in which she slowly rotated her hips as the
audience shrieked with delight. The force of the counter-canon pervaded the
College of Arts as popular tastes redefined official notions of national culture.

Economic factors were also influential in the college's contradictory attitude
toward *kukata kiuno*. The faculty of the college formed a group called Bagamoyo
Players, which, in addition to working on theatre for social change and various
development projects, also provided entertainment for expatriate or business
functions. Disparagement of the popular troupes' counterinvention aside, the
Bagamoyo Players was quick to participate in erotic performances to suit its
audience's expectations. When the Bagamoyo Players performed for the National Cashew Association in the elite Kilimanjaro Hotel in Dar es Salaam,
the women performed a dance that depicted female initiation, in which the older
women taught *kukata kiuno* to the young initiate.[13] Before the dance began, the
women pretended to chase away the men in the group, scolding them for peeking
at a "woman-only" dance. This tactic called even more attention to the numerous
European, African, and Asian men in the audience, who watched as the initiate
gradually learned the movement until she closed her eyes in ecstasy, gyrating
slowly to the cheers of the other women. Granted, this version of *unyago* was
enacted in the private confines of one of the most expensive hotels in the city and
did not signify the public sphere to the same extent as the college's auditorium or
Vijana Social Hall. Nevertheless, the performance demonstrated the Bagamoyo
Players' willingness to put aside official ideas of the appropriateness of sexuality,
particularly if their meager faculty salaries would be supplemented in the process.

It should be noted that neither Bagamoyo Players nor the students performing *lizombe* replicated the versions of *ngoma* found in the performances of
TOT, Muungano, and Mandela. In both cases, men were excluded from the stage,
meaning that women demonstrated their sexuality in the spotlight without being
subordinated to a male partner in a simulated act of intercourse. These performances delineated a unique compromise between state directives and official
tastes—in other words, the college produced a counterinvention with a difference.

In the mid-1990s, an additional force entered the *ngoma* landscape to reshape the dominance of southern dances. In the section that follows, I theorize the
influence of international tourism upon *ngoma* as a *re*invention of tradition.
Tourism is linked to nationalism as a hegemonic force that reworks popular
conceptions of *ngoma* to suit new audiences and shifting political needs.

REINVENTIONS

An examination of Tanzanian *ngoma* would be incomplete without a discussion
of tourism, given that the increased emphasis on the tourist economy in the wake
of socialism's demise. As Siri Lange points out, "Tanzania's cultural bureaucrats
have realized that the idea of building a national culture on the many ethnic
dances did not work out, but they can still use dance as a symbol to the outside
world" (1995, 66). The need for a symbol to the outside world has markedly
increased since the state prioritized tourism in an attempt to compete with
neighboring Kenya, which has long dominated East African tourism. In 1997,
three *ngoma* troupes formed with the express purpose of playing for tourists; their
names—Simba, Serengeti, and Kilimanjaro—corresponded to three major tourist

attractions: lions (*simba*), Serengeti National Park (a favorite safari destination), and Mount Kilimanjaro. As implied by their choice of names, they carefully marketed themselves for a growing tourist audience. During my fieldwork, members from these groups approached me with the boast that their work was more traditional than Muungano, TOT, or Mandela. Aware of the Western preference for "authentic" dances, they assumed that their claims would pique my interest.

These companies were, however, more likely to challenge the tourist gaze rather than satisfy it. The invasion of mass tourism was still relatively new to Tanzania, and local producers of tourist art were yet to become familiar with typical Western expectations of the "performative primitive," an evocative phrase coined by Dean MacCannell (1992). Furthermore, the legacy of Tanzania's historical emphasis on social relevance pervaded even tourist art. These factors coalesced in productions that did not fit typical descriptions of tourist performance that seem to depend upon tropes of the "savage male" and "erotic female" (see, for example, Balme 1998; Desmond 1997). Seldom did I see stereotypes of the primitive savage played out in tourist performance; instead, the restrained, subdued quality of Tanzanian tourist performance seemed more appropriate for an audience of cultural officials than for tourists. Because of this subdued, de-sexualized quality, I have categorized tourist *ngoma* as a reinvention of tradition since it *returned* to the invention of tradition put forth by the state.

For example, Lange tells of a troupe's performance at a tourist hotel, in which the announcer boasted that none of the dancers were from the places where the various *ngoma* had originated. Lange writes that "he had internalized the governmental policy of nation-building and de-tribalizing, happily ignorant of the fact that the tourists probably would have been more excited to hear that what

Figure 11. One of Mandela's male dancers, wearing black face paint for the *limbondo* dance of southern Tanzania. The "performative primitive" is more likely to be found in popular performance than in tourist performance.

they were about to see was the such and such tribe performing their authentic esoteric dances" (1995, 18). Although troupes had become more savvy about tourists' preferences since the period of Lange's research in the early 1990s, disruptions of these expectations continued to proliferate during my fieldwork. As revealed in a Swahili newspaper article (*Nipashe* 1997a), for example, Serengeti also participated in the rhetoric of nation-building. The leader of Serengeti, after boasting to the reporter about the number of times his troupe had performed in tourist hotels, proceeded to criticize TOT and Muungano for perpetuating European culture (*uzungu*)—unlike his own troupe, which he claimed preserves *utamaduni*. His investment in participating in anti-colonial discourse demonstrated the troupe's alignment with cultural nationalism, even though fellow Tanzanians were hardly the targeted audience.

This discursive bleeding of nationalist discourse into the domain of tourism is not surprising, considering that the performance of nationalism also demands staged authenticity. MacCannell writes that "tourism is not just an aggregate of merely commercial activities; it is also an ideological framing of history, nature, and tradition; a framing that has the power to reshape culture and nature to its own needs" (1992, 1). This same definition could easily be applied to nationalism, given Nyerere's revision of the African past to conform to socialist ideals and the legislation of tradition enacted by the Ministry of Culture. The ideological framing of both nationalism and tourism require the containment of tradition into a realm of purity, supposedly uncontaminated by modernization and Westernization. Christopher B. Balme identifies the peculiar irony in the "aporia of the tourist gaze, which on the one hand appears to demand authenticity and on the other works to deauthenticate anything which comes into its field of vision" (1998, 64–65). This irony can be likened to the invention of tradition, a phrase which itself encapsulates the underlying contradiction of cultural nationalism.

This intermingling of tourism and nationalism was most clearly discerned in the performances of gender in tourist *ngoma*. Since Western notions of African authenticity include stereotypes of the eroticized and/or passive African woman, the tourist economy seemed unlikely to disrupt the sexual stereotypes performed in the counterinvention of *ngoma* discussed above. The rendition of the female initiation ceremony performed by the Bagamoyo Players for the Cashew Association, which was staged for foreign visitors as well as local elites, provides one such example of this eroticization of the female body. This exception aside, however, I did not see stereotypes of either the savage male or erotic female played out; instead, the tourist choreography tended to revert to the de-sexualized movements preferred by the state. For example, the troupe Simba performed a version of *sindimba* that was far more restrained than anything I had seen performed by the popular theatre companies. Although the characteristic *kukata kiuno* remained the defining movement of the female dancers, it was greatly subdued, and the usual segment in which the male dancers "try out" the females was discarded. Furthermore, the female dancers did not conform to conventional standards of attractive female bodies as defined by the West. In each of the groups mentioned above—Bagamoyo Players, Simba, Serengeti, and Kilimanjaro—the female dancers embodied a variety of physical shapes and ages. While this variety apparently pleased the Tanzanian male gaze, it undoubtedly proved a challenge to Western tourists.

Muungano's own fumbling attempt to cash in on tourist dollars provided a striking example of this intersection between nationalist and tourist performance.

In December 1996, Muungano tried to secure a contract at Nyumba ya Sanaa (House of Arts), an arts and crafts shop catering to tourists located next to the Sheraton Hotel. They managed to produce one performance on December 3, for which the admission fee was 3,000 shillings ($4.20), three times the cost of their usual performances in neighborhood bars. For this occasion, they eliminated plays from the program, realizing that tourists would be unable to follow the Swahili dialogue. Despite these attempts to conform to a tourist aesthetic, however, they (inadvertently) managed to defy the expectant tourist gaze at every turn. Muungano retained its boisterous and unwieldy quality of its popular performances, with the sound system turned up to top volume despite the intimacy of the performance space. As a result, pained *wazungu* clapped their hands over their ears throughout the show. The Sheraton building looming overhead was unable to dampen Muungano's exuberance; as a result, Muungano failed to secure the coveted contract.

The intermingling of popular culture and the reinvention of tradition meant that Muungano's representations of gender were everything *but* what is usually expected in a tourist performance. For example, an abrupt de-sexualization of *ngoma* signified the discursive meshing of tourism and nationalism described above. Muungano went a step further than the group Simba and dropped *sindimba* from the performance altogether; indeed, the ubiquitous *kukata kiuno* did not make a single appearance throughout the evening. They did, however, include their vigorous and eye-catching version of *bugobogobo,* the harvesting dance often performed at the College of Arts previously described. In addition to the use of twirling hoes, Muungano added a segment in which the male and female dancers marched with wooden guns, followed by a "gender war" between the men and women enacted through hand-to-hand combat. Instead of the eroticized African woman, Muungano served up images of female soldiers insisting upon their rights. They finished the evening with a round of *taarab,* which typically caused a stampede of female fans onto the stage to dance and tip the singer. Instead, my fellow *wazungu* seemed more amused by the singer's elaborate sequined gown than impressed by her powerful stage presence.

Michael Denning has argued that in late capitalism very little cultural production survives other than in the form of commodities (1990, 9), an argument that seems applicable in the age of the "new," market-driven Tanzania and the commodification of *ngoma* throughout official, tourist, or popular spheres. The Muungano performance, however, provides a reminder of the ways in which *ngoma* exceeded the limits of commodification. As the next section illustrates, moments that invited identification rather than alterity also counteract the notion of commodification as an indefatigable force.

CHOREOGRAPHIES OF RESISTANCE

The following examples of ruptures in the *ngoma* narrative fall into two categories—those *ngoma* performances in which ethnic identities are celebrated rather than commodified, and those in which female agency is explored. This division recalls Bhabha's point that marginal communities are focal points of anxiety in the construction of a homogenized nation. The "either-or" pattern of these examples—either ethnicity *or* female agency is celebrated—serves as a reminder of the systemic control in which *ngoma* is embedded, for I never found the two disruptions integrated in a single performance.

Those moments in which *ngoma* provided a forum for the celebration of ethnic identity stand out in my memory and serve as powerful reminders of the unique role that this performance tradition served for marginalized ethnic groups. Often, in the creative hands of TOT and Muungano, southern *ngoma* such as *lizombe* and *sindimba* became affirmations of ethnic identity instead of portrayals of the primitive other. These moments were especially startling in the performances of TOT given its usual emphasis on urban sophistication and modernization. Despite this overriding agenda, the majority of the TOT dancers identified as Makonde or Ngoni. Individual ethnic identities among the performers were quite capable of complicating the troupe's ideological stance.

In June 1997, TOT announced a special dance contest between the Ngoni, represented by *lizombe,* and the Makonde, represented by *sindimba.*[14] Although the company did not include enough Ngoni and Makonde performers to stage "authentic" versions of the dance, they compromised with the announcement that the drummers for each version were of that ethnicity. It quickly became difficult to see the dancers due to the crowds of spectators swarming onto the stage to tip or dance alongside them; occasionally, some spectators would mock the movements, signifying their allegiance to the rival ethnic group. None of this mockery contained hostility; indeed, the sense of celebration and enthusiasm that pervaded the bar during this contest was unparalleled.

TOT's dance contest could, however, be interpreted as an attempt to channel ethnic identities into carefully contained modes of expression. Once both dances had been performed, the emcee promised that the winner would be announced at the performance the following week. Not surprisingly, no winner was ever declared. The designation of a victorious ethnic group would have contained connotations of tribalism, thus disrupting TOT's rhetorical support of national unity.[15] Indeed, this celebration could have been allowed precisely *because* of the marginalized status of the Ngoni and Makonde; T. L. Maliyamkono dryly notes that groups such as the Makonde are expected to speak their languages in public "but it only takes one Chagga or Haya [economically advantaged ethnic groups] to do so for others to conclude that 'this is tribalism'" (1995, 45). Southern ethnic groups are perceived as especially impoverished and therefore bear no threat to the nation-state. But even with these considerations in mind, the intensity of audience participation suggests that spectators seized the potential of performance to reclaim ethnic identities and refuse the homogeneity of nationalism.

Muungano went a step further and staged a contest between races instead of ethnic groups. During a performance at the College of Arts in Bagamoyo, Muungano incorporated a dance contest into *masewe,* a storytelling dance in which the narrative is intermingled with singing and dancing.[16] In this story, a male traveler returning to his home village came across a dancing contest between white and African women. A white woman, signified as a tourist by her brief shorts, was coaxed onto the stage and instructed to follow the lead of the Muungano dancer, who enacted the movement of *kukata kiuno* to the shrieks of the audience. The bewildered tourist awkwardly wiggled her hips, fulfilling her role as racial other in comparison to the smoothly erotic moves of her African rival. Through an affirmation of racial stereotypes of the "natural" superior musical and dancing ability of Africans, the contest invited Tanzanians to identify with the Muungano woman, who was loudly cheered.[17] Muungano cleverly reversed the tourist gaze by transforming the typical tourist watching an African dance into a spectacle for the consumption of the Bagamoyo audience. As in the previous example, Muungano used the framework of a contest to trigger a sense of identification, allowing difference to be explored and celebrated.

In both cases, however, *gender* difference remained binarized, with the women positioned as subordinate to the men. In the dance contest between the Ngoni and the Makonde staged by TOT, the dancers of *sindimba* enacted a short comic skit in which two male dancers attempted to use their skill to seduce a woman. The woman was played by a cross-dressed male, precluding the participation of a female performer in a moment when she could have displayed her own comic skills. Moreover, the racial challenge posed in Muungano's version of the dance contest was enacted on the site of the eroticized female body—dancing, as usual, *kukata kiuno.*

With the notable exception of the rifle-wielding women in Muungano's *bugobogobo,* the passivity of female dancers was a trope repeatedly affirmed in the *ngoma* of the urban popular stage. Anne McClintock states categorically that "[a]ll too often, the doors of tradition are slammed in women's faces" (1995, 385). In the case of *ngoma,* the door seems quite thoroughly slammed in the faces of the women performers and spectators. As if in response to these networks of control, they turned to other segments of the popular performance such as *taarab* as a more fluid and accessible form of artistic and cultural expression.

Yet a dismissal of urban *ngoma* as yet another example of appropriation and capitalist commodification does not account for the potential of agency in the moment of live performance. Amidst the sexual stereotypes, I witnessed some striking, albeit few, examples of the potential of using tradition to carve out agency. Although this potential was frequently curtailed in *ngoma* in the interests of authenticity, the following examples indicate that the female dancers were quite capable of maneuvering within this rhetoric.

Two examples of this potential that I witnessed occurred at the College of Arts among the third-year students. These students enjoyed more creative freedom than the first- and second-year students, who were graded on their ability to adhere to a formalized choreography. In a "Friday show," a student performance that was assembled every two weeks, the third-year female students performed *mganda wa kikutu,* one of the "canonized" *ngoma;* incidentally, *mganda* was the only canonized *ngoma* that retained its socialist Swahili lyrics. In the previous versions of *mganda wa kikutu* that I had observed, it began with all of the dancers, both women and men, leaping into the air in a rare display of joint athletic ability. Then, however, the choreography separated into designated male and female movements, especially in the segment in which the socialist lyrics were sung. During this segment, the women usually mimed gathering grain while singing praises to Nyerere. They called out in unison "*Kujitegemea!*" (Self-reliance) and exited while rotating their shoulders in a sensual movement. Once the women had exited, the men formed a line and left the stage while performing explicit pelvic thrusts.

In their experimental version, the female students, Mwajuma Gumbo, Joyce Hagu, and Deograsias Ndunguru, transformed *mganda wa kikutu* into an all-female dance.[18] In the process, they claimed all of the movements as their own; for example, after calling out "*Kujitegemea!*" they performed the distinctly masculine conclusion and thus fulfilled the rhetoric of "self-reliance" through the boldness of their experiment. Cross-gender play was not atypical in Tanzanian performance; for example, in the urban popular troupes, men occasionally cross-dressed as women for comic effect, as in the example of *sindimba* in TOT's dance contest. At the college, the students often cast themselves across gender lines in class projects due to shortages of either sex. Even in the midst of these examples of cross-gender casting, this version of *mganda* was unique since the female students fully inhabited the male movements in *ngoma*. In addition, they did not separate themselves into male and female dancers but encompassed all of the movements, challenging the careful gender distinctions that characterized *ngoma* choreography.

It should be noted that the Friday shows were usually "in-house" with the audience consisting mostly of other students; I doubt that the women would have been allowed to perform this version in an official occasion such as the Workers' Day celebration or at the annual National Arts Festival. A more striking example of female agency is the third-year dance majors' version of *masewe*, called "Issue," which *was* performed on several public occasions, including the 1997 festival. The three students (Robert Ajwang', Deograsias Ndunguru, and Aloyce Makonde) worked with their teachers Basil Mbatta and Luiza Maganga, both of whom were former members of the National Dance Troupe, to create their own expanded version of the dance. In the process of transformation, it became a vehicle of power for Ndunguru, the only woman among the three dance majors.

As explained by Mbatta (1997), *masewe* was typically used by older women to educate young girls during initiation. He implied that the dance was not originally an initiation dance that was then "exposed" to the public, but that it had a dual function as a means of public entertainment, when it was danced by both sexes, and as private instruction. Even when it functioned as public entertainment, the storyline included a lesson or warning; for example, if a male villager was abusing his wife, the storyteller might relate a story about a villager beating his wife until she died. As explained by Mbatta, *masewe* exemplified the intersection of entertainment and efficacy that characterized the historic role of *ngoma*.

In order to reflect the historical and cultural role of *masewe* in female initiation and pedagogy, Mbatta cast Ndunguru as the storyteller and adapted a storyline that was used to teach the initiates about childcare. The plot, which tells of a woman searching for a cure for infertility, integrates two common themes in traditional stories: the woman unable to bear children and the traveler making a journey throughout Tanzania. In search of a cure that will give her a child, the female protagonist of the story travels through Tanzania toward the southern region of Mtwara, where she is told she will find a Makonde *mganga* (healer) equipped with the medicine she needs. She experiences a loosely connected series of adventures along the way, many of which are connected with motherhood. For example, when passing through Bagamoyo, she comes across several women weeping in sympathy for their sons undergoing their own initiation (*jando*), which involves circumcision.[19] Another frequent theme in her adventures is that of cleanliness; for example, she encounters several children who at first appear to be washed, but closer inspection reveals that their backs are dirty. Apparently this brief incident would be interpreted as a lesson that children should be thoroughly bathed.

Eventually, the woman finds the Makonde *mganga* who provides her with the needed medicine. He warns her that she must never wash the infant nor let rain strike him. She readily agrees and immediately gives birth to a son, who is named Katope (an allusion to *matope,* or mud) in reference to the unwashed child's appearance. Tragedy strikes when rain abruptly begins to fall, and the woman frantically tries to dodge the raindrops to protect her child. The first few times I saw this *ngoma* performed, the story quite abruptly ended at this point.[20] While Ajwang' and Makonde sang a lament, Ndunguru informed the audience that she was too tired to continue. I was told that they wanted to leave the story at its climax without a resolution, which was an acceptable way to conclude plays and dances at the college.

In the course of telling the story, Ndunguru spoke of the woman in the third person, but she frequently assumed the woman's character through her actions. For example, she held the new baby out with pride to the audience and other dancers, and she searched desperately for refuge from the rain in the story's conclusion. When describing the mothers weeping for their initiated sons, Ndunguru abruptly fell to the ground and mimicked their cries. Her easy movement through a range of characters and her command of the story meant that Makonde and Ajwang' were continually responding to her lead throughout the dance. Ndunguru, herself a charismatic performer with a strong voice, inhabited her role as storyteller with authority and presence.

Although three other students were incorporated into the dance when *masewe* was selected for inclusion in the 1997 National Arts Festival, Ndunguru remained the undisputed leader.[21] For the festival performance, Mbatta expanded the ending: after the mother loses Katope to the rain, she returns to her husband, who scolds her and drives her into the streets. The new ending was meant to warn parents about the dangers of arranged marriages (Mbatta 1997). Apparently, the new version demonstrated that arranged marriages would result in the unhappy end of *masewe,* in which the courageous woman who had traveled throughout the country is transformed into a forlorn abandoned wife.

Ndunguru, however, had other ideas. At the time of the festival, Ndunguru, Ajwang', and Makonde had all graduated; as a result, Ndunguru perhaps felt freer to subvert her former teacher's choreography. When the husband, played by Omari Mwarape, began scolding Ndunguru for losing their son, she responded by pushing him to the floor, startling even Mwarape since Ndunguru had told no one of her plan. As the audience cheered with delight, Ndunguru then pulled a child from the audience onto the stage and admonished Mwarape, mocking him for acting no older than this child. The *ngoma* ended with a female dancer seizing the moment and proving her improvisational skill. In a showcase of Tanzanian culture, Ndunguru refused to be contained.

The female students at the college walked a precarious tightrope in trying to push boundaries; on the one hand, they were encouraged to push gender constraints through learning to play musical instruments and perform acrobatics; on the other, they were cast in subordinate roles in *ngoma* to uphold the college's role as the savior of traditional culture. Although tensions between what is perceived as tradition and modernity permeate Tanzanian society, these female students were unique insofar as the tension was played out in the public realm of performance. Given these contradictory messages, it is little wonder that *masewe* served as such a striking example of female subjectivity since it was a moment in which agency and traditionalism were not at odds.

In conclusion, this study returns to the domain of urban popular culture to explore a final example of female subjectivity—that of Salma Moshi, a famous figure in the Dar performing arts scene. Moshi's career in the performing arts began in the 1980s when she was working as an accountant for Dar es Salaam Development Corporation (DDC). In 1983, she took over the management of the parastatal's cultural troupe, DDC Kibisa, which became one of the most successful theatre companies in Dar es Salaam. In 1987, she founded her own company called Ujamaa (Moshi 2001a). In an attempt to give Ujamaa a competitive edge, Moshi became the only woman in the country who danced with snakes, earning a nationwide reputation as the "snake woman" (*mama wa nyoka*) in the process.[22] She was particularly famous for writhing on the floor with her "bosom friends" (in Moshi 2001b) in an act brimming with intersections of sexuality, nationalism, and feminism.

Moshi herself calls attention to her sexuality as a key feature of the performance. Her press materials are dominated by two types of photographs: those in which her body entwines with those of the snakes, and those in which she "kisses" a snake. Moshi freely makes coy remarks in reference to the kissing in interviews, describing the smoothness of the snake's tongue tickling her lips in vivid terms: "It is part of the game that arouses curiosity in the people and once inside I feel its forked tongue exploring, but I don't feel fear" (Moshi 2001b). She also notes that her "intimate [human] associates" fear kissing her (Moshi 2001b). This invocation of sexuality could be read as substituting the stereotype of the demure traditional woman for a primitively erotic one—more dangerous, perhaps, but one that can still be pigeonholed and dismissed. Her act could be categorized as an example of primitive female sexuality on display for consumption, embracing the "bestial sexual license of the African" (Bhabha 1994, 66) that I referred to in the opening of this chapter in a literal sense.

Moshi's version of the performative primitive, however, was challenged through an artful articulation of nationalism and ethnicity. Snake dancing is considered a tradition of the Sukuma/Nyamwezi people of Lake Victoria; if Moshi claimed to come from this tribe, her skill and daring would be chalked up to her innate ethnic knowledge and would solidify notions of primitive forms of artistic expression. Instead, Moshi refuses to mention her tribe, dodging the question with a nationalist stance: "I like to be known as a Tanzanian" (Moshi 2001b). In this silence, Moshi's last name would read as Chagga—the tribe known for its wealth and education as the antithesis of more traditional tribes such as the Sukuma and Makonde. As such, her name flew in the face of primitivist stereotypes in the national imagination.

These connotations would be also challenged through Moshi's emphasis on snake dancing as a *learned* skill: she repeatedly notes that she learned snake dancing through the tutelage of a Sukuma snake dancer (Moshi 2001b). Instead of accessing her "innate" understanding of snake dancing through her ethnicity, Moshi assembled a body of knowledge that she deliberately sought out as a savvy businesswoman trying to ensure the commercial success of her troupe. This knowledge exceeds the isolated act of dancing to include a wealth of information: Moshi also catches the snakes, raises them, and treats snakebite. In conversations with reporters, she repeatedly demystifies the process of raising and catching snakes through her detailed explanations about the different methods, as well as ways of curing snakebite (Moshi 2001b). She counteracts her sexuality with detailed technical knowledge, casting herself as an expert in a male-dominated field.

She also characterizes herself as a feminist: in the name of women's equality, she braves the dangerous world of snakes. She plans to make a videotape of her work in order to encourage women to attempt work that is usually considered only for men (Moshi 2001b). She also spoke proudly of her husband and children's support of her occupation—providing an alternative model of familial politics in which she could freely pursue her unusual calling. Like Ndunguru, Moshi acts as a protagonist writing a new script of Tanzania through exploiting the potential of tradition as a means of exploding stereotypes of domesticated women. In this particular counterinvention, Moshi might have been playing the role of the savage female, but she manipulated this image on her own terms.

Before I spin off into romanticized constructions of Moshi as a voice of feminist resistance, it should be noted that her audience had become fairly exclusive. In the heyday of the popular theatre when Moshi competed against Mandela and Muungano in the bars and social halls of Dar es Salaam, her daring rendition of tradition provided a powerful alternative to the displays of *kukata kiuno* in *lizombe* and *sindimba*. In the wake of the consolidation of the commercial theatre companies that occurred in the early 1990s, however, Moshi turned mainly to tourist performance in order to make a living (Moshi 2001a). Instead of performing for her fellow citizens, this showcase of female agency plays out before the gazes of privileged foreigners in a venue that resonates with objectification. Although her performance would forcefully challenge Western notions of passive African women, her self-promotion as "the only woman snake dancer in Africa" means that her nuanced articulation of Tanzanian ethnicity is lost in such a context.[23] Her versions of staged authenticity would be readily commodified and consumed as primitive sexuality.

Although these moments and examples caution against a categorical dismissal of *ngoma,* they also invoke the issues that make *ngoma* a site of vexation and unease. Ndunguru and Moshi enacted their challenges of gender norms in the relatively isolated venues of the College of Arts and tourist performance; meanwhile, on the urban popular stage, spectators work to reclaim ethnic identity in a challenge to nationalist homogenization. This distinction recalls the oscillating tension between gender and ethnicity, serving as a reminder of the threat that "tribalism" and female identity pose to the nation. It seems that one cultural "sore zone" (Herzfeld 1997, 27) could be safely challenged without censure, but never the two shall meet through the performance of *ngoma.*

A brief note of historical context further problematizes the sense of agency that Ndunguru and Moshi so vividly display. As historian Susan Geiger argues, women's dance groups played a central role in promoting the nationalist movement prior to independence in the 1950s. Geiger believes that the link between women's *ngoma* and nationalism is due to the status of *ngoma* as "[a] culturally approved place for the expression and further development of this solidarity among urban coastal women" (1987, 22). She elaborates upon this connection in a passage that delineates the unique qualities of women's dance groups:

> [U]nlike most male-dominated organizations which continued to be based
> on the exclusionary principles of tribal, regional, or religious affiliation, the
> women's *ngoma* groups already embodied nationalist principles. They were
> trans-tribal in composition; they accepted all women willing to dedicate them-
> selves to the group and recognize the authority of its leaders; and they were
> fully aware of the critical unifying force of Swahili as a common language.
> (1987, 15)

In a later work, Geiger used this evidence to launch a critique of postcolonial dismissal of nationalism as a Eurocentric or patriarchal construct, noting that these claims to the "universal truth about nationalisms" cannot account for "the contours of Tanzanian nationalism, especially when . . . viewing women not simply as recipients or bearers of nationalism, but as among its major progressive creators" (1997, 13). Geiger's work bears powerful testimony to the vitality of *ngoma* in the nationalist movement—a vitality beside which the individual experiments of Ndunguru and Moshi tend to pale. In a similar vein, studies of contemporary rural *ngoma* are filled with references to its potential as a mode of female empowerment (Mwakalinga 1994; Swantz 1995), in which the agency of the collective at least temporarily displaces layers of social and cultural oppression. These examples bear witness to *ngoma*'s ability to "address not only individual rights and freedoms, but also the interests of communal and cultural solidarities" (Nyamnjoh 2002, 112). This perspective clarifies that in the context of urban popular performance, the radical potential of *ngoma* has been effaced.

It is difficult not to conclude this chapter on a pessimistic note. With the exception of the isolated examples discussed above, the economy of the stereotypical smiling, hip-swaying woman effectively contained female dancers in nationalist and/or urban popular culture. To return to Bhabha, he cautions against using the stereotype as "the scapegoat of discriminatory practices," describing it as "a much more ambivalent text of projection and introjection, metaphoric and metonymic strategies, displacement, overdetermination, guilt, [and] aggressivity" (1994, 81–82). The anxiety and desire that circulates around womanhood throughout these various inventions, counterinventions, and reinventions serve as a powerful reminder of the potential of *ngoma;* however, it is a potential that has been successfully subdued. As a result, the "African Woman" almost disappears from view, overshadowed by her leaping, aggressive, or comic male counterpart— but her smile remains intact.

FOUR

Popular Drama and
the Mapping of Home

On July 5, 1997, Tanzania One Theatre (TOT) performed in an expatriate and tourist nightclub in an affluent area of Dar es Salaam.[1] Instead of its usual exuberant routine of skits, acrobatics, dances, and songs, TOT confined itself to performing a series of *ngoma* as a concession to the largely European audience, intermingled with a few African and Asian Tanzanians. The event predictably unfolded into a sanitized, generic performance that invoked stereotypical images of traditional rural Africa upon which the tourist economy depends.

An intriguing moment occurred, however, once TOT launched into *imborokoi*, a dance of the Maasai ethnic group.[2] A few minutes into the dance, an elderly Maasai woman, who had been quietly selling beadwork in a corner, abruptly claimed center stage when she closed her eyes and began to sing along with the TOT dancers. Both Tanzanian and foreign spectators reacted with visible delight. "Look, they are taking her home," my associate Robert O. Ajwang,' one such delighted Tanzanian, said to me. Indeed, she seemed transported across space and time to what I assumed *was* her home, and a picture of a rural village removed from the turmoil of industrialization automatically came to my mind. At the time, I was struck—even charmed—at the power of *ngoma* to invoke Tanzanian rural roots in a European-style nightclub.

In retrospect, however, this moment seems ripe for unpacking the complex overlapping of a postcolonial metropolis, hinterland, and home. To be "taken home" is one of the highest compliments that can be paid to a *ngoma* dancer or musician in an urban setting. The phrase implies that the movements are danced and the lyrics are sung to such an authentic degree (*kama ukweli*, "like the truth") that the spectator is transported across time and space to what is indeed a rural village removed from the turmoil of industrialization. This image of mine cannot be labeled as only the product of a Western mindset; it was also cultivated through several months of listening to urban Tanzanians rhapsodize about the peace and quiet of their home villages. These homes were invariably opposed to the crime and bustle of Dar es Salaam in a classic opposition of city and country.

In *The Country and the City,* Raymond Williams historicizes and unpacks the British notion that the country represents peace, innocence, and simple virtue, in contrast to the city, which signifies learning, communication, and light (1973, 1).[3] When he turns his attention away from England toward colonial and neocolonial nations, he finds a strikingly similar polarization of city and country (279–288). In a homogenizing gesture at odds with his nuanced analytical approach, he theorizes that the force of imperialism caused the former colonies to "follow, internally, the lines of the alien development" (286). With this statement, Williams falls into the usual academic pitfall of categorizing colonized subjects as meekly following Europe's lead.

Despite such criticisms,[4] Williams's observations prove surprisingly salient in a Tanzanian context. The persistence of this urban/rural dichotomy is particularly interesting given developments in Tanzanian urban migration. Williams describes postcolonial migration patterns in classic terms of rural-to-urban, in which a "displaced and formerly rural population" moves toward "intensely overcrowded cities" (1973, 287). In the case of present-day Tanzania, this typical trajectory is increasingly reversed. As Aili Mari Tripp explains in her study of Dar es Salaam, the sustained economic crisis that began in the 1980s strengthened the already powerful links between rural and urban spheres, "[binding] the futures of urban dwellers inseparably to those of their rural kin" (1997, 52). The sharp decline in real wages necessitated the need to maintain the *shamba* (farm) in the village in order to supplement urban wages with food; as a result, the imagined boundary between rural and urban living has been replaced with a revolving door (53). In the midst of these fluid boundaries, the rural/urban divide held firm with a stubbornness that raises questions concerning cultural stakes and national anxieties.[5]

This chapter explores the intersection of the rural/urban dichotomy and the politics of gender in popular drama. Female characters in *maigizo* regularly conformed to certain stereotypical behavior that depended upon their rural or urban identity. Rural women were invariably stalwart, faithful, and honest in contrast to their collective urban "other," who paraded their lustful or illegal behavior across the stage. An unpacking of this dichotomy reveals the ways in which these stereotypes overlapped with nationalism. State discourse and popular culture colluded to maintain the fiction of a city/country duality and, subsequently, a coherent national identity.

The historical moment of democratization ensured, however, that this nationalist script was subjected to improvisation. The second part of this chapter addresses three fascinating ruptures in the national fabric. Two plays, TOT's "Control Yourself" ("Ushinde Moyo Wako") and Muungano's "Such Matters" ("Mambo Hayo"), used the controversial topics of rape, AIDS, and female circumcision to produce a moment of crisis in which traditional/modern and rural/urban dichotomies were at least temporarily overturned. The third rupture consists of the character Mzee Jangala, a recurring figure in Mandela's plays, whose mixture of crudity and rage not only embraced national stereotypes of the traditionalist, rural male but also marked a moment of excess and exaggeration that strained the underlying nationalist code to the breaking point. In the process of destabilizing the postcolonial equation of "masculine" city and "feminine" country, these narratives and characters challenged essentialist constructions of the primordial home and, concomitantly, notions of gender. Such moments reclaimed the discourse of democratization to carve out alternative nations in which peripheral spaces and marginal figures assumed center stage.

GEOGRAPHY, GENDER, AND HOME

Nostalgia permeates Julius K. Nyerere's theoretical musings on African socialism. He locates his vision of an egalitarian, democratic, socialist society in the precolonial past: "We, in Africa, have no more need of being 'converted' to socialism than we have of being 'taught' democracy. Both are rooted in our own past—in the traditional society which produced us" (1968b, 12). This nostalgic quality was, however, reserved for the past; rural villages of the present were lamented for their collective state of poverty and even chided for their refusal to modernize: "Les [*sic*] us go to the villages and talk to our people and see whether or not it is possible for them to work harder" (30). In contrast to the harsh realities of rural Tanzania, the primordial past was more malleable and thus suited to Nyerere's discursive approach. His romanticized depiction of the traditional past calls to mind definitions of *synthetic* nostalgia, which "mourns for what is missing from the present" and thus depicts the past as distanced and contained (Strathern 1995, 111).

What makes Nyerere's political theory so fascinating is how this nostalgic yearning for a fictional past crystallized in radical socialist policy. In a classic example of what Rijk van Dijk has termed *syncretic* nostalgia, in which "the longing for a past and its evocation with present social reality" are blended "*to create* a specific route of empowerment" (1998, 156), he translated traditionalist rhetoric into legislation that resettled several million rural Tanzanians in planned socialist villages from 1967 to 1977.[6] Nyerere conceptualized the socialist village as a communal society where peasants shared the land, the produce, and the profits. He also sought to integrate far-flung rural citizens into the modern nation-state by providing them with access to schools, dispensaries, and agricultural extension workers. Nyerere's strategic rehabilitation of the rural village carved out an alternative path between polarized notions of the modern European nation-state and traditional African society. The concept of syncretic nostalgia foregrounds the transformative potential of nostalgia as a tool in politicized projects such as nation building.[7]

This potential was, however, curtailed in the hands of government officials. The initial promise of Nyerere's policy of *ujamaa* degenerated into aggressive attempts to bring recalcitrant villages into the state's fold. When segments of the rural population proved resistant to Nyerere's scheme of resettlement, the government turned to blatant displays of force. According to eyewitness testimony gathered throughout the country, people's homes or food supplies were destroyed to ensure the villagers' capitulation (Coulson 1982, 250–252). In order to conform to Nyerere's primordial vision, villages were uprooted and relocated in an act that epitomizes van Dijk's comment that nostalgia is about *selective* yearning and therefore is about power (1998, 156).

Similar to the complexities of *ujamaa,* the field of popular drama contained multiple layers of nostalgia, transformation, and subjugation. In their full-length plays, Muungano and TOT avoided the problematic realities of contemporary, impoverished Tanzanian villages by representing them only through emissaries, the male and female migrants who showed up on Dar's doorstep to pursue wealth and prosperity. (The unique case of Mandela, which frequently used village settings, is explored in the final section of this chapter.) These migrant characters inevitably bore the rural trappings of naïveté, honesty, and eagerness, displaying the perceived moral superiority of their traditional background. The female characters in particular were flattened into a rural stereotype; simply to costume a woman in *khanga* signified her kindness and marital fidelity. The conspicuous absence of the village and the persistent stereotypes of rural characters could be explained as a manifestation of synthetic nostalgia and the urge for containment and control. These stereotypes serve as a reminder of the anxieties that circulate around tradition, which is not merely a figment of a fictionalized past but persists as a complex reality. As the bastion of tradition, the village was subjected to containment and control.

A careful analysis of these female characters reveals, however, that Muungano's and TOT's interpretations elide simple categorization. On the one hand, these anxieties consistently revolved around the female characters, who served as a kind of Maginot Line between traditional/modern and rural/urban divides. Their dramatic function as "boundary-markers" entailed a flattening of female subjectivity and agency. On the other hand, the ambiguities of tradition itself, which straddles precolonial time and rural space, meant that this divide could also be destabilized and overturned. The nostalgic glow of the precolonial past inevitably clashes against the harshness of the rural, impoverished present. Simultaneously romanticized and scorned, the village provides a focal point for this sense of tension, serving as both the place of truth, *ukweli,* and the place of backwardness, *ushenzi.* At the risk of locating transformation in the fissures of narrative ambivalence and thus erasing distinct and specific modes of oppression and resistance,[8] the plays of Muungano suggest that the conflicted world of tradition did indeed carve out a space of female agency.

Before proceeding to an exploration of the plays, a brief discussion of postcolonial feminist theory helps to clarify the ways in which power, gender, and nostalgia intersect and overlap. Anne McClintock explains that in order to resolve the tension inherent in the Janus-faced postcolonial nation, which attempts to straddle both the traditional past and a modern future, the contradiction is figured in terms of gender: "Women are represented as the atavistic and authentic body of national tradition (inert, backward-looking and natural), embodying nationalism's conservative principal of continuity," whereas men "represent the progressive agent of national modernity (forward-thrusting, potent and historic)" (McClintock 1995, 359; see also Kandiyoti 1994). In a similar move, Partha Chatterjee usefully identifies the home as the internal nation-space in which "woman" serves as the national bearer of spiritual values, placed in opposition to the male and material world (1993, 119–121). Although both scholars link the postcolonial woman with the perpetuation of tradition, McClintock casts her in the shadows of the past and Chatterjee locates her in the confines of the home. In this dual framework, the village assumes a distinctly feminine form.

The geography of the city, however, is defined by men. In *Nomadic Identities: The Performance of Citizenship,* May Joseph refers to urban migrants as "travelers within the national imaginary," noting that they "are often produced as weak or inauthentic subjects, wanting in their public displays of citizenship" (1999, 155). In light of McClintock's and Chatterjee's work, I would extend Joseph's argument and suggest that *women* serve as the inauthentic urban migrants since postcolonial nationalist discourse situates the authentic woman as rural and traditional. Within this framework, the village serves as an object of precolonial pride when associated with womanhood.[9] This analogy surfaced in TOT's *ngoma* performance in the nightclub previously described. At first, the traditional Maasai woman was more or less ignored in her anomalous role as a female urban migrant clinging to her ethnic ways. Only when she was figuratively transported to the rural village via the music did she invoke delight and approval from the Tanzanians in the audience. At this point, she conformed neatly to the gendered paradigm, creating a permissible moment for nostalgic remembrances of home. In a similar vein, the 1967 Arusha Declaration, a defining document of Tanzanian nationalism, trumpets this traditional woman/modern male dichotomy in a prime example of how gender and nation are entwined. In a section entitled "Hard Work," the declaration proclaims categorically that rural women are the most industrious workers in Tanzania. The document then adds: "The energies of the millions of men in the villages and thousands of women in the towns . . . are at present wasted in gossip, dancing and drinking" (Nyerere 1968b, 245), thus implying that only urban men and rural women are authentic citizens who uphold national virtues. As the declaration indicates, the hard work of nation building depends upon the rural woman to carry out her preordained social role as the axis of the nation-state.

Muungano, which carefully emphasized the rhetoric of traditionalism in its performances, provides a useful starting point for the exploration of popular drama. Its ideological stance, which held up tradition as a panacea for Tanzania's ills, would theoretically translate into a fairly rigid stance in which rural women are summoned as the paragons of authenticity. Instead, however, Muungano produced contradictory and complex plays in which rural female characters adhered to notions of conventional morality but also managed to exert their will.

Muungano's play "The Landlady" ("Mama wa Nyumba"), which related the tale of a naive young man who migrates to the city, provides a representative example of this complexity.[10] Soon after the young man arrived in the city, the assertive landlady seduced him. When his rural wife joined him a few months later, she soon realized her husband was having an affair, although she did not know with whom. In a letter to her grandmother in the village, she requested that a spell be cast on her husband's lover. Instead of retreating to the village, she drew upon traditional practices as a way of fighting back and remaining in the urban sphere. Although stereotypes of the innocent female from the village abounded in Muungano's works, these migrants also employed traditional *practices,* such as witchcraft, as a crucial medium for agency and subjectivity. These practices were not only encrusted with the past in the sense of synthetic nostalgia but also served as a resource to negotiate the complexities of the present.

The representation of urban women, however, reveals the limits of Muungano's interpretation of nostalgia. These characters invariably served as inauthentic citizens who needed to be purged from the nationalist landscape. When the landlady, who exemplified the stereotype of the modern, lustful, urban woman, sought to poison the wife, she was duly punished when she accidentally drank the poison and died a melodramatic death on stage. The landlady was typical of the corpses who occasionally appeared in Muungano's plays, the majority of whom were urban women.[11] This unusually harsh treatment was suggestive of the anxiety that this figure provoked and also helps to ensure that only traditional— and therefore "natural"—women will be rewarded. In this particular play, for example, the rural wife triumphed as the play ended with her rival dead at her feet and her appropriately contrite husband restored to her side.

In contrast to Muungano's romanticism, the cynical world of TOT seldom allowed rural women to achieve a desirable end. Instead of a place of nostalgic return, the village and its inhabitants were transformed into objects of ridicule. Village inhabitants no longer acted as stalwart representatives of the moral nation but instead were distanced through the lens of comedy as buffoons. Peals of laughter greeted fresh, wide-eyed arrivals from the village who readily performed their backwardness through eating candy wrappers or cowering in fear from Dar's snarl of traffic. In these moments, the village was depicted as anachronistic space, removed from the newly cultivated sophistication of the urban dweller and homogenized as uncouth.

Van Dijk's work on nostalgia helps to clarify the potentially radical nature of this trend. He calls attention to the tendency of certain postcolonial movements such as African Pentecostalism to *reject* nostalgia and utterly dismiss the traditions of the past: "In this case, the past is not made powerless . . . nor is it turned into a resource of empowerment. . . . Instead, the past is ruptured" (1998, 157). He argues that this rupture produces "the moment of instant rebirth," which "is seen as the power base from which new future orientations are constructed" (158). Although van Dijk's use of the term "power base" serves as a reminder that political agendas pervade these moments of rebirth, he helps to clear fresh theoretical space by positioning this rupture in the formation of postcolonial subjectivity instead of dismissing it as a reactionary symptom of a modernizing mindset.

In a similar vein, TOT's mockery of the village paves the way for new conceptions of Tanzanian identity that embrace the future rather than yearn for a fictional past. In this framework, urban women are freed from the trappings of conventional nostalgia and can successfully pursue individual agendas rather than bear punishment for their deviation from established national norms. A particularly fascinating play, TOT's "The Good People" ("Wema Waponza"), is suggestive of this sense of potential. Like Muungano's "The Landlady," "The Good People" also tells the story of a wide-eyed *washamba* couple who migrates to the city with the assistance of a wealthy benefactor.[12] TOT's analogous version of the landlady was the benefactor's lustful wife, who initiated an affair with her new male houseguest. But instead of following Muungano's example and killing her off in the final moments of the play, TOT allowed the adulterous wife to triumph. In order to secure complete freedom to pursue her new affair, she hatched a scheme to have her husband framed for illegal drug possession and thrown in jail. Then, to demonstrate the extent of her malevolence, she left their infant daughter with her jailed husband, blithely abandoning her to the appalling conditions of a Tanzanian prison. Like Muungano, TOT reified the notion that the urban woman was unnatural since she refused to "go home" to the primordial past. In TOT's world, however, she was allowed to revel in her inauthenticity rather than be censured.

As in the plays of Muungano, however, TOT perpetuated a sharp delineation between rural and urban women. Although TOT's urban female characters were allowed to triumph, their traditional counterparts were consistently punished as stubborn throwbacks to an atavistic era. In "The Good People," soon after the village couple arrived in the city, they exchanged their village rags for sleek Western clothes. The male migrant made a Cinderella grand entrance in his new attire, swaggering proudly across the stage in his baseball cap and fancy sneakers. The wide-eyed *mshamba* male was instantly transformed into the suave city slicker; the ease of his transformation indicated that he was simply falling into the appropriate mold. For his wife, however, the uprooting was more traumatic.

Unlike her husband, she proved unable to adapt to the manipulative ways of the city. Instead, she retained her naïveté and meekness, made all the more vivid in comparison to her husband's sleek urban lover. When the wife discovered the extramarital affair, the husband responded by mocking the scars on her legs that were caused by a plow. In her case, city clothes only temporarily concealed the geographical marking of her rural body; the Cinderella transformation was reserved for men. As a figure of the past, the rural woman exists in what McClintock calls "a permanently anterior time within the modern nation," barring her from the possibility of fighting back in the urban domain (1995, 359). Accordingly, the wife returned to the village in seeming defeat and did not appear for the remainder of the play. For these characters, the demarcation between city and country solidified into a rigid boundary. This pattern suggests that rural space and traditional past still haunted TOT's modern, urban world, triggering a unique version of anxiety that singled out the traditional female as the irritant that must be purged.

These conflicting tendencies are not surprising in light of theories of nostalgia and displacement, which have called attention to the need for romanticized depictions of home coupled with the desire for affirmations of the new, perhaps bewildering life. It is noteworthy that none of the plays I saw in Tanzania even used the term *ujamaa* in reference to villages. To do so would have historicized and politicized the village, lending it a specificity that would defeat its purpose as a generic backdrop to serve these contradictory needs. In the process, female characters also became generic, serving as markers of national identity rather than fully inhabiting the complexities of African subjectivity. These patterns of homogenization reaffirm country/city, male/female hierarchies and serve as reminder of the layers of anxiety that the female citizen-body provoked.

In the midst of these hierarchies and stereotypes, however, a sense of ambivalence troubled the performance of urban womanhood. Although Muungano often punished these characters, the plays also provided context for their actions or made them relatively sympathetic to the audience. In "The Landlady," for example, the scheming urban lover invoked sympathy in her direct addresses to the audience in which she forlornly confessed her love for her tenant. In another *igizo*, the husband left his unfaithful wife and remarried; in the concluding scene, the ex-wife came to his wedding in tears. When the guests and her former husband treated her with scorn and mockery, she responded by singing a plaintive *taarab* song about her unhappiness.[13] The ending included a note of moralizing since the adulterous woman was clearly punished, but at the same time she was portrayed sympathetically in contrast to the cruel wedding guests. A more political note was struck in an especially well-received *igizo* titled "On Account of Greed" ("Kwa Ajili ya Tamaa"), in which a sister attempted to murder her brother in order to seize their father's inheritance, which, as dictated by customary law, was the sole property of sons and not daughters.[14] Although the sister was clearly meant to be perceived as deserving of punishment—indeed, she was killed at the end of the play—the *igizo* reminded the audience of the laws that denied her of her share of the inheritance in the first place. Shades of complexity helped to destabilize the nationalist codes that consigned her to the realm of stereotype.

Female spectators in the audience readily seized and expanded upon these moments of complexity. During the early 1990s, most of the women in the audience left after *taarab,* which at the time preceded the *igizo* (Plane 1995, 56). As a result, the audience for *maizigo* consisted mostly of male spectators. As its popularity intensified, however, *taarab* was rescheduled as the crowning event of the evening. This alteration in the schedule ensured that women outnumbered male spectators throughout the performance. Their presence dominated the *maigizo,* since they tended to be far more participatory than male spectators through *kutunza* and calling out advice to the female characters. By taking command of the performance, these spectators challenged representations of urban womanhood and pushed the boundaries of the nation to include themselves in its scope.

Overt expressions of sympathy for urban female characters played a key role in these moments of nation transformation. In Muungano's "On Account of Greed," several female spectators filed onto the stage to slip money into the sister's hand as she lay dying after being shot by her brother.[15] Although the performers often worked a "sob scene" into the *igizo* to encourage this tradition of *kutunza,* the female spectators determined which characters deserved their sympathy and coins. Their expressions of sympathy could exceed the act of giving money; for example, in the *igizo* about the unfaithful wife who was mocked at her former husband's wedding mentioned above, one female spectator angrily intervened in the action by pushing one of the scornful guests. In a sense, these acts intervened in the overlapping webs of morality, nationhood, and nostalgia that excluded them from authentic citizenship.

These female spectators continue to be implicated in three specific interventions that I explore for the remainder of this chapter. Although ambiguity and excess invariably pervade popular performance, two specific plays created by TOT and Muungano reflected a sense of moral panic in a particular historical moment when foreign imports began flooding the urban Tanzanian market and thus intensified usual conditions of ambiguity that pervade the formation of postcolonial subjectivity. In the process of wrestling with this anxiety, the companies redefined concepts of nostalgia and cleared the way for new paradigms of womanhood.

NEW TERRAINS

During the period of my fieldwork in Tanzania, a wave of concern over what was perceived as a "sudden" prevalence of rape swept through the country, as reflected in both state discourse and the popular press (*Mzalendo* 1997; *Guardian* 1997a, 1997c, 1997d; *Sunday Observer* 1997). These expressions of concern typically depicted rape as a symptom of moral decay precipitated by an invasion of European and U.S. cultural products.[16] The wave peaked in July 1997, when the Tanzania Media Women's Association (TAMWA) organized a highly publicized symposium for the Members of Parliament to lobby for law reform on a variety of issues relating to women's rights (TAMWA 1997). Despite the range of issues that TAMWA addressed, the press seized upon rape as *the* issue of the symposium. Journalists lamented rape as a sign of societal decay and ignored the practical strategies for combating the problem that the organization was trying to address.

The symbolic usage of the raped woman is endemic throughout postcolonial nationalist writings. Typically, as Ania Loomba notes, "racial and sexual violence are yoked together by images of rape, which in different forms, becomes an abiding recurrent metaphor for colonial relations" (1998, 164). This nationalist narrative, which elides the material presence of the raped woman, suggests that once the colonial invaders are removed, the daughters of the nation will be safe. In the context of Tanzania in the 1990s, however, this fixation indicated that rape continued to function as a metaphor for the nation—the daughters of which were once again in danger.

This danger stemmed from Tanzania's social upheaval during the 1990s. In the process of shifting to a market-driven economy, the Tanzanian government lifted numerous import restrictions, which resulted in a flood of Western films, television programs, and pornography into the urban sphere. Although these products were eagerly consumed, they also exacerbated anxiety over protecting an essentialist notion of culture from the imperialism of the West. In the midst of national transition, rape surfaced as a convenient focal point of this anxiety. During a time when national identity was increasingly contested and redefined, the figure of woman, who symbolized the pure, essentialized core of the traditional Tanzanian self, became vulnerable to cultural rape in the national imagination.

This cultural anxiety played out on the Tanzanian stage as well as in the press. The College of Arts presented several plays that explored the issue of rape, most of which perpetuated the classic cultural nationalist paradigm that defines womanhood as the domain of tradition. For example, one such play, produced by the third-year students, related the story of the traditional village girl who ventured to Dar es Salaam. Once she began wearing blue jeans and going to discos, she was raped by her brother-in-law as if in punishment for refusing her ordained traditional role in upholding the nation.[17] This play exemplified Mary Layoun's concern that "the violation of rape is evoked in a scheme of things in which women are pure, moral, powerless; men are impure, aggressive, and powerful" (1994, 72). As a "pure," modest girl from the village, the girl in the play did not resist the rape, and her wealthy brother-in-law remained unpunished—and in power—at the end of the play.

On the popular stage, TOT's "Control Yourself" provided a startling reversal of this conventional treatment of rape. In this instance, the crisis of national identity was ultimately a *productive* crisis through challenging the dichotomy of traditional woman and modern man. Although the search for female subjectivity in a play that situated women as victims is admittedly problematic, I argue that through a refusal to defer the problem of rape onto the Western other, the victims in this play were defined not only as daughters in need of protection but also as citizens deserving of their rights.

"Control Yourself" conceivably reached more Tanzanians than any other play in 1997. After the play's opening performance on June 6, 1997, TOT performed it in at least seven different neighborhoods throughout the city and in nearby towns of Chalinze and Mlandizi over the next two months.[18] The following November, they performed "Control Yourself" in the city of Mwanza before an audience of thousands as part of a competition with Muungano. Usually, TOT discarded its plays after a few performances and moved on to a new scenario; seldom did I see one of their plays performed more than twice. In this instance, however, they were openly proud of this play and chose to revive it whenever they performed in a new location. TOT's transgressive moment was not an isolated case but was repeated multiple times over the course of six months.

The timing of "Control Yourself" was especially apt, since in late July TAMWA organized the symposium for the Members of Parliament discussed earlier. A debate about rape took place in the parliamentary hall that perpetuated the cultural nationalist argument that the West was to blame. Miniskirts and the recent introduction of television were hotly debated as causal factors; then, one parliamentary member pointed out "an example of some tribes whose women walk half naked but the men of the tribe do not rape them" (TAMWA 1997, 11). In other words, accusations against women's supposed immodesty were deflected with a nostalgic construction of a "tribal" space where sexual violence did not occur. As such debates were waged in the seat of government and in the press, "Control Yourself" provided an alternative perspective within a comical frame.

TOT's emcee, Felix Sawala, typically introduced "Control Yourself" with the qualifier that, unlike the usual comedies that TOT presented, this particular play addressed "serious matters" (*mambo mazito*) in Tanzanian society. Yet, the opening scene, in which the characters Richard and Stumai got married in a frenzied wedding filled with obscene jokes and break dancing, did not hint at these "serious matters." Sawala's introduction notwithstanding, the numerous sexual references and frenetic electronic music set up "Control Yourself" as a screwball comedy. The serious matters were delayed until the second scene, in which an intoxicated Richard and a friend assaulted a young woman on the street and carried her offstage to rape her. Even in this scene, the comic tone continued through Richard's exaggerated portrayal of intoxication.

The aftermath of the rape was not shown. Instead, Baba Swaumu, the elderly father of Stumai, and a male friend entered, excitedly discussing the rape that had just occurred in their neighborhood. The friend glanced at Baba Swaumu's hat, the type commonly worn by East African Muslim men; in a daring reference to homosexual male rape, he commented, "You think that hat will protect you?" (*Unadhani kofia hiyo itakusaidia?*). The two of them vowed to walk always in a pair to forestall the threat of rape. Although comically presented, this scene touched upon a deep-seated anxiety in Tanzanian male culture, which has become increasingly prevalent as homosexuality becomes more difficult to "blame" on Western or Arabic influence.[19] "Control Yourself" was the only play I saw that referred to the possibility of male rape, which complicated the usual gender connotations of the rape victim as female and thus disrupted the metaphorical use of womanhood as a symbol of cultural vulnerability.

Richard then committed a second rape, this time within the confines of his home. He assaulted his sister-in-law Mbilimbi, who was temporarily serving as his housegirl while the pregnant Stumai stayed with her mother. After a brief monologue in which Richard expressed his sexual frustration in his wife's absence, he called in Mbilimbi, who was portrayed as a plain, asexual young girl dressed in *khanga*. As he quizzed her about the housework, she responded in a tired monotone. When Mbilimbi mentioned that she made the bed, Richard announced his desire to inspect her skill at bed making and unceremoniously dragged her offstage. A few moments later, Mbilimbi emerged, holding her groin and crying. In the midst of her exaggerated sobs, she shrieked that her entire body hurts from the rape. The wife, Stumai, coincidentally returned at this very moment with her new baby daughter (represented by a bundle of *khanga*). When she found out that Mbilimbi was raped, she slapped Richard hard and proclaimed a divorce on the spot; meanwhile, Mbilimbi simply observed her sister's rage.

The two sisters then arrived at the home of their father, Baba Swaumu, who lived alone since the divorce from *his* wife, which was depicted in the opening wedding scene. He launched into a tirade when informed of the assault, shouting,

Figure 12. The character Mbilimbi tells the audience she has just been raped by her brother-in-law.

"The government won't stand for this!" (*Serikali haitaendekeza!*). He urged them to report it to the police and offered to look after the baby, his new granddaughter, in the meantime. After his two daughters left for the police station, Baba Swaumu playfully made faces and tickled the baby. He commented on the baby's resemblance to her grandmother, his former wife, and became somewhat agitated. He patted her bottom, giggled, and murmured "*wowowo,*" a sexual reference to women's buttocks. Then, he abruptly carried the baby off-stage with the explanation that she needed changing. The audience heard the baby's cries through the sound system intermingled with Baba Swaumu's gasps; it was immediately understood that the baby was being molested. When the crying cut off, Baba Swaumu re-entered, holding the baby with an exaggerated expression of shock. Once his daughters returned from the police station, Swaumu quickly slipped out the door. Stumai dissolved into wailing when she realized that her baby was dead, which attracted the attention of several neighbor women. When they gathered around Stumai to provide comfort, one spotted blood on the baby's thighs and departed to inform the police.

The two courteous and efficient policemen intermingled with the audience, asking spectators if they had recently seen Baba Swaumu and Richard. When the two men were apprehended with the assistance of the audience, who called out their location to the police, the neighbor women punched and kicked them in a brief display of unrestrained rage. Richard and Baba Swaumu were then lined up together on the stage, and one of the women called out to the audience, "What should we do?" (*Tufanyeje?*). The audience immediately seized the opportunity to shout out their suggestions, which ranged from killing them, burning them, or simply taking them to jail. The police and the community of women did not differentiate between the rapist and the child molester; instead, both were treated as equally monstrous, which implied that Mbilimbi was no more at fault than the infant. In their attempts to stir up societal outrage over rape, TAMWA often linked the rape of young women with child molestation in order to challenge attitudes of blaming the victim. With this ending, TOT graphically illustrated this argument.

In a coda to the play, Swaumu's shocked and bewildered friend asked the audience, how could Baba Swaumu be a rapist? He insisted that he himself would never do such a thing—"I do not rape!" (*Mimi sibaki!*) were his final words as he leaves the stage. The defensiveness of his tone consistently prompted the audience to warn him not to be so sure. This final statement served as a reminder that the issue remained deeply embedded in society and could not be contained through the imprisonment of Richard and Baba Swaumu. In later performances, the actor added a line in which his character began to wonder if Baba Swaumu was planning to rape *him* next. As mentioned earlier, this reference to male homosexual rape complicated the female gender typically associated with rape victims. In re-invoking this threat in the closing moments of the play, however, Swaumu's friend detracted focus from the three actual victims (all of whom have been female) onto himself and thus defined rape as a problem experienced by men. This ambivalent ending positioned him as both a potential rapist *and* a potential victim in a dissolution of boundaries.

In refusing simple answers, "Control Yourself" defied simple interpretations. TOT clearly meant it to be received as a serious play; in addition to introducing it as such, Sawala often asked the audience if they understood the message once the play had ended. On evenings when the laughter seemed especially unrestrained, he would add that although many spectators laughed, others were reduced to silence; his tone of voice implied that the silent spectators had responded "appropriately." Despite the serious subject matter, however, the play was filled with comic elements such as Richard's exaggerated drunkenness that encouraged the audience's laughter. This contradiction between the troupe's stated intent to present a serious play and the comic techniques that were used is difficult to explain. One could argue that if the audience's laughter and the actors' comic performance were signs of belittling victims of rape, the play itself can be disparaged as misogynist. The conclusion, however, cautions against a simplistic reading of this laughter as indifference, since the comic presentation did not extend to the rapists' treatment once they were caught or to the spectators' reactions when they were asked for suggestions.[20]

In grappling with the complexities of this issue, "Control Yourself" used the crisis of rape to encourage new explorations of gender identity, transgressing the nationalist paradigm that defines women as the "keepers" of precolonial tradition. This argument is partly based on a somewhat problematic consideration of what Jenny Sharpe has called "what it means to be rapable" (1994, 226), meaning that in the context of this play, "being rapable" was not meted out as punishment for refusing traditional norms. The first woman, though nonseductive in her clothes and manner, was dressed in modern clothes and was walking alone in the city after dark. Mbilimbi, however, dressed in *khanga* and dutifully fulfilled her responsibilities in the confines of the domestic space. In the cultural nationalist paradigm, Mbilimbi would be safe; in TOT's, rape permeated all such constructions and left females of all ages and backgrounds vulnerable.

This pattern, on its own, was not particularly empowering. It could even be argued that in nationalist discourse, African traditionalism in all of its homogeneity at least affords a protective space, if not a liberating one. But in the final scene when the two rapists were kicked and punched, the formerly passive Mbilimbi joined with the neighbor women to express her anger and overturned the nationalist paradigm that inscribes the traditional woman as meek and submissive. Dualities of rural tradition and urban modernity fell away in an onslaught of rage that enabled the female characters to unite. Mbilimbi seemed incapable of expressing anger against her rapist in the aftermath scene; instead, she passively watched as her sister reacted on her behalf. Then, through the strength of the local female community, she transgressed notions of traditional behavior and assaulted Richard.

The targets of this rage, Richard and Baba Swaumu, also exceeded stereotypes and encouraged a recognition of rape as a societal problem that cannot be blamed on external factors. As a young, rich, modern Christian, Richard stood in opposition to Baba Swaumu, an elderly, poor Muslim. Between the two of them, they managed to cross boundaries of class, religion, and age, all of which were significant identity markers in Tanzanian society. Baba Swaumu committed the more heinous action of the two in committing incest with his infant granddaughter and killing her in the process; as such he fulfilled stereotypical notions of Muslim men as less "civilized" than Christian ones. At the same time, the narrative closure punished them both equally, regardless of the different parameters of the crime and the contrasting backgrounds of the characters.

These characterizations of both rapists and victims removed rape from the realm of metaphor and located it as an internal problem, disrupting society from within. In the world of the play, rape could not be deferred to the West. The rapists were hardly a nebulous other to the victims; instead, they were brothers-in-law, neighbors, and grandfathers. Such treatment nudged the issue of rape out of the realm of a metaphor tossed around in societal discourse into a problem that demanded both local and national solutions. TOT called upon state and subjects alike to combat the crime, as the moment in which the police enlisted the audience's help in tracking down Baba Swaumu signified. Although the characterizations of the two caring and efficient policemen recalled the complicit relations in which TOT and the state were enmeshed, the play also showed the state rising to the challenge—albeit belatedly—of protecting its female citizens.

Another play that addressed rape, which was produced at the state-sponsored 1997 National Arts Festival in Bagamoyo, provides a useful comparison.[21] In this play, the victim, who was seductively dressed in Western clothing, wore a tight black dress at the moment of assault. The performers turned to the audience after the rape scene and requested solutions from the audience. Many spectators assumed the attitude of blaming the victim, claiming that the woman's tight dress provoked the rape. The performers responded with the point that in the precolonial era, women wore little clothing and were not raped; hence, rape was a result of colonial influence and *not* the woman's fault. Although this argument deflected blame from the woman, a refusal to consider the distinct possibility that rape existed long before the arrival of the Europeans played into the nostalgic stereotype of traditional woman as pure and unviolated, creating a precolonial utopia where sexual violence supposedly did not occur. A disturbing corollary to this view is that since a return to the precolonial era is not possible, rape is subsequently inevitable. This particular play, performed in a showcase of national culture, fit neatly into a cultural nationalist framework that idealized the realm of tradition regardless of its repercussions for women.

In contrast, "Control Yourself" recast this official discourse and pointed the way to an alternative nation, one in which rape was *not* inevitable. The cautiousness of this sentence, however, precludes a categorical closure to this discussion. Rape was not *prevented*—it was simply "not inevitable." The play complicated the concept of "home" but left the female characters unmoored without a positive alternative in sight.

Muungano's play "Such Matters" did provide this alternative. Muungano created this play in November 1997 for the occasion of an elaborate series of competitive performances with TOT. Like "Control Yourself," this play was unusually well crafted in honor of the competition, which was staged in three regions of the country.[22] For thousands of spectators, Muungano produced an unwieldy but daring play about female circumcision, rape, and HIV. In locating this triad of controversial topics in the village sphere, Muungano wrenched the romanticized traditional village from an imaginary past and placed it squarely in the complexity of a postcolonial present. Along with "Control Yourself," this play stood out as one of the most complex and original plays that I saw throughout my field research.

The topic of circumcision was broached in the opening of the play, which began with the sound of drumming. This symbolic sound of tradition heralded the entrance of several village characters singing and dancing, their gaiety clashing with the attitudes of two sullen-looking young girls dressed in black. The women began to chant, "Cut, cut, do not be afraid" (*Kata, kata, usiogope*). This ambiguous phrase could have referred to the dance movement of *kukata kiuno,* which means "to cut the waist" and supposedly mimics the movements of heterosexual intercourse; indeed, one of the female villagers joyfully began to demonstrate this movement to the sullen initiates. On a more subtle level, it could have referred to the actual cutting that was about to occur. After the female villager finished demonstrating *kukata kiuno,* the male lead dancer held up a razor blade and proudly announced that he had circumcised seven other girls with the same blade. The drumming, the initiation ritual, and the village setting intertwined to create the proverbial traditional scene.

At this point, so-called modern concerns abruptly intruded into the primordial past. One of the village women, played by the famous *taarab* singer Khadija Kopa, immediately and loudly protested that he would surely contribute to the spread of AIDS. As the villagers scoffed at Kopa's character, a few women restrained one of the initiates. The male lead dancer reached to lift her black cloth; at this point, the initiate began to shake violently in a state of spirit possession and screamed that the blade carried AIDS. In the shocked hush that followed, the second initiate, apparently inspired by her peer's outburst, stood up and launched into a long-winded monologue in which she condemned initiation rites with the claim that girls are taught certain sexual positions that contribute to the spread of AIDS.

This rapid succession of speeches defied the usual parade of meek rural women and outspoken urban ones that are typically found in *maigizo;* instead, the characters drew upon a multitude of tactics to delay the violation of the female body. As the "Queen of *Taarab,*" Kopa's reputation exceeded her rural character; indeed, her appearance on stage caused a stir of excitement among the spectators in all three rounds of the contest. Kopa was notorious for her frank sexuality and many lovers and thus represented the epitome of the modern and supposedly lustful urban woman. In positioning the urban woman as the savior of

Figure 13. The *mganga* (traditional healer) enacts a celebratory ritual dance prior to the act of circumcision. The two initiates are sitting on the ground.

these girls, the play invoked a problematic framework that equated modernization with female liberation. Kopa, however, performed alongside two lesser-known actresses who were easily subsumed into the roles of young rural women. In a strategic move similar to that of the rural wife in Muungano's "The Landlady" described above, one of these initiates called upon the traditional means of spirit possession as a means of resisting the circumcision. This strategy refutes the notion that modernization is equated with female empowerment, for it depicts tradition as a resource rather than simply as a means of oppression. Her companion took the opposite tack by casting her protest in a Western development framework. Her reasoning that traditional sexual education contributes to the spread of HIV reflects the work of Western researchers seeking to blame the rapid spread of HIV in certain African countries (including Tanzania) on "exotic" heterosexual practices (Patton 1992). This monologue transformed the fearful initiate into a mouthpiece for these disturbing stereotypes of African sexuality as constructed by the West. The combination of these various strategies coalesced in a triumvirate of postcoloniality: the first initiate represented the traditional village, Kopa signified the postcolonial city, and the second initiate stood for the Western metropolis. All three facets coalesced in an attempt to forge the girls' escape.

For the moment, they were successful. Once the second initiate finished her speech, the play deferred the situation by delving into the issue of rape. Several villagers dragged a struggling man into the clearing, and a sobbing young female character stammered out that he had attempted to rape her. This character served as the sole example in the play of the stereotypical passive rural woman—who, as a symbol of African tradition, required protection from the violations of modern Western society. In an ironic disruption of this national icon, however, a cross-dressed male actor played the sobbing young girl. This disruption was not conscious on Muungano's part: their young-looking actresses were already cast in the part of the initiates, so the troupe turned to a young-looking male actor to play the role. But in the context of this complex play, this male actor foregrounded the articulate and outspoken women around him.

Instead of creating a primordial utopia where sexual violence supposedly did not occur, "Such Matters" positioned rape as a societal issue that the local community must address instead of depicting it as an inevitable by-product of urbanization. This contextualization of rape *within* the village in "Such Matters" exploded the rural/urban dichotomy through its deconstruction of rural safety and peace. The commanding Kopa and a young man in drag were offered in place of the vulnerable rural girl as representatives of the "new" postcolonial village.

Although this rural/urban collapse could have easily led to confusion, Kopa guided the play to a surprisingly optimistic conclusion. In her powerful voice, she stated that both the government and society must fight against such matters (*mambo hayo*); the "matters" apparently included rape, female circumcision, and AIDS. In calling on the state, she located the issues within the nation as a whole—a nation that could no longer depend upon the feminized village as a protected home, safe from the turmoil of modernization. She did not, however, defer the issues to the state as a means of resolution, for she concluded with a dramatic proclamation that called upon community action as well: "Such matters—we must stop them!" (*Mambo hayo, tuache!*). The villagers picked up this final statement and turned it into a song with the same melody as the opening music. The villagers exited in a mood of celebration—this time, with the two initiates joining in.

In these two plays, TOT and Muungano used the transnational issues of AIDS and rape to foreground the infiltration of rural and urban spheres. Since the global order depends upon a carefully defined hierarchy of center and periphery,

Figure 14. The villager played by Khadija Kopa lectures the audience about the dangers of violence against women. The foiled rapist is sitting on the ground; his intended victim is to the right of Kopa.

challenging the parameters of city and country *within* the Third World nation could facilitate a reconfiguration of systemic power in the metropolitan world. Granted, as plays in which urban and rural female bodies were under attack, they can easily be categorized as yet another manifestation of "diffuse anxieties about the moral and material health of nations [taking] root in women's bodies" (Comaroff and Comaroff 1999, 31). In Muungano's play, however, the dismantling of home did not leave the women helpless. Unlike the female characters in TOT's "Control Yourself," the initiates and the (almost) rape victim escaped unscathed, unmarked, and ready to be transformed.

On a more pessimistic note, it could be argued that the violation did not occur because national borders remained uncrossed. Never, for example, were female characters permitted to travel to Europe; that privilege was reserved only for upper-class men. In the only play I saw in which a female character was granted this freedom, her wealthy husband literally carried her off the stage as if to demonstrate her vulnerability outside the nation's borders.[23] Such moments served as a reminder that migration *outside* the nation denoted an economic and gender privilege from which a majority of the population was excluded. Even for political refugees, transgressing the national border was an act that called for censure. A 1996 Muungano play entitled "Tribalism" ("Ukabila") told a melodramatic story set in Burundi about a Tutsi woman married to a Hutu man.[24] To avoid ethnic slaughter, they fled to a Tanzanian refugee camp. In the borderland of this camp, the pregnant Tutsi woman was brutally slashed with a panga; in contrast, her husband was physically unharmed. Removed from the containment of village and nation, the unhomed female body literally came apart.

Such moments of violence provide a stark reminder of stakes concerning citizenship and national identity. Although the female initiates in "Such Matters" escaped unscathed, they are outnumbered by the number of urban women and the female refugees who were "killed off" in the final moments of Muungano's plays. In the world of TOT, even a female infant could be subjected to rape and murder. These graphic acts of violence resonate with Julie Skurski and Fernando Coronil's discussion of the undercurrents of hostility contained in the postcolonial city. In a thoughtful interrogation of Williams's *The Country and the City,* they point out that the location of the postcolonial city between the periphery of the rural hinterland and the centrality of Europe creates "relations of ambiguity" that complicate local attempts to read these cities as lands of progress and modernization as dictated by the imperial model (1993, 232). To define this process of "double articulation," they write:

> The postcolonial city is defined domestically as a civilizing center in relation to the nation's primitive countryside. Yet since both country and city are located in the "country," or the global hinterland of the metropolitan centers, they are subsumed within an internationally inclusive category of backwardness and colored by the hostile meanings associated with the colonized. (1993, 232)

In effect, this "double articulation" works as double marginalization since postcolonial city *and* country sink into the morass of backwardness and hostility. For the Tanzanian rural woman, "double articulation" could as easily be read as double confinement since she is trapped within the domestic space and anterior time of the traditional rural home.

Through Mzee Jangala's attitude of relentless hostility, Mandela strikes another cautionary note in this optimistic tale. Because of its radical performance of villagehood that exceeds frameworks of nostalgia, the company has been largely absent throughout this discussion. Instead of relying upon gender codes to uphold the rural/urban divide, the blustering character of Mzee Jangala adds a critical element of class rage. Mandela does not distance the village through comedy or romance; instead, it delves directly into the village itself and portrays the masses of ordinary Tanzanians left to languish on the periphery despite the rhetoric of the free market (*soko huria*) and democratization. Mzee Jangala's tirades sound a powerful warning against attempts to theorize Tanzania's political transition to a democratized system of government as part of a teleological narrative of empowerment.

TOPOLOGIES OF ANGER

The subtitle for this section was inspired by Célestin Monga's *The Anthropology of Anger: Civil Society and Democracy in Africa,* in which he theorizes "the vicious legacy of anger" as a manifestation of systematic oppression, arguing that "anger must be considered as a factor in political instability and democratic sustainability" (1996, 5). The character of Mzee Jangala in Mandela's *maigizo* captured this legacy and refuted romanticized ideas of democratization and liberalization. In the course of the approximately fourteen plays of Mandela that I saw in 1997, Jangala chased after a wayward daughter with a machete, regularly showered his long-suffering wife with verbal abuse, threw his father-in-law out of his household, and "mooned" his son. The relentless stream of invective seemed to compress the rage of an entire community into this single character.

It is particularly significant that this rage was embodied in the *mshamba* male. Bakari Mbelemba, who played Jangala, conceived the character as a recalcitrant traditionalist who refused to "go with the times" (*kwenda na wakati*) and accept new technology and ideas. To return to the theories of McClintock and Chatterjee previously discussed, Jangala refused to fulfill the appropriately masculine role in upholding the nation through embracing a modern, industrial future. As the traditional, rural male, Mzee Jangala stood out as an anomaly in the nationalist code. Accordingly, he played his role as inauthentic citizen to the hilt, as each play produced another facet of his crude and vulgar behavior. Instead of personifying supposedly positive aspects of traditional village life, such as respect toward family and industriousness, Jangala seemed to embrace the Arusha Declaration's condescending attitude toward the "wasted" men in the village. Like the diabolical urban females in TOT, Jangala reveled in his inauthentic status as the *mshamba* male. Unlike these "unnatural" women, however, Mzee Jangala established a sense of familiarity with audiences as his outrageousness was grounded in specific and recognizable problems.

The village itself was the locus of Jangala's most insurmountable obstacle of poverty. Unlike TOT's and Muungano's preference for urban settings, Mandela regularly located scenes, if not entire plays, in the village. Instead of depicting the village as a democratic forum where solutions could be found, as in Muungano's "Such Matters," Mzee Jangala's village served as a quagmire of impoverishment and decay. The brutality of economic survival transformed the "traditional African family" revered in Nyerere's writings into an inchoate mass of selfishness. Jangala kicked out his father-in-law because he was unable to pay the rent, displaying an utter lack of respect that was clearly meant to shock the audience.[25] When his son announced that he had received a scholarship to study at the prestigious Makerere University in Uganda, Jangala's main response was not pride; instead, he began to wrangle some of the scholarship money for himself.[26] Familial love or even affection seemed thoroughly absent as family members were valued only for the economic advantages they possessed.

Jangala's ethnic identity grounded the characters' overwhelming poverty in a specific context. Although Mandela followed the usual custom of popular theatre and left the village unnamed, Jangala's accent located it in southern Tanzania among the Makonde, a southern ethnic group viewed with a certain amount of suspicion for what is perceived as a strong loyalty to traditional practices. For example, in a classic colonialist trope of "savage" Africa, Makonde men are widely regarded as fierce. Although Jangala's rage affirmed these popular conceptions, the plays never allowed the audience to forget that this feral quality was borne out of desperation. Given the exclusion of the southern regions from the country's march to economic progress as measured by Western standards, the region provided a fitting backdrop for Jangala's rage against the seemingly insurmountable obstacle of poverty.[27] Violence, poverty, and ethnicity coalesced to make Mzee Jangala exceed the identity of the awkward *mshamba* and become *mshenzi*, a term that roughly translates as "uncivilized" but also contains connotations of fierceness.[28]

Neither did the city provide a path of escape. Several plays focused on a son or daughter of Mzee Jangala who had migrated to the city presumably in hopes of a better life. Not only did these children continue to struggle for economic survival, but they also faced the threat of HIV/AIDS. Upon contracting the disease, they became the brunt of parental anger on one end and institutional coldness on the other, as one play in particular vividly illustrated.[29] Mzee Jangala's young, HIV-infected granddaughter showed up at his home, deserted by her mother and needing shelter. Incensed at his daughter's immoral lifestyle— and upset at the additional expense that his granddaughter would incur—Jangala proceeds to track down the mother in a city hospital where she is wailing over the death of her lover from AIDS. After delivering a series of insults, Jangala leaves her with her daughter, deserting both daughter and granddaughter to their fates. The medical personnel are similarly immune to their suffering. In the final tableau, as the mother continues to wail, the impassive doctor tells the nurse that he is leaving for the day. Neither the institution of the traditional African family nor that of modern medicine could be relied upon to provide alternatives to suffering.

Regardless of their location, all of Mandela's characters were united through their poverty and struggle against seemingly insurmountable obstacles. In the Arusha Declaration, Nyerere identified poverty and disease as two major national threats (1968b, 14); Mandela effectively dramatized both. A particularly evocative moment occurred in "This Condition" ("Hali Hii"), which told the story of Jangala's son, Mashaka, migrating to the city and eventually dying of AIDS.[30] Upon engaging the services of a prostitute, Mashaka informed her that although he would give her only 500 shillings for sex with a condom, he would give her 5,000 shillings without. The prostitute, clearly torn and even anguished about this choice, turned to the audience and plaintively asked for advice—a question to which the normally boisterous audience did not respond. This moment captured the intersection of poverty and disease, communicating a sense of despair that crossed rural/urban divides.

Monga argues that anger stemming from systematic oppression is frequently translated into political attitudes and actions: "Throughout Africa, people are invading the political arena in an (often furious) attempt to get their will finally taken into account by the leaders, and ethical ambition is expressed through explosions of anger" (1996, 10). In this vein, one could link Jangala's rage to a harsh critique of the nation that forcefully explodes any lingering romanticism that situates the village as peripheral to the nation-state. The process of deconstruction invites the possibility of *re*construction—by placing the village center stage, the power relations of center/periphery are potentially transformed. But this interpretation raises a host of questions: Who is allowed to express this anger? How is the anger productive? What alternatives are suggested? These questions help to complicate what Monga himself admits is a determinedly optimistic approach about the potential of anger as a force for social revolution (1996, 11).

In the case of Jangala, his anger should perhaps be described as a force of domestic violence since his wife and children frequently bear the brunt of his rage. It is noteworthy that Jangala never directed his anger against institutions of the state. Indeed, such institutions were conspicuously absent from Jangala's world; unlike the plays of Muungano and TOT, police characters rarely made an appearance in the company's *maigizo*. The plays revolved around Jangala's extended family, none of whom were immune from his anger. His sons who migrated to the city were inevitably caught up in this pattern, as they were typically as abusive to women as their father, Mzee Jangala, was to his long-suffering wife. The class rage of the male characters was meted out on both subservient traditional women and urban prostitutes, causing differences between rural and urban women to collapse.

Rarely did these women resist. Regardless of their status as daughters, wives, or lovers, whether they hailed from rural or urban backgrounds, they were united in their passivity. "Where Should She Stay?" ("Akae Wapi?") provides a representative example of this subservience.[31] After the young woman was deserted by her husband, her parents refused to claim her as a member of their household since they lacked the money to support her. They insisted that the husband's parents (including Mzee Jangala) assume responsibility, and most of the play consisted of an argument between the girl's parents and her in-laws. The deserted wife was mostly silent throughout the play; indeed, at one point, her parents and in-laws literally pushed her back and forth across the stage. The performers wished to drive home the seriousness of the woman's plight through emphasizing the bleakness of her situation; however, her utter lack of agency perpetuated the notion that women are unable to survive on their own. Of the three main theatre companies, Mandela was regularly singled out for its negative representations of women among faculty and students at the University of Dar es Salaam and the College of Arts;[32] I suspect that this pattern of female submission was a major factor in this perception.

These critiques of Mandela's gender politics, however, did not account for the ironic form of egalitarianism that its plays contained, as both sexes were equally trapped in the politics of oppression. Regardless of whether they are sons or daughters, almost all of Jangala's children met distressing fates. His daughters either contracted AIDS or were condemned for becoming pregnant outside of marriage; similarly, his sons either contracted AIDS or were condemned for making a lover pregnant. On the rare occasions when Jangala provided schooling for his children in order to improve their chances of economic success, he was rarely rewarded. In one such play, his daughter became pregnant and was expelled from school; in a second play, his son became insane as a result of witchcraft, presumably for refusing to pay back the money that Jangala borrowed for his education.[33] When faced with such obstacles, Jangala's fury did not distinguish between sons and daughters; all were targets of his rage.

Only one character in Mandela's plays managed to triumph over poverty.[34] Jangala's son, Kidole, succeeded in winning a scholarship to study at the prestigious Makerere University in nearby Uganda. Despite Jangala's attempts to thwart his son's plans through wrangling some of the scholarship money for himself, Kidole went on to study at the university. He returned at the end of the play as a successful university student to find the family squabbling over the remaining amount of the scholarship money he had set aside for them. A model of poise, Kidole proceeded to condemn their actions; his calmness provided an effective counterpoint to his father's bluster. On the one hand, the character of Kidole, whose dignity struck a unique note in Mandela's usual melody of cynicism and rage, suggested that the desperate world of Jangala was not a predetermined fate. On the other hand, it is significant that Kidole must leave Tanzania altogether in order to escape this fate. In the world of Mandela, the entire country has become a quagmire that swallows up opportunities to succeed.

But to focus on the existence of dignity in particular characters perhaps relies too heavily on Western ideals of individualism. What Monga provocatively calls the "collective consciousness" in Africa helps to clear space for conceptualizing the dignity of Jangala's *community* as a force for the re-building of civil society. The term *baraza,* a Swahili word for "council," was frequently invoked in Mandela's plays, as Jangala's outrageous actions and those of his children usually provoked a crisis that called for Jangala's relatives and neighbors to intervene in an attempt to find a resolution. When Jangala kicked his father-in-law out of the house for being unable to pay rent, for example, this community showed up on Jangala's doorstep and demanded that he allow his father-in-law to return. A *baraza* could be called in the city as well as in the village, which indicated that this sense of community pervaded rural and urban spheres alike and thus could not be contained as a "traditional" feature of village life. The persistence of this community as a social force was vividly illustrated in the final tableau of the play in which the unplanned pregnancy of Jangala's daughter was revealed. As Jangala chased her off the stage, shouting his rage, the rest of the community pursued Jangala, chastising *him* for the child's upbringing. The *baraza* ensured that Jangala's rage was not isolated and thus operated as a force of constraint. The power of this gaze might explain why Jangala shouted obscenities and "mooned" his own children but consistently stopped short of physical violence.[35]

Admittedly, the council invariably failed to find a resolution. Unmoored from the conventional anchor of tradition and the promise of modernity, the endings of Mandela's plays usually lacked closure. Instead, the characters continued to carry on with the various domestic quarrels, and a mood of mutual hostility usually prevailed. Although these endings could be explained as yet another manifestation of Mandela's cynicism, they also signified a collective refusal to concede and thus could be interpreted as a sign of strength. One of the few plays that did provide a sense of closure was "This Condition," the final scene of which consisted of the funeral of Jangala's son who died of AIDS. Emptied of his usual rage, Jangala sat silently and motionless throughout the funeral. His defeated attitude clarified the connection between anger and strength. Even in this rare moment of surrender, Jangala roused himself in the final moments of the play, turning to the audience and asking harshly, "Tomorrow, who will be in the coffin?" His challenging tone provoked an angry response from the men in the audience who clearly took offense at Jangala's implication that their fates were sealed. The mood of hostility again prevailed, this time between the spectators and Jangala. "This Condition" provided a powerful reminder that Mandela's characteristic lack of resolution stemmed from a collective refusal to submit.

Mandela's cynicism helps to explain the company's refusal to follow its rivals' lead into promising directions and new terrains, and why it did not produce a play that was the equivalent of TOT's "Control Yourself" and Muungano's "Such Matters." What the plays of all three companies had in common, however, was that the strength of community would not be denied. Of course, to invoke the term *community* is a potentially homogenizing move since it overlooks the violence of exclusions within that community despite its egalitarian connotations. But the clarion call to the community to find the rapists in TOT's "Control Yourself," Muungano's optimistic demand that the state and the community band together to fight against rape and HIV/AIDS, the ubiquitous *baraza* in Mandela—these moments gestured toward a messy, vibrant democratization defined on a local level as opposed to a hegemonic concept imposed by the West. In a forceful reclamation of the term *democracy,* Monga writes that "the democratic project in sub-Saharan African has not been perceived by the people as a cultural fetish used to disguise famine, misery, and suffering. Rather, they see it as a means of expressing citizenship, confiscated and perverted by decades of authoritarianism" (1996, 10). I believe that this chapter reveals the way that the theatre companies of Dar es Salaam also participated in the rejuvenation of the democratic project.[36]

These moments help to create a new poetics of nationalism that exceed tired binaries of rural tradition and urban modernity. In the wake of massive social change, the complexities of Tanzanian history that seethed beneath the "peaceful" village of Tanzanian nationalist discourse were increasingly revealed. These retellings of nationalism in crisis resonated with Mary Layoun's suggestion that in and through such narratives, "we can sense the palpable longing for, the faint imagining of, other not-yet-articulable communities; other ways of producing sexual, familial, and social relations; other ways of knowing and living differences" (1994, 64–65).

People might have continued to "return home" when the *ngoma* were performed, but it was a home that was beginning to imagine the Maasai women, urban landladies, and wide-eyed *washamba* within their midst.

PART THREE

Contesting the Nation

FIVE

Culture Wars

TOT versus Muungano

When local acquaintances in Dar es Salaam learned of my interest in urban popular theatre, I came to expect the question "Which do you like best—Muungano or TOT?" The plethora of companies that dotted the theatrical landscape in the 1980s had consolidated into a rivalry between the old-fashioned, traditionalist Muungano and the modern, trend-setting Tanzania One Theatre (TOT). The expansive networks of *utani* and *mashindano* were reduced to a binaristic, oppositional force; not even Mandela was acknowledged as a contender for the "best" company. TOT's and Muungano's monopolistic hold of the popular theatre scene stood out as an anomaly in a post-socialist era teeming with contestation and debate.

East African competitive performances are generally theorized as affirmations of the status quo, in which intergenerational, interethnic, and/or class tensions are brought to the fore only to be defused in the process. In his introduction to *Mashindano! Competitive Music Performance in East Africa,* Frank Gunderson sums up this pattern in his description of the "harmonizing force" of *mashindano* (2000, 16), which serves as a means of "community formation and solidification, bringing and holding individuals, clans, voluntary associations, ethnicities, and nation-states together in both traditional and creative new ways" (15).[1] Although this framework is reminiscent of what Jonathon Glassman terms the "safety valve" interpretation (1995, 164), which posits festive and ritual performance as a contained space in which societal tensions can be expressed and purged, East African societies readily provide cultural-specific evidence that grounds these claims in a social context. The concept of *utani,* or joking relationship, which binds together relatives, clans, or ethnic groups in a "peculiar combination of friendliness and antagonism" (Radcliffe-Browne 1940, 196) provides a particularly famous example of an indigenous custom that uses the seemingly paradoxical notion of antagonism and opposition to create a sense of shared identity. Such practices lend contextual weight to arguments for the communal nature of *mashindano* and evade the usual Western pitfalls of homogenizing African ritual and performance as uniformly conservative practices that uphold societal norms.[2]

The specific case of the TOT/Muungano competitions provides even more compelling reasons for being categorized as a unifying force. As surrogates of national culture, TOT and Muungano were complicit in sustaining the hegemony of the state, which maintained a latent presence throughout their boisterous and freewheeling performances in Dar's social halls and bars. Once they began producing elaborate competitive events on an annual basis in 1994, this latent presence became especially pronounced through the appearance of official guests and judges.[3] These representatives of what Achille Mbembe calls "officialdom" (2001) would conceivably operate as a dampening force upon the creative improvisations on national culture that usually characterized popular performance. In addition, TOT and Muungano had an economic motive for maintaining a sense of equilibrium, since the "heat" (*joto*) of their rivalry helped to ensure large audiences. Given that thousands of Tanzanians readily paid a tripled admission price of 3,000 shillings ($4.20) to see the competitions, the companies had little interest in triggering unrest and attracting the censure of the officials who granted permits for such events.[4] Complicity and economic gain were key factors in this version of *mashindano* that played upon audiences' fierce loyalties without triggering open conflict.

Nevertheless, an exploration of the TOT/Muungano rivalry should also examine how the *staging* of conflict and antagonism sparks new meanings and ideas. Glassman, who researched festivals and dance competitions on the Swahili coast in the nineteenth century, observes that "far from serving as mechanisms for the mediation and resolution of conflicts, festive rituals *became* impregnated with tension and often turned violent" (1995, 163, emphasis added). In contrast to Bakhtin's famous suggestion that festivals in which rules are temporarily overturned ultimately reaffirm the social order (1981), Glassman argues that conflict was produced, rather than defused, in the moment of performance. Although the TOT/Muungano rivalry did not erupt in actual violence, an underlying tension shaped the form and content of the competitive performances themselves. The complexity of the medium, the agency of individual performers, and the sense of ownership on the part of their fans culminated in multifaceted events in which contradictory and even conflicting agendas coexisted.

The current socioeconomic situation further complicates the notion of competitive performance as a harmonizing force. TOT's surge in popularity indicated that the company no longer depended upon the old rivalry to help stir up fans and command loyalty. As Muungano's survival became increasingly threatened by TOT's access to wealth and political power, it was forced to call upon a multitude of strategies and invent new ones simply to remain in the playing field. In a climate of uncertainty, the stakes had become particularly high, and the time was ripe for traditional standards of decorum to be overturned. Whereas Gunderson theorizes music competitions as "a place where community values are displayed, remembered, reinforced" (2000, 15), TOT and Muungano produced a site in which such values were also complicated, contested, and, at least temporarily, overturned.

An elaborate competition between TOT and Muungano that played out in three specific performances in October and November of 1997 provides rich terrain for a nuanced reading of *mashindano*. The first two rounds, which took place in Dar es Salaam and the nearby town of Morogoro, trod the well-worn paths of affirmation and unification. In these showcases of national culture, the opposition between the traditional Muungano and the modern TOT was carefully upheld. Even within these two rounds, however, spectators and performers began to push against the boundaries of containment and consolidation. Once the companies moved to the northwestern city of Mwanza for the third and final round, the oppositional force of TOT and Muungano gave way to a reconfiguration of national identity in the venue of competitive performance. This particular performance provided an exciting moment where the unique combination of collaboration and contestation coalesced to produce a nation-in-the-making that unfolded before thousands of rapt citizen-subjects.

COCKS VERSUS QUEENS

In response to the frequent question concerning TOT and Muungano, "Which do you like best?" I learned to say that I liked Muungano's *maigizo, ngoma,* and *sarakasi* and TOT's *muziki wa dansi* and *taarab.* This statement consistently received approving nods of agreement—approving, I think, because I was affirming the constructed identities of these two troupes that circulated throughout Dar es Salaam. This categorization reaffirms the positioning of the traditional Muungano versus the modern TOT—a binary that, in its very essentialism, seems fundamental to the construction of Tanzanian identity. Michael Herzfeld points out that the construction of national identity consists of "processes of reification and essentialism as well as challenges to these processes" (1997, 26). This process of reification was perpetuated by both the popular press and the troupes themselves, as demonstrated through the flurry of media attention that the troupes received during the weeks preceding the 1997 contest.[5]

Journalists often used TOT's *kwaya* and Muungano's snake dance to demarcate the boundary between the two troupes. In an account of the 1994 contest between TOT and Muungano in Dar es Salaam, "the cultural clash of the century," the reporter sets off *kwaya* against Muungano's snake dance. He describes the warm reception of "veteran crooner" Komba in *kwaya* and then writes: "Komba's Muungano counterpart, Norbert Chenga, did not go on stage. But his snakes did, levelling matters with TOT's choir singing supremacy by drawing many cheers as the 'snake eaters' performed their antics" (*Daily News* 1994).[6] This opposition of *kwaya* versus snakes also surfaced in the media attention that preceded the 1997 contest. One writer claimed that for Muungano to sing *kwaya* is like fighting a battle with stones inside a glass house, and that for TOT to dance with snakes is like planting rice in a desert (*Mfanyakazi* 1997; see also *Majira* 1997a). In other words, the contamination of these identities was deemed both unsuitable and nonproductive.

Not surprisingly, this particular dichotomy of the snake dance and *kwaya* conformed neatly to what is generally perceived as the polarities of tradition and modernization. Muungano's snake dance, in which a dancer dressed in a headdress, grass skirt, and rattles shuffled rhythmically around the snake, integrated audience participation, a celebration of tradition, and a sense of danger. As the drummers began the repetitive beat of the Sukuma snake dance, a large wooden box that contained two snakes was carried onto the stage. The dancer, Abbas Ahmed, dressed in a grass skirt, headdress, and ankle rattles, lifted the snakes out of the box and attempted to calm them through slow, shuffling dance movements. The "dance" itself was a relatively minor part of the performance, which consisted mainly of Ahmed frightening the audience by permitting the snake to slither close to the edge of the stage. Invariably, children shrieked and spectators scattered, knocking over sodas, beers, and chairs in their haste. After a few minutes of this mayhem, Maulidi Domingo, the emcee, invited audience members to hold the snake on stage, where a photographer stood ready to document their bravery. Through the snake dance, Muungano transformed *ngoma,* a symbol of tradition, into a participatory moment that held the spectators captive with suspense.[7] A particularly revealing moment occurred during a performance in December 1996 when a thoroughly annoyed snake bit a female spectator.[8] In response, Chenga whisked her backstage and placed what was called a "Sukuma black rock" over the bite to draw out the poison. The incident not only illustrated Muungano's ideological stance of taking indigenous practices such as traditional healing seriously, but it reminded audiences of the enduring power of tradition to produce material effects.

In contrast to Muungano's peon to tradition, TOT's *kwaya* conveyed an attitude of modernization through the content of the songs and the staging. Komba, dressed in a two-piece gray suit, and his fellow singer, Gaspar Mapunda, sang songs pervaded with development rhetoric accompanied by a female chorus dressed in matching mono-colored dresses. Komba, the composer of the songs, focused primarily on the glories of Tanzanian culture, the importance of science and technology, and environmental issues. Prior to singing "Mazingira" ("Environment"), Komba often delivered a brief lecture about the dwindling number of forests in Tanzania—a tactic that situated *kwaya* securely in the context of development and modernity. The two men were flanked by a chorus of women, who wore low-cut dresses and slit skirts as if to sugarcoat the educational content of the songs. Although Komba's talent and the elaborate dresses of the female chorus retained the audience's attention during this part of the performance, *kwaya* was characterized by a sense of restraint that clashed with the participatory, democratic atmosphere of Muungano's snake dance. The praise of modernization, diminished level of audience participation, and general atmosphere of restraint shored up *kwaya*'s status as "civilized" and refined.

This categorization positioned the traditional Muungano against the modern TOT in a classic binary that calls forth Tom Nairn's oft-cited description of the Janus-faced nation. He compares the nation to the two-faced Roman god Janus, who stood above gateways looking both forward and backward: "Thus does nationalism stand over the passage to modernity.... As human kind is forced through its strait doorway, it must look desperately into the past, to gather strength wherever it can be found for the ordeal of 'development'" (1977, 348–349). Using Nairn's framework, one could theorize the forward-looking TOT and the backward-looking Muungano as a Janus-faced figure standing in the gateway of nationalism, a pillar of support for the status quo. The duality between tradition and modernization also resonates with Swahili scholar Peter Lienhardt's notion that a binary opposition helps to unify a variety of fragmented populations (1968, 16), a theoretical formulation later echoed in David Maybury-Lewis's more expansive argument that dualistic practice throughout world cultures "seeks to institutionalize the balance of contending forces in order to maintain that harmony in society" (1989, 14). Nationalist discourse and indigenous customs join together in support of *mashindano*'s potential for unification and resolution.

The notion of "unity through binary," however, overlooks the distinctly privileged status of TOT. Decades of cultural nationalist rhetoric notwithstanding, tradition is judged distinctly inferior to what are perceived as emblems of modernization.[9] Moreover, the binarism of TOT/Muungano extends beyond that of tradition and modernization to include connotations of gender. Partha Chatterjee (1993) and Anne McClintock (1994) have theorized tradition as a feminized domain in contrast to the modern, "outside" world controlled by men. In this regard, *kwaya* could be positioned as "male" not only on a literal level through its spotlight on a male singer but figuratively through its connotations of modernization. Although Muungano's snake dance does not conform to the notion of femininity quite so seamlessly since the snake dancer was also male, the company can be configured as "female" through its traditionalist stance. As such, its subordinate position to the masculine TOT is reaffirmed.

TOT's masculinity even pervaded the musical form of *taarab,* which usually served as a showcase for female singers. TOT's ranks included several talented female *taarab* singers—indeed, the rivalry itself supposedly originated as a feud between Nasma Khamis of TOT and Khadija Kopa of Muungano, who exchanged a series of fierce insults through *taarab* songs in 1993.[10] However, TOT began to redefine the genre of *taarab* in 1994 when Komba lured Ally Star, a male *taarab* singer and a long-standing member of Muungano, to join his company. To this day, Star remains one of TOT's main selling points due to his tremendous popularity. Star's youthful appearance and trendy, "hip" renditions of *taarab* music fit neatly into TOT's alignment with masculinity and modernization. As counterpoints to Muungano's trademarks of the snake dance and Kopa, the "Queen of *Taarab,*" TOT highlighted Ally Star and *kwaya* as the self-proclaimed "Rooster of Africa."[11]

TOT can also be figured as upper class. Although Muungano's battered stage furniture and worn curtain backdrops were hardly unusual in Dar es Salaam, they did convey a sense of poverty in comparison to TOT's well-equipped stage. Moreover, Muungano relied upon simple *khanga* and T-shirts as costuming for *ngoma,* whereas TOT could afford to create unique and elaborate costumes for a single dance. The most powerful visual symbol of TOT's wealth consisted of the elaborate Bose sound system, which figured prominently in publicity photos and radio advertisements. This collection of bass guitars, keyboard, and stereo speakers—rumored to have cost about $65,000—vividly displayed TOT's access to CCM's financial resources. Indeed, TOT's economic privilege extended beyond the trappings of the performance to the performers themselves, since TOT often succeeded in luring away Muungano's best performers with the promise of higher salaries. Through political, economic, and patriarchal terms, TOT upheld its supremacy on a number of fronts.

This polarizing of the troupes defined the parameters in which their rivalry was played out. In the weeks preceding the contest, Komba and Chenga began circling each other for the upcoming battle through the medium of the popular press, and reporters delighted in recording each one's various boasts and jibes. In taking on TOT as an opponent, the disenfranchised Muungano was forced to draw upon a variety of tactics, while TOT simply reiterated its marks of privilege. One of Chenga's main strategies was to single out TOT's new instruments as a point of attack, telling reporters that although TOT owned the instruments, its musicians lacked the talent to play them properly. He claimed that if Muungano had access to those instruments, they would make their fans tremble with excitement (*Dar Leo* 1997c). Chenga also undercut TOT's financial privilege with the claim that TOT could only win the contest if the judges considered costumes instead of artistic ability (*Uhuru* 1997)—an acerbic comment upon TOT's ability to create expensive and flashy costumes for each of their different acts. These references to TOT's expensive costumes and instruments suggested an attempt to establish an alliance with those audience members who would have identified with its impoverished state.

In response to Chenga's jibes, Komba openly acknowledged TOT's financial privilege. Komba shrugged off his rival's comments and simply referred to the instruments' cost, as if the expense alone should ensure TOT's victory (*Uhuru* 1997; *Dar Leo* 1997c). In a blunt reference to Muungano's poverty, he announced that TOT had only agreed to the contest in order to help Chenga pay his performers' wages (*Uhuru* 1997). These comments implied that TOT's financial security was equivalent to artistic superiority and evaded the fact of CCM's financial backing. In an especially insulting statement, Komba also informed reporters that the final ingredient needed to make TOT complete was to hire Chenga himself as a snake dancer (*Nipashe* 1997b; 1997c). The appropriation of Muungano's defining act and the leader himself would erase the company's very existence. CCM maintained its status as "number one" through a massive consolidation of power; Komba's responses implied that TOT was following its sponsor's lead.

This exchange of insults took an intriguing turn when Komba publicly observed that Chenga had recently shaved off his hair, which is widely perceived as sign of practicing witchcraft (*Dar Leo* 1997b). He noted that he had heard Chenga intended to cast a spell that would cause TOT's singers to shake and their instruments to stop working. In addition to affirming Muungano's traditionalist reputation, this comment suggested that Chenga was forced to resort to these practices in the face of TOT's superiority. On his part, Chenga might have been referring to witchcraft when he stated bluntly that on the day of the contest, TOT's instruments would burn (*Majira* 1997b). Like the rural female characters in Muungano's plays who called upon the resources of witchcraft, Muungano implied that it was quite capable of drawing upon traditional practices in its drive to win. Interestingly, Komba countered with a reference to his Ngoni ethnicity as a sign of his ability to defend TOT from any spells (the Ngoni people are supposedly well versed in matters of witchcraft). The wealthy, modern Komba could invoke a multitude of privileges that ensured his victory; at the same time, his Ngoni ethnicity allowed him to hold his own with Muungano on the traditional terrain as well.

Given Muungano's disenfranchisement in the TOT/Muungano equation, it is tempting to position Muungano as the rebellious underdog. Throughout this exchange of insults, however, Muungano faithfully retained its nationalist stance. Even its strong points of *ngoma, maigizo,* and *sarakasi* paid tribute to the state's previous attempts to maintain national troupes devoted to each of these three forms. In contrast, TOT focused upon the forms of *muziki* and *taarab,* both of which the Ministry of Culture had categorized as "foreign." A member of Muungano tried to criticize TOT on these cultural nationalist grounds with the claim that TOT had failed to follow national guidelines for theatre as set by the National Arts Council through their emphasis on *muziki.* Komba waved aside this criticism with the simple comment that TOT "honors" (*kuenzi*) Tanzanian culture and promotes national art (*Dar Leo* 1997a)—an argument easily "proved" by the refrain of *utamaduni* throughout TOT's musical acts. Instead of maneuvering, negotiating, and countering the invention of tradition, TOT did as it liked and defined the results as national culture with the force of CCM to back up its claims.

At the same time, the hint of violence in Chenga's comments regarding the burning of TOT's instruments perhaps conveyed a sense of desperation in the face of TOT's arrogance. The opposition of Muungano and TOT was becoming increasingly strained through the relations of inequality, which threatened to upset the sense of equilibrium that the binary maintained. The intensity of Chenga's comments served as a reminder of the potential for conflict that bubbled just beneath the surface of this seemingly genial tradition of *mashindano*. For the time being, however, this potential for conflict was contained within the carefully designed parameters of rounds one and two.

CULTURE CLASH 1997

Given the intensity of the exchanges between Komba and Chenga through the press, the 1997 contest seemed slated to erupt into an open display of conflict. Instead, the first two rounds maintained an unusual sense of decorum that seemed more designed to please the Ministry of Culture than the enthusiastic fans. Government officials were appointed as judges of the event as if to remind the companies to toe the nationalist line. As is explained later, this presence of the state was effaced in the Dar es Salaam competition and was practically nonexistent in Mwanza. Nevertheless, through the domestication of their normally boisterous performances, Muungano and TOT conveyed their intention to play along as expressions of official culture and therefore became complicit in this revamping of popular performance.

A brief discussion of historical context helps to explain this transformation. During the 1994 TOT/Muungano contest, an isolated example of conflict occurred when Ally Star, who still belonged to Muungano, stopped singing and announced that he was joining TOT. In response, the "frenzied spectators" erupted, and police intervened to bring the ensuing fracas under control (*Daily News* 1994). Although the police cut short the conflict before violence occurred, this incident is reminiscent of Glassman's assertion of the potential for violence that festive rituals possess (1995, 163).[12] Here, through the medium of the police, the state moved quickly to restore order when the audience became unruly.

As if to preclude a repeat of this event, the presence of the state became explicitly marked for the second competition, which was produced in 1995. The competition marked the jubilee of CCM (Lange 2000, 71); as such, the entire event was subsumed under the aegis of the state as an official celebration. In a seemingly blatant display of collusion with the state, TOT created a play that praised the police for fulfilling their duty to Tanzania (*Mwananchi* 1995). On its part, however, Muungano articulated a voice of resistance through a play that directly criticized the government for caring only about the upcoming elections instead of the citizens (*Mwananchi* 1995). Not only did Muungano use the venue of a political celebration to voice this challenge, but the company also chose an especially sensitive time since the first multiparty elections were only a few months away. This unusual foray into political criticism undercut the competition's official alignment with the state and signified the societal tension that lay beneath the celebratory rhetoric.

For the 1997 competition, new stage configurations were a key factor in creating an atmosphere of restraint. The first round took place at Vijana Social Hall—a site in which official and popular cultures had long overlapped.[13] Because Vijana Social Hall belonged to the youth branch of CCM, it provided a source of funding for the party. The hall was also a coveted performance space among Dar es Salaam theatre companies and bands due to its large size and proximity to public transportation. For the purposes of the contest, the ramshackle performance hall had been transformed. Instead of using the low, crumbling stage, TOT and Muungano each constructed a high raised stage, both suitably decorated for the occasion with balloons, streamers, and palm branches. These high stages made it difficult for spectators to intervene in the action and therefore limited the high degree of audience participation that usually characterized performances at Vijana. Action shifted easily from one stage to the other—a sharp contrast to the usual performance style in which each transition is punctuated with a lengthy pause. The combination of fluid action and raised stages colluded to create a sense of restraint more characteristic of the relatively sedate College of Arts than of the lively Vijana.

For the next two rounds of the contest, which were held in the massive sports stadiums in Morogoro and Mwanza, the spectators were even more removed from the action. A wide, paved track that ran between the stages and the stands created a chasm between the actors and audience that obliterated the usual intimacy that characterized these performances. In Morogoro, the stadium seating was divided into sections for TOT's and Muungano's fans; in the neutral ground between the two sections, a "high table" was set up for the attendance of several members of Parliament. The representatives of the state served as a buffer zone between the two sides and provided the final touches on the orderly and officious atmosphere.

The content of the performances also suggested that the popular performance was being "tamed" into official submission. In the rounds held in Dar es Salaam and Morogoro, the unique patter of TOT's and Muungano's emcees was replaced with a neutral announcer who blandly introduced each act. Meanwhile, the battling Chenga and Komba remained on the edges of the crowd away from the audience's view. Their subdued behavior deflated expectations of an open display of the conflict that had simmered for weeks through the press. In a more explicit move, the snake dance and *kwaya* were omitted from the lineup. The exclusions of Muungano's and TOT's defining acts threatened to transform the performances into a generic version of national culture that eliminated the troupes' specific identities and minimized the spectators' enthusiasm.

To some extent, the reconstruction worked. In contrast to the usual boisterous atmosphere that pervades popular performance, a degree of decorum persisted throughout the contest, and the usual parade of cross-dressed men, pythons, and frenzied brawls was excluded from the stage. Nevertheless, the deep-seated ideological investments of the two companies would not be denied. Despite the removal of the snake dance and *kwaya*, the demarcation between the democratic, traditionalist Muungano and the restrained, modern TOT were strategically sustained.

Although Muungano's first entry in the contest, the notorious "waist-wriggling" *lizombe*, was strangely subdued,[14] its second *ngoma*, the *tokomile* of the coastal Zaramo, showcased Muungano's ability to reinvigorate ideas of tradition through a democratic lens. A few months earlier, TOT had created a characteristically "modern" version of *tokomile*, transforming it into a complicated dance drama and using its electronic instruments as an accompaniment.[15] As if in direct challenge to this version, Muungano's interpretation used only drumming for music, as well as the *zumari*, a kind of coastal horn. To provide an edge of novelty, the *taarab* singer Khadija Kopa participated in the dance. When she danced in the first round, numerous female spectators immediately pressed onto the stage to tip. The excitement that the contest generated seemed to erase the usual reticence of female spectators, who tended to avoid participating in *ngoma* due to its connotations of *ushenzi* ("uncivilized" behavior). This tipping soon evolved into actual dancing alongside the Muungano female performers in the only time I saw women join in *ngoma* with unrestrained enthusiasm. Many of them danced the steps with assured skill, signifying their Zaramo identities. Kopa's participation created an overlap between *ngoma* and *taarab* that coalesced in a moment in which Zaramo women dominated the stage. In Muungano's creative hands, *tokomile* became a celebration of coastal and female identity.

TOT responded with a celebration of CCM. Its political alliance manifested itself in its usual surreptitious manner through the Nyakyusa dance called *ling'oma*.[16] Like the traditions of *mganda* and *beni, ling'oma* is based on German military formations; as such, the male performers wear white military-style shorts, dress shirts with neckties, and play kazoos. Terence O. Ranger quotes an informant of *beni* who could have been describing TOT's version of *ling'oma:* "This was a clean dance because everyone wore good clothes.... at daybreak they looked as clean as if they had not been dancing at all" (in Ranger 1975, 72). Unlike the loose *khanga* and ankle rattles worn by the *ngoma* dancers of Muungano, TOT had procured expensive, elaborate costumes of all-white, Western fashions trimmed in red. The men were divided into two groups, or "ranks": those who wore red neckties with their white shirts and shorts, and those who donned red sashes and shoulder tassels in imitation of military uniforms. Although *ling'oma* is by custom an all-male dance, TOT also introduced female dancers, who modeled feminine versions of the "clean" costumes just described. The women were costumed in white high-heeled pumps and white straight skirts with a red belt; they also carried starched white handkerchiefs. As if to parody Western ideals of womanhood, they barely moved in their heeled pumps except to wave their white handkerchiefs daintily through the air. These starched white uniforms seemed especially crisp and orderly when compared to Muungano's loosely tied, colorful *khanga* worn in *lizombe*.

With this interpretation of *ling'oma,* TOT presented *ngoma* as commensurate with the agenda of CCM. In a particularly blatant move, TOT inserted a few lines of Swahili into the Nyakyusa lyrics in which the company launched into a condemnation of corruption in the government, singing, "Let's stamp out corruption" (*Tuzime rushwa*). Given that anti-corruption was a favored slogan of CCM in the multiparty era, used to counter accusations that they maintain power through illegal means, this moment signified a covert promotion of CCM packaged in fancy costumes and slick choreography. Even the starched white cleanliness of the costumes conveyed a none-too-subtle message of the "cleanliness" of CCM. Within the contained parameters of the contest, TOT proved quite capable of disseminating its political agenda.

In contrast to the "cleanliness" of TOT, Muungano's performers literally reveled in dirt. In honor of the occasion, Muungano created an entirely new *sarakasi* act for which the performers deserted the high raised stage in favor of a pole erected in the center of the audience space. Throughout all three rounds of the contest, the acrobats performed various daredevil stunts in which they dangled from the pole or balanced on top of it. As a result of the pelting rain that fell throughout the performance in Dar es Salaam, their jumpsuits became

Figure 15. TOT performed *ling'oma* in all three rounds of the competition. This Nyakyusa dance, like *beni* and *mganda,* was originally inspired by colonial military formations.

increasingly streaked with mud as if to celebrate the connotations of *uchafu* (dirt) that their ideological embrace of tradition contained.

In the first two rounds of the competition, the *maigizo* provided a particularly vivid illustration of opposing ideologies. Muungano's relatively serious play, which took place in a village, explored the controversial topic of the ritual of female circumcision, whereas TOT's comic play focused on an upper-class urban male. In a synecdoche of Muungano and TOT's "culture clash," rural, impoverished women squared off against a wealthy, upper-class man. Since Muungano's contribution of "Such Matters" ("Mambo Hayo") was thoroughly discussed in the previous chapter, a brief summary of the plot will suffice. Instead of the usual urban tale of domestic intrigue, "Such Matters" told the story of a village ceremony of female initiation. Kopa, playing the role of one of the village women, tries to halt the ceremony, insisting that such practices contribute to the spread of HIV/AIDS. In the midst of this layered discussion of rural tradition and global disease, the issue of rape also enters the scene with the revelation that another young girl of the village had been attacked. In the play's conclusion, Kopa calls upon local communities and the government to bring a halt to "such matters"–including HIV/AIDS, rape, and domestic violence.

Its significance in the context of the TOT/Muungano competition lies in the company's complex treatment of rural women. Typically, the village was depicted as isolated from the upheavals of modernization, so therefore it would theoretically escape the attendant evils. This play demonstrated that Muungano's embrace of traditional ideology did not preclude the group from a critical examination of oppressive practices such as female circumcision; moreover, its frank discussion of the spread of AIDS in the village broke down the dichotomy of urban and rural spheres. The play also served as a showcase for Kopa as the outspoken advocate for women's rights who denounced the ritual. Through her multiple appearances in *ngoma, maigizo,* and *taarab,* her charismatic presence provided a through line of female strength that threw TOT's parade of female stereotypes into sharp relief.

Whereas Muungano treated rural concerns in a thoughtful, critical manner, TOT chose the comic route in the creation of "The Shame of Money" ("Fedha Fedhaha"). The focal point of the play was the wealthy Richard, whose lavish use of money dominated his interactions with his family and neighbors. In the opening scene, a mother, accompanied by her crying daughter, demanded that Richard's daughter apologize for hitting her child at school. Richard ignored her complaints and offered her some money, which the offended mother refused. This interaction was the first of many in the play in which Richard bought his way through life. He gave his daughter 20,000 shillings ($28) just to go to the beach with friends; also, instead of attending a funeral, he told his wife just to send cash. Finally, he knocked over a tray of hard-boiled eggs from a vendor and refused to apologize; instead, he overpaid for the broken eggs. Tragedy struck when his daughter, after returning from the beach, abruptly fell ill and died. Richard and his wife prepared to receive visitors for the *msiba,* a customary gathering that precedes the actual burial in which neighbors and relatives visit to express sympathy and contribute money to the cost of the funeral. Although various neighbors responded by coming to the *msiba* and contributing money, they all made increasingly bizarre excuses when Richard invited them to the burial that afternoon. Richard was reduced to tears at the realization that no one would come to his daughter's funeral. Finally, the egg seller and the mother from the first scene lectured the now-contrite Richard on the consequences of living his life by the rules of money.

The play drew a contrast between the foolish upper-class father figure and the wise, poverty-stricken characters who taught him a lesson. Given that TOT was "upper class" in comparison to Muungano, the unflattering depiction of Richard could be interpreted as TOT's attempt to distance itself from its own privilege. The spectators, who undoubtedly would have identified with the characters of the impoverished egg seller and the mother, were encouraged to laugh at Richard, who was portrayed in an exaggerated, over-the-top manner in contrast to the relatively naturalistic interpretations of the lower-class characters. Even the scene in which he mourned his daughter was made comical through the actor's exaggerated nose blowing, and the audience obligingly laughed at his tearful antics.

At the same time, TOT carefully maintained its usual ideological stance of patriarchal and class privilege. The mother and the egg seller existed only to point out the error of Richard's ways; in the end, their lower-class status remained firmly in place. Moreover, despite his foolishness, the father was the undisputed head of the household; no one dared to defy him since he maintained the household's wealth. His obedient and subservient wife never questioned his instructions on how their money should be spent nor challenged his readiness to spoil their daughter. Even though the daughter's "tough" appearance and behavior made her a potential rebel of the family, she was transformed into a model of submission in front of her father. Through the guise of urban comedy, TOT's investment in structures of power remained intact.

Within the carefully contained atmosphere of round one, the interlocking dualities of TOT/Muungano, tradition/modernization, male/female, and upper/

lower class held firm. Although the removal of the snake dance defused the potential of disorder and audience participation, Muungano sustained the chaotic spirit when its acrobats crossed into the audience space and staged an especially vigorous, mud-splattering *sarakasi* act. Muungano also compensated for the lack of audience participation through its staging of *tokomile,* which stands out as one of the most striking performances of *ngoma* I saw throughout my fieldwork in terms of the intensity of female participation that it inspired. Whereas the repeated appearances of the charismatic Kopa added to the diversity and excitement of Muungano's performance, TOT's female performers faded into the blandness of uniform submission. As if to call attention to its sense of entitlement, TOT's elaborate sound and music equipment served as the background for a series of male singers and characters secure in their position of masculine privilege.

In the spirit of "unity through binary," the division between TOT and Muungano was clearly holding firm. As is characteristic of East African competitive performance (Nyoni 2000, 253), a victor was never identified despite the many speculations in the press about which troupe would win the contest. The declaration of a winner would theoretically upset the sense of equilibrium that the tension between the two companies maintained. Although inequalities and ambiguities permeated the TOT/Muungano rivalry, indigenous custom and official interests coalesced to ensure that the two companies formed a pillar of nationalism that upheld the status quo.

As the final round in Mwanza suggests, however, this sense of unity invoked by this rivalry was precarious. Although the more boisterous and disjointed elements of the popular performance were held in check during the first two rounds of the contest, moments of excess still managed to test the parameters of order and restraint. In the third and final round in Mwanza, this sense of restraint disintegrated to reveal the instabilities and contradictions that permeated the TOT/Muungano rivalry. In a tale of broken-down buses and failing generators, these lines of demarcation between TOT and Muungano were destabilized and overturned.

MWANZA INTERVENTIONS

In the 1997 competition, Muungano and TOT joined forces in the recasting of *mashindano* as an official event. The restrained quality of the performances in Dar es Salaam and Morogoro, reflected in the stage configurations, presence of government officials, and the content of the various acts, signaled the transformation of the competitive performance into a "safe" money-making venture that walked a line between pleasing fans and government officials. In this context, the potential of conflict and resistance would theoretically be defused.

But to categorize these events simply on the basis of overt conflict—either its presence or absence—does not account for the potential of competitive performance to produce new meanings. Historically, *mashindano* in Tanzanian popular theatre has served as a force of innovation rather than consolidation. When factories and branches of the army co-opted existing dance societies in Dar es Salaam as cultural troupes in the 1970s, the grassroots network of *utani* in which these dance societies operated was redirected rather than suppressed. As a result of the cultural troupes' enthusiastic attempts to "outdo" one another through additional acts, the vaudeville style of Tanzanian popular theatre was created.[17] Moreover, an understanding of these competitions must take into account the role of spectators, who use the tradition of *mashindano* to express individual loyalties and tastes regardless of official attempts to create a contained atmosphere. The *mashabiki* (fans) provide a reminder that the historical roots of *mashindano* extend far deeper than postcolonial attempts to co-opt them.

Despite the official facades of the performances in Dar es Salaam and Morogoro, the vitality of *mashindano* could not be suppressed. Despite careful planning, the prosaic factor of weather in the Dar es Salaam performance challenged attempts to tame the tradition of *mashindano*. Rain poured intermittently throughout the performance and turned the Vijana grounds into a sea of mud. As a result, the official guests did not venture to the contest, and their absences were filled by the intensity of loyal fans. In front of both stages, particularly ardent fans danced and cheered mindless of the mud and rain throughout each of the multiple acts. Even among those who preferred to huddle under umbrellas, many marked their allegiance by carrying small flags, red for TOT and green for Muungano.[18] Their forceful presence challenged efforts to create a contained atmosphere that discouraged conflict.

Even in Morogoro, where the competition was particularly orderly and officious, the audience members proved an unpredictable element. Whereas the fans seemed equally divided in Dar es Salaam, this sense of equilibrium yielded to a distinct majority for TOT once the contest shifted to Morogoro, with twice as many fans crowding TOT's side as that of Muungano. The disproportionate number of TOT fans can be attributed to a month of training in Morogoro once the company had received their new sound system and instruments. During this period of training, TOT held public performances in Morogoro town, cultivating a strong local following that turned out in great numbers at the competition to see "their" troupe perform. Perhaps in order to compensate for their smaller numbers, the Muungano fans were especially vocal in their catcalls and jeers of TOT's performers. For example, during TOT's relatively lengthy *ngoma* of *kibati,* they began loudly complaining that the storyteller was monopolizing the stage.[19] Although the TOT fans were markedly subdued in comparison to those of Muungano, their sheer numbers made TOT look more powerful than ever, and the catcalls and jeers from Muungano's side seemed ineffectual and weak.

Interestingly, TOT itself produced a crack in the carefully controlled atmosphere of the Morogoro performance. As if to disregard the parameters of the contest, TOT restored its defining act of *kwaya,* which marked a significant change from the first round.[20] After singing about the environment and the importance of *utamaduni,* Komba moved into political territory with the third and last song: "The Neighbor's House Is on Fire" ("Nyumba ya Jirani Yaungua Moto"), which metaphorically referred to the self-destruction of opposition parties. In the context of the contest, however, the "neighbor's house" referred to Muungano, which cast the troupe in the same light as the self-destructing political opposition. This analogy became especially poignant in the week following the third round in Mwanza, when I saw a poorly attended rally for the opposition party CUF (Civic United Front). The similarity between the sparse crowds for CUF and the sparse crowds for Muungano did not bode well for the fate of either in the multiparty era (this political rally is discussed in more detail below). TOT's tactic of consuming a disproportionate amount of stage time effectively diminished Muungano's presence.

In the third round, Muungano was almost eliminated. Whereas previous competitions were confined to one or two rounds, the 1997 version expanded to include a third round in Mwanza, Tanzania's second-largest city, located in northwest Tanzania. The first two rounds of the 1997 contest maintained a sense of decorum, but the official facade began to disintegrate in Mwanza as a result of the fundamental inequities between the two troupes. As TOT's arrogance and Muungano's desperation intensified, the unspoken rules of the contest were increasingly ignored.

Even before the contest officially began, Muungano's troubles gave forewarning that the competition was to take an unusual turn. A week before the Mwanza contest, which was scheduled for November 1, the members of TOT leisurely traveled second-class by train and arrived in the city two days beforehand. In contrast, only Muungano's *sarakasi* performers had managed to arrive on the morning of the contest, which was scheduled to begin around 2 PM that afternoon. By that time, however, the remaining members, who were traveling by bus over dirt roads through central Tanzania, had not arrived. Meanwhile, expectant crowds had already begun to gather in Kirumba Stadium.

In the two previous rounds, challenges and insults between the troupes had been coded through performance conventions such as *kwaya,* which worked to suppress the potential of an open display of conflict. Komba, however, dispensed with this formality and used Muungano's lateness to promote TOT. He gave a welcoming speech to the crowds in which he boasted that TOT had worked hard to arrive in Mwanza two days early, whereas Muungano was nowhere to be seen. His speech sidestepped issues of privilege since he did not acknowledge CCM's financial backing that enabled the troupe to arrive in advance. Komba had the resources to buy expensive train tickets, whereas Muungano had to scramble for transportation funds. According to gossip I picked up from the performers, Komba had lent Chenga 250,000 shillings ($336) to buy third-class train tickets, but Chenga used the money for funeral expenses when one of the members tragically died of malaria shortly before they were due to leave for Mwanza.

Even the setting of Kirumba stadium proclaimed TOT's privilege. Because the stadium was owned by CCM, the slogan, "CCM Preserves Our Unity" ("CCM Idumishe Umoja Wetu"), was painted in enormous letters along the rim of the stadium. Audience members could clearly see this stark reminder of the party's systemic power throughout the performance. Moreover, TOT promptly seized the gap left by Muungano's absence and used it to the troupe's advantage. Instead of the "nonpartisan" emcee used in the previous two rounds, TOT's emcee, Felix Sawala, took control of the show, using Muungano's empty stage as the platform for his introductory patter as if claiming it as TOT's territory. The visual symbols of TOT's dominance did not bode well for Muungano's fate.

Meanwhile, Muungano's utter *lack* of privilege was on prominent display. Throughout the performance, Muungano's manager periodically reassured the crowd that the rest of the company was on its way. With each speech, the crowd heightened their expressions of displeasure, and spectators began to jeer at him when they saw him walking toward the stage. Muungano managed to regain some favor through three *sarakasi* acts, which were interspersed throughout TOT's program. The skill and daring exhibited through the acrobats' tumbling, contortionism, and pole-climbing succeeded in keeping Muungano's presence visible instead of completely erased. But despite their best efforts, this particular performance continued to act as a showcase of TOT's power, framed with the ever-present reminder of CCM's backing along the stadium's rim.

Figure 16. While waiting for the rest of the company to arrive in Mwanza, Muungano's acrobats attempted to keep the spectators entertained.

In a striking turn of events, however, this showcase did not contain TOT's usual promotion of modernization and patriarchy. The constant deferral of Muungano's arrival threw TOT's scheduled program into disarray, and it was at this point when the company's ideological base began to crack. At first, it seemed feasible that the remaining members of Muungano would arrive within a few hours. In order to stall for time, the troupe added extra acts, some of which disrupted TOT's self-promotion as the paragon of trend-setting style.

For example, TOT performed an additional *ngoma* after the usual offerings of *ling'oma* and *kibati.* They chose to perform *tokomile,* the same Zaramo dance that Muungano had performed in Dar es Salaam and Morogoro. Although this particular choice suited the demands of the moment since TOT's version was fairly lengthy, the dance also signaled an abrupt break from the troupe's usual contest fare since it paid homage to the realm of tradition that TOT usually maligned. The opening of the *ngoma* depicted a dance contest in which a male and female dancer displayed their skill before their fellow villagers. Meanwhile, a man and woman, costumed as ragged *washamba* travelers, passed through the audience, chatting with various spectators along the way. When they heard the drumming, the man wanted to join the contest and dragged his protesting female companion to the stage. The music eventually overcame her reluctance, and she enthusiastically threw herself into the dance. Her male companion, overcome with sexual desire at the display of her skill, pulled her to the ground. In response, she simply pushed him away and returned to her dancing. She became the focal point of the dance drama as her skill in dancing blotted out her awkward, *mshamba* self. Although this celebration of rural tradition veered in the direction of stereotypical primitivism, the enthusiasm with which TOT's performers executed the dance conveyed an affection and respect that was usually excluded from its stage. In addition, *tokomile* provided a startling twist on the usual gender politics of *ngoma.* As the dance progressed, the woman's movements became increasingly uncontrolled until, in the grip of a sexual frenzy, she shoved herself violently against the buttocks of one of the male dancers. Her assertive sexuality

Figure 17. In the Mwanza competition, the TOT performers created a procession through the audience during the southern dance *tokomile.*

challenged the usual *ngoma* narrative in which the smiling, hip-swaying woman was pursued and "tried out."

Another interesting twist occurred in TOT's choice of *maigizo.* Still trying to stall for time, TOT replaced "The Shame of Money" with the more lengthy play "Control Yourself" ("Ushinde Moyo Wako"), which addressed the issue of rape. Like "Such Matters," this play was a focal point of my discussion in the previous chapter as a play that challenged the nationalist dichotomy of tradition and modernization. In the course of the play, Richard, an upper-class Christian male, rapes a young woman on the street and his sister-in-law. His Muslim father-in-law, Baba Swaumu, molests his infant granddaughter, who dies as a result. Like Muungano's "Such Matters," the play ends with a call to the community and the state to fight the problem of rape. The relevance of "Control Yourself" in the context of the competition is that TOT replaced "The Shame of Money," a comedy about the problems of an upper-class male urbanite, with a play that contained a sensitively portrayed social message related to gender. This *igizo*—one of the most complex and intriguing plays I saw throughout my stay— complicates TOT's usual self-performance as the patriarchal authority intent on the consolidation of CCM's power. Like the version of *tokomile,* "Control Yourself" seemed more characteristic of Muungano instead of TOT and there- fore marked another disruption caused by Muungano's delay. Ironically, "Con- trol Yourself" was itself disrupted when the electricity went out, causing the *igizo* to ground to a halt for half an hour while TOT's members hooked up its gen- erator. When the play resumed, the story had lost momentum, and the spectators did not experience the emotional impact that characterized previous productions I had seen. It seemed somehow fitting that TOT's attempt to explore serious dramatic material was undermined by difficulties with the very technology that was its mark of privilege.

In the end, all of these efforts to stall for time came to naught. After "Control Yourself" had ended, Muungano's manager finally admitted to the displeased crowd that the troupe's vehicle had broken down in the neighboring region of Shinyanga. Since the Muungano members would not arrive until after midnight, the contest was postponed until the next day. When I spotted several of Muungano's performers the following morning, their obvious exhaustion and ill humor led me to speculate that a victory was beyond their reach, especially considering TOT's advantage that had been seized the day before.

I also expected that the crowd would be smaller, since the high entrance fee of 2,000 shillings ($2.80) was charged again for the second day. Instead, thousands returned to throng the stadium in time for the contest's opening act. Unlike the two previous contests, the audience was not divided into TOT and Muungano sections, and very few red or green flags were waved. Mwanza had no apparent allegiances to either troupe and seemed quite ready to forgive Muungano of its fiasco on the day before. Despite TOT's apparent lead, the city remained a fresh battleground to be won.

It seemed at first that Muungano was not up to the task. Instead of opening with its own version of *tokomile,* which had proved so popular with female spectators in the first round in Dar es Salaam, the troupe retreated to ordinary *ngoma* fare. They performed the coastal *kibunguu,* a stately dance that emphasizes repetitious, graceful movements for both women and men. The anomalous choice of *kibunguu,* which was often used as a warm-up act in Muungano's regular performances, implied that the repercussions of Muungano's lateness began to be felt. Kopa was apparently too tired from the journey to assume the starring role in *ngoma* that she played in the previous two rounds, so Muungano was forced to fall back on *kibunguu* as a poor substitute. Muungano did manage to recover some of its usual glory with *sindimba,* and the audience screamed in startled delight at the many sexually charged moments of the dance.

Throughout the first few hours of the contest, such screams of delight marked the extent of the audience participation. Although the crowd vocally expressed its appreciation during the *ngoma,* TOT's *achimenengule,* and Muungano's *sarakasi,* no one ventured to either stage for *kutunza* (tipping) until Komba's *kwaya.* Komba did not perform *kwaya* on the previous day, because, as he explained to the audience, he wanted to save it for the actual contest. During his second song, "The Neighbor's House Is Burning," people showed their approval by flocking to the stage to give Komba money in the first obvious display of appreciation throughout the evening. This appreciation exploded into a moment of ardor during the third and last song, which consisted of TOT's standby of "*Utamaduni.*" "*Utamaduni,*" which contains the ubiquitous message of exalting the glories of Tanzanian traditional culture, was usually politely received by audiences. In this case, however, people swarmed to the stage and began to dance wildly. The fervent enthusiasm of the crowd created a startling moment in which the binaries began to crack.

In another abrupt shift of tone that was becoming par for the course in the Mwanza competition, this moment of passion was immediately contained. Once the final notes of "*Utamaduni*" had faded and the dancing spectators had returned to their seats, Komba introduced Chenga to the crowd. Chenga stood on Muungano's simple stage with their battered instruments; opposite him, Komba stood against a background of TOT's elaborate equipment and well-dressed *kwaya* female chorus. The moment seemed designed to highlight Muungano's poverty; even Chenga's simple batik shirt clashed with Komba's expensive two-piece suit. A poised, controlled Chenga explained in formal Swahili to the audience about Muungano's difficulties of the night before. He apologized for the inconvenience, and added that Muungano would perform an additional show in Mwanza Hotel for those who would care to see it. His comments and manner operated within the parameters of restraint that had been laid out in the two previous rounds—parameters that now seemed designed to keep Muungano in a subservient position to TOT.

At this point, Chenga's carefully polite tone abruptly changed, and he called out that even though TOT has all the money, "Muungano is still the best!" (*"Muungano ni nzuri kuliko zote!"*). For the first time in all three rounds, Chenga dispensed with decorum and called attention to the financial advantage that served as the foundation for TOT's success. In response, the crowd immediately erupted into sustained cheers. The same crowd that had expressed its fervent support for TOT during *kwaya*—moments before Chenga's speech—now just as readily declared its support for the "burning house" of Muungano. This seemingly fickle quality of the spectators was aligned with the general atmosphere of the performance. In Dar es Salaam and Morogoro, the fans held firmly onto their respective allegiances. In Mwanza, however, the allegiances were subject to the sudden shifts that characterized the performance as a whole.

Muungano's forceful declaration of this "underdog" status permeated its next offering. Because of Kopa's exhaustion, the company replaced "Such Matters" with a play that focused on a poor, urban young man who cannot escape from the harsh realities of the city and thus strengthened the troupe's alignment with the *walalahoi* of Tanzania. In the opening, the impoverished Braco and his mother were arbitrarily kicked out of the upper-class home where they worked. In the next scene, a young boy wearing expensive sneakers asked the audience for directions to the TOT/Muungano contest. A "hoodlum" (*mhuni*) spotted the boy and matter-of-factly killed him for his money and sneakers. Braco entered as a passerby and kneeled by the boy's body, at which point he was discovered by a policeman, who promptly declared Braco's guilt and dragged him to jail.

In an elaborate trial scene, the judge, who was the same man who fired Braco and his mother in the opening scene, sentenced him to thirty years of hard labor. His dying mother was carried to the prison to bid him farewell. She died in her son's arms, and Braco sang a *taarab* song to express his sorrow. At every turn, the hapless Braco seemed doomed to unfairness and mistreatment. Unlike the other three *maigizo* that had been presented during the contest, this one was bleak and lacked resolution. Moreover, it was the only *igizo* that called attention to the harsh lives of the urban poor. The bitter tone of the play called attention to the parallel between Muungano and the destitute, luckless Braco.

In the end, however, the seemingly luckless Muungano managed to have the last word. Once Muungano's *igizo* had concluded, the remainder of the contest consisted of *taarab*. In a clear demonstration of Kopa's superior fame, several spectators left after her performance. Since *taarab* did not enjoy the same degree of popularity in Mwanza as it did on the coast, the spectators were less invested in watching the entire finale of *taarab*. Despite this relative lack of interest, many had heard of the notorious Kopa and stayed long enough to see her perform, which meant that her singing was the concluding act for several spectators. She sang, *"Jeuri hiyo huna,"* which roughly translates as "You can't bully me." "Whom would you be able to hurt?" the song asks.[21] The song implied that TOT was incapable of violence—unlike Muungano.

It should be noted that this underlying sense of violence did not erupt into open rebellion, and the spectators left the stadium without becoming directly involved in the staging of conflict. What they had experienced, however, was a transformation of conventional models of nationalism and unity that depended upon polarizing terms. The circumstances of the final round disrupted TOT's relentless affirmation of the status quo, and the TOT/Muungano opposition became unmoored. Even their roles as exemplars of national culture were forgotten as they focused on winning over the stubbornly elusive Mwanza spectators. This sense of fluidity resonates with what Homi K. Bhabha terms the "third space," a discursive space in which "we may elude the politics of polarity and emerge as the others of our selves" (1994, 39).

The utopian tone of Bhabha's phrase in this context does not seem misplaced. It is useful to consider Benedict Anderson's famous concept of the nation as an imagined community, "imagined because the members of even the smallest nation will never know most of their fellow-members . . . yet in the minds of each lives the image of their communion" (1983, 15). In a sense, the TOT/Muungano competition helped to construct an imagined community among the audiences in Dar, Morogoro, and Mwanza. Although they might not ever know their fellow members of this sub-community of fans, the common experience of the TOT/Muungano performance forged a national link among them.[22] This connection does not, however, fit Anderson's description of "communion," which calls forth images of a fixed, soothing religious ritual that unites various factions through the economy of sameness. In contrast, TOT and Muungano produced a dizzying array of conflicting and merging alternative nations that forcefully reminded the audiences of those citizens—from the urban poor to rape victims—located on the margins of society. These layers of contestation carved out an alternative version of imagined community, one that overturned the notion of unity as a homogenized whole. In this light, the audience's fervent response to Komba's singing of *"Utamaduni"* could perhaps be interpreted as an enthusiastic embrace of the transformative version of Tanzanian national culture that was unfolding before their gaze.

It is tempting to end the chapter here, on this positive, even celebratory, note. Nevertheless, post-performance events challenge my interpretation of the Mwanza competition as a site of transformation. After the last *taarab* song was performed at around 10 PM, TOT immediately boarded a bus that brought the performers to the harbor, at which point they sailed across Lake Victoria for a CCM campaign in Kagera region. It was during this campaign that TOT's power emerged from hiding and provided a forceful reminder of the effectiveness of TOT as a weapon for CCM. In one of the rallies, the opposition party CUF was holding a rally alongside CCM.[23] CUF's only offering consisted of political speeches spoken into a megaphone. Meanwhile, the approximately fifty members of TOT, with their expensive costumes, their "American system" of sound equipment, and an electrical generator, set up camp alongside CUF. Predictably, the CCM/TOT crowd dwarfed the CUF gathering, which seemed small and weak in comparison. The CUF candidate was the only one running against the CCM candidate, and the odds were excellent that the CCM candidate would win the seat (which he subsequently did the following week). Despite the party's likelihood of victory, CCM took no chances and paid for the considerable costs of transport, food, and housing for fifty people so that they could sing for half an hour at each rally. TOT's nation-wide popularity ensured a full house for this extravagant promotion of the dominant party.[24]

The campaign, in which hundreds of rural spectators displayed their devotion to CCM, allowed TOT's assertion of power to continue unabated. During the evenings of their visit to Kagera, TOT put on shows for the town's entertainment that returned to the usual lineup of variety acts. For these performances, TOT invariably included "The Shame of Money," which could pessimistically be interpreted as the restoration of TOT's ideological stance of patriarchy and wealth as the foolish father repeatedly exerted his control. The excoriations of rape in "Control Yourself" and the powerful rural female in *tokomile* had disappeared, only to be replaced by figurative reminders that CCM was indeed number one.

When I conducted additional research in Dar es Salaam in 2001 and 2004, I found that not only were CCM—and TOT—"number one," but that their joint grip on popular consciousness had strengthened. In the intervening years, TOT's popularity had surpassed that of Muungano; in a tacit concession to TOT, it was understood that the two troupes were no longer rivals. As I discuss in my conclusion, a victor had emerged at the turn of the millennium.

SIX

A Victor Declared

Popular Performance in the New Millennium

At the Bagamoyo College of Arts, I was frequently told that unlike Western audiences, Africans do not expect happy endings. This statement has haunted me throughout the writing of this book as I struggle against an academic version of a happy ending in which the theatre companies triumph over the hegemony of the state, the ruling political party, and the forces of neoliberalism. This struggle has culminated in a pattern in which I emphasize the potential for social transformation in popular performance but then backtrack on my own argument as I explain how this potential became mired in the sociopolitical realities of postcolonial Tanzania. After exploring alternative *ngoma* narratives in chapter 3, for example, I noted that these new directions are produced through individual agency as opposed to the more formidable power of the collective. In chapter 4, I described the formation of promising new versions of nationhood in "Such Matters" and "Control Yourself" but then used a discussion of Mzee Jangala to show that the "new" Tanzania continues to operate on the systematic disenfranchisement of the rural poor. Although the TOT/Muungano competition in Mwanza produced a rupture in TOT's usual performance of power, as discussed in chapter 5, TOT immediately reestablished this power through a celebrated campaign tour for a CCM candidate. This pattern marks my attempt to excavate the creativity and agency of these companies but also to avoid the academic pitfall of glamorizing popular culture as a mode of empowerment and transgression.

My findings when I returned in 2001 would seem to dash any remaining hopes for a happy ending. In May of that year, I arrived in Dar es Salaam with the confident anticipation that I would resume my weekly schedule of attending performances five nights a week, alternating among TOT, Muungano, and Mandela. Instead, I was hard pressed to find even a single performance, let alone resume my previous schedule of five performances weekly. The performances I did see struck me as faint copies of their former ebullient selves. The vaudeville-style performances that intermingled music, drama, and acrobatics had been considerably consolidated in order to carve out additional time for *soukous* music. Even the performance traditions that remained conveyed a sense of lethargy, particularly in the performances of Muungano and Mandela. Upon my return to the United States after this particular visit, I watched videotapes of performances in 1996 and 1997 to reassure myself that I had not been lulled into a romanticized vision of Tanzanian popular theatre through the distance of time and space but that other forces were indeed at work.

One could easily strike an elegiac note about the future of Tanzanian popular theatre, given that several actors deserted the theatre companies for the more lucrative opportunities that a burgeoning television industry offered. Even the theatre artists in Tanzania spoke forebodingly about the decline of popular theatre. "The arts are dying" (*Sanaa zinakufa*), Captain Komba told me flatly (2001). Given my emphasis on heterogeneity and complexity of the popular performance as a gateway to transformation, its diminished quality suggests that the potential of popular theatre as a venue for grassroots democratization, a forum of civil society, or a mode of alternative nationhood was not only unfulfilled but teetered on the brink of extinction. Instead of exploration and contestation, the popular theatre in 2001 suggested consolidation and defeat.

I believe, however, that the reasons for this change exceed the lure of the television industry. As I have sought to demonstrate throughout this book, the straddling of official and popular culture created a rich terrain that allowed levels of innovation and creativity to reach new heights. The strength of the companies' *engagement* with the dynamics of nationalism ensured that multiple interpretations of postsocialist Tanzanian identity played out on the popular stage. The dynamics of nationalism, the historical moment of democratization, and the indigenous force of *mashindano* coalesced in such disparate moments as erotic dance, annoyed pythons, and songs about environmentalism. Creativity and innovation intensified as state and theatre collaborated in the production of new meanings and alternative identities.

The current lack of engagement with the nation-state leads me to speculate that the variety of manifestations on the popular stage—collaborative, alternative, and strategic—have all collapsed into the economy of homogeneity. The variety of emotional tones among the troupes—such as the bitterness of Mandela and the cynicism of TOT—were abandoned for the frenetic beat of *soukous*. In this conclusion, I return to the themes of democratization and nationhood to explore the ramifications of this unhappy ending for the diminished potential of popular theatre to articulate the complexities of Tanzanian lives, identities, and concerns.

Although this line of argument evades the pitfall of the happy ending, the alternative is also problematic. To write pessimistically about this diminished potential could ascribe to a narrative of nostalgia in which I mourn the popular theatre of the 1990s. Van Dijk's comment that nostalgia is about selective yearning and therefore is about power (1998, 156) serves as a reminder of the political repercussions of this narrative. To emphasize the lost potential would be to subscribe to a narrative of defeat and thus collude with international stereotypes of sub-Saharan Africa as a quagmire of hopelessness. It would also discount the significance of what the performances are *saying* about the specific historical and political moment. Even in a subdued state, the performances proliferate with nuances and contradictions. In an attempt to do justice to these layers of complexity, this conclusion seeks to understand the meanings of Tanzanian performance at the turn of the millennium.

DEMOCRATIZATION FATIGUE

An editorial published on the *Guardian* website (2005) lamented: "Work, work, work, they say, makes John a dull boy. By the same stretch of thinking, we can, plausibly, say CCM, CCM, and CCM . . . makes democracy a dull affair." Despite the initial excitement which greeted the shift to multipartyism in the early 1990s, the 2000 and 2005 elections indicated that the status quo has thoroughly reasserted itself. After making promising gains in the 1995 election, the opposition parties descended into confusion as leading politicians "hopped" from one party to another. The most noteworthy example occurred when Augustine Mrema, a touchstone for opposition to CCM, defected from NCCR-Mageuzi to join the Tanzania Labour Party in 1999. As the opposition faltered, CCM moved to consolidate its power. In the 2000 election, NCCR-Mageuzi lost all fourteen parliamentary seats won in 1995. Overall, the four opposition parties won only nine seats, down from the twenty-two seats won in the 1995 elections (Martin 2000). Moreover, President Mkapa handily won re-election with over 70 percent of the mainland electorate. Despite predictions to the contrary (*East African* 1999), even the death of Mwalimu Nyerere in 1999 did not shake loyalty to the party. In the third multiparty election held in November of 2005, the CCM candidate, Jakaya Kikwete, won with 80 percent of the vote, which the *Nation* called "the highest figure ever attained by a presidential candidate since the re-introduction of multi-party politics in 1992" (2005). The stability, or what might be interpreted as the dullness, of CCM reigns.

TOT also reigns. When I left Tanzania in December of 1997, I had expected—perhaps hoped—that additional "opposition" troupes would proliferate and challenge TOT's supremacy on a variety of fronts. During the transitional phase to multiparty democracy, the performances of TOT, Muungano, and Mandela could be theorized as a vigorous debate over the directions of nationhood in a post-socialist era. As TOT consolidated its hold on popular tastes, however, the vigor of the debate diminished. Even the famous TOT/Muungano competitions, in which dueling versions of nationhood played out before thousands of citizens, had become a relic of the past. Although TOT had long proven itself the ascendant, more powerful company, its rivalry with Muungano implied a sense of connection and continued engagement in the terms of a national debate over tradition, morality, and democracy. Now detached from its traditional *mtani* (rival), TOT isolated itself from the usual boisterous fray of *mashindano*.

A striking addition to TOT's usual paraphernalia literalized the company's ascendant status. In addition to its usual signs of wealth—the shiny red minibus and expensive musical equipment—TOT had procured a semi-truck painted the CCM color of bright green in order to facilitate its ability to tour and thus spread the CCM message throughout the country. In addition to serving the prosaic function of transporting equipment, the truck could also be converted into a high stage for performances. In comparison to Mandela and Muungano, TOT had always been especially fond of performing on raised stages, presumably in order to show off its musical equipment. With the addition of the truck, TOT achieved permanent elevation even when performing in the open countryside.

A series of relocations in the city's network of social halls and bars reflected the changing dynamics of power. Vijana Social Hall, a particularly prized venue because of its location and size, had traditionally served as the Saturday night venue for Muungano throughout the 1990s. In 2001, the prestige of Vijana had

Figure 18. TOT's female performers prior to a performance for the anniversary of TAZARA train station. They are gathered in TOT's minivan. Khadija Kopa, the "Queen of Taarab," is the woman seated at the far right.

been awarded to TOT, which claimed the hall on those Friday nights when they were not on tour. As if to acknowledge the changing of the guard, Vijana experienced a transformation of its own. The large, crumbling, low stage that proved so inviting to audience participation was replaced with a high, freshly painted stage. The rowdy Saturday night performances of Muungano were replaced with the relatively restrained musical acts of TOT, suitably barricaded by a line of microphones along the edge of the stage.

Meanwhile, Muungano and Mandela were increasingly estranged. In its search for alternative venues, Muungano secured a new Saturday night venue in Mbagala called Kwetu Bar. In a similar fashion, Mandela relocated to the neighborhood of Gongo la Mboto on the outskirts of Dar. A failure to pay the electricity bills in its home base of Tukutane Bar in Buguruni meant that the electricity had been shut off; the members gave little indication that they expected to resume its performances at Tukutane in the near future. Although all three companies regularly performed in various far-flung neighborhoods throughout the city, these new locations did not provide either company with secure footing. Both companies lacked a strong fan base in these new neighborhoods, and audiences were sparse at the performances I attended. Whereas TOT's success had skyrocketed, Mandela and Muungano struggled to maintain a semblance of appearances.

The last few weeks of my stay in 2001 literally resounded with TOT's power. On July 4, 2001, the vice president of Tanzania, Omar Ali Juma, unexpectedly died. The government declared two weeks of official mourning, during which all performances were forbidden. Only "serious" tunes were allowed to be played on the radio stations, which meant that the airwaves were filled with

American country music, love songs, and a song that Komba composed in Juma's honor. While Muungano's and Mandela's performers bitterly endured a considerable loss of receipts, TOT recorded a mourning song for the departed official that played incessantly on the radio stations. It should be noted that Komba's composition cannot be categorized as a token political gesture; its poignancy brought people to tears. The song exemplified the strategic ways in which TOT's political power, artistic ability, and emotional connection with its fan base intertwined.

The weakening of Muungano and Mandela was not the only manifestation of a deteriorating popular theatre culture. Its diminished quality was also reflected in the reduction of the forms of expression. The unique composition of dance, music, drama, and acrobatics contained within a single performance were rapidly disappearing; the next section seeks to understand the ramifications that this aesthetic shift entails.

NOSTALGIC RETURNS

The consolidated performance was not, in itself, a new development. TOT anticipated the trend in the mid-1990s when it cultivated a relatively seamless performance through the exclusion of *sarakasi,* the compartmentalization of *ngoma,* and the growing emphasis on *muziki wa dansi.* Its slick performances stood in sharp contrast to the unwieldy nature of Mandela's and Muungano's shows. Previously, I have theorized TOT's streamlining tendency as reflective of its political agenda. That is, in order to rehabilitate CCM's image as the "old guard" and cultivate its appeal among younger and urban voters, TOT adopted a more polished and streamlined approach that domesticated the sprawling nature of Tanzanian popular performance. By 2001, however, Muungano and Mandela had also moved in this direction, marking a major transition in the aesthetics of popular performance. Each form contained a micro-narrative of appropriation and re-appropriation, invention and counter-invention; the assemblage of these forms within a single performance paid tribute to the complexities of Tanzania's precolonial, colonial, and postcolonial history. In discarding these forms, the companies were not simply reducing expenditures or refocusing their energies—I believe they were revisioning the concept of Tanzania itself.

TOT had intensified its efforts in streamlining and consolidating. In order to conserve time for expanded musical acts, TOT discarded *maigizo* completely. Aside from *muziki,* the remaining forms seemed more like afterthoughts than artistic expressions. The *ngoma, kichekesho,* and *kwaya* were squeezed into a time span of about an hour. In a performance at Friends Corner Hotel in Manzese, Komba sang a few *kwaya* songs and then announced abruptly, "It's six o'clock. Time for *taarab*" (*Ni saa kumi na mbili. Ni wakati wa taarab*).[1] This regulated schedule discouraged opportunities for audience participation and improvisation and thus diminished the transformative potential that the performances contained. The forms that remained lacked originality and complexity; for example, TOT's performance of *ukala,* the Zigua hunting dance, simply replicated the choreography of the College of Arts. This choice was especially startling considering that the theatre companies in Dar had long mocked the College of Arts for the perceived dullness of its *ngoma.*

Interestingly, this lack of originality seemed to be a deliberate choice. TOT's ranks included some of the most famous actors and dancers in the city.

One of its performers, Hamza Kassongo ("Mzee Vumbi"), was one of the most famous actors in Tanzania; moreover, he had frequently contributed his play-writing talents to some of TOT's most interesting *maigizo,* most notably "Control Yourself." TOT's considerable command of resources and talent suggested a deliberate snub of the richness of Tanzania's theatrical past. Komba's categorical statement that "the arts are dying" conceals TOT's contribution to this gradual death. Although TOT did not shun these forms completely, its relative lack of effort and the regulated schedule ensured that they were contained and margin-alized.

Mandela's new configuration marked a strained attempt to follow TOT's example. Mandela's unwieldy conglomeration of *vichekesho, ngoma, maigizo, sarakasi, taarab,* stage show, *kwaya,* and *muziki wa dansi* was replaced with a nondescript show in which *ngoma, vichekesho,* and *muziki* were the lone survi-vors. It is particularly noteworthy that two of its most vivid acts—*maigizo* and *sarakasi*—were missing from the lineup. In the case of *maigizo,* its removal meant that Mzee Jangala no longer appeared on Mandela's stage. Since Jangala's anger at the harshness of rural life had honed Mandela's sardonic, bitter edge, its cynical stance faded once the form was removed. Although conversations with Mbelemba and other performers indicated that *maigizo* was discarded in order to clear space for *muziki,* the disappearance of *sarakasi* occurred through an act of sabotage. In 2000, Chenga hired all of Mandela's acrobats and thus robbed the company of *sarakasi* and drastically depleted Mandela's ranks. In response, the group abandoned *sarakasi* altogether in a gesture of surrender rather than training or recruiting new acrobats. The absence of the crude Mzee Jangala and the innovative *sarakasi* acts smoothed Mandela's characteristic rough edges and produced a relatively generic show. Like TOT, Mandela had discarded the tri-partite model of nationalist performance forged in the 1970s that depended on drama, *ngoma,* and acrobatics. Only *ngoma* survived, mainly in hopes of ap-pealing to *wazungu* tastes and thus securing a touring engagement in Europe as opposed to a sense of cultural loyalty. Unlike TOT, however, Mandela lacked the resources to pull off the slick and polished look. Instead, the company appeared to be drained of energy.

Muungano at least partly resisted the trend. The company maintained its old-fashioned brand of nationalism as *ngoma, sarakasi,* and drama continued to be performed. In an ironic comment on the vagaries of Tanzanian performance, cultural nationalism—usually considered a homogenizing force—helped to main-tain a semblance of multivocality on Muungano's stage. What is even more ironic is that this diversity was maintained at Mandela's expense when it lured Mandela's male performers away. In light of my depiction of Muungano and Mandela as op-position parties, Muungano's poaching could be compared to the self-destructing moves of the political opposition parties, which seemed more concerned in at-tacking each other than in attacking the formidable monolith of CCM.

And like the opposition parties, Muungano continued to founder. Even though most of the format remained intact, its lackluster shows displayed scant evidence of its former energy and creativity. "What happened to Khadija Kopa?" I asked one of Muungano's performers in an undertone during *taarab.* "Left for TOT." "Where are the snakes?" I asked Chenga after vainly waiting for their appearance. "Sleeping," was the reply. Although Kopa herself would not com-ment on the reason for her defection to TOT (2001), it seemed obvious that Komba had offered her a salary she could not refuse. As for the snakes, although they had not followed Kopa's lead and "defected" to TOT, the absence of the snake dance seemed to unmoor the company. The dances had typically produced one of the most exciting moments of Muungano's performances, generating an intensity of audience participation that exemplified the potential of "tradition" as a means of creating vibrant theatre. The snakes' slumber was emblematic of a general malaise that had descended upon Muungano's performances.

Malaise is, of course, rather limited as a theory of popular performance. A more productive and revealing approach is to consider the impact of the diminished role of drama in the performance texts. Whereas each company had included both *vichekesho* and *maigizo* in past performances, Mandela and TOT now confined themselves to half-hearted renditions of *vichekesho,* and Muungano performed only *maigizo.* In a discussion of what Barber terms the *potentiality* of Yorùbá plays, she notes that "every moment and every level of production is a site of creative potentiality" (2000, 9); in other words, the flexibility of unscripted plays allows the performers to respond instantly to changes ranging from their own lives to the local political scene to global events. Although popular music serves as a powerful venue for articulating critiques of the current sociopolitical climate, dramatic forms such as *maigizo* and *vichekesho* contain a wider range of potentiality since they are not limited to beats of the music and lyrics of the song.[2] Differences in age, religion, ethnicity, class, and sex provided a point of departure for the creation of plots in which children rebel against their parents, rape victims strike back, and impoverished Muslims struggle to survive. These struggles were inhabited and explored, instead of simply narrated, alongside a continual stream of vocal and embodied participation from the audience. Theatre, with its ephemeral, immediate, collaborative quality, offers "a site at which to think through questions of the signifying body" (Dolan 1993, 426); or, to invoke Bhabha's notion of the "in-between," the stage provides "the terrain for elaborating strategies of selfhood—singular or communal— that initiate new signs of identity, and innovative sites of collaboration, and contestation, in the act of defining the idea of society itself" (1994, 1–2). *Vichekesho* and *maigizo* articulated those moments in which new identities are continually forged and reinvented, and their absence minimized opportunities for experimentation.

The absence was not, however, being filled with silence. Instead, a craze for *soukous* music was actively displacing the free-for-alls of *vichekesho* and the domestic melodramas of *maigizo.* One might argue that the companies' detachment from the old-school model of cultural nationalism has provided them with a sense of freedom to focus on appealing to an urban public's insatiable desire for the Congolese sound. But as I explain in the next section, I suspect that *soukous* cannot be theorized as *detached* from national identity but instead reflects a major shift to a *cosmopolitan nationalism* that draws upon musical strengths to strengthen its international presence. This shift is perhaps reflective of Tanzania's renewed determination to reach beyond its borders and intervene on the East African stage.

COSMO NATION

Since the late 1980s, Congolese popular music has regularly appeared on the popular stage. Muungano's band, for example, played *soukous* as background music during acrobatics, and it served as a key feature of Mandela's stage show.

TOT's *achimenengule* provoked a mild controversy when it was introduced over whether or not it was "authentically" Tanzanian since it was obviously influenced by Congolese music. Its presence was, however, overshadowed by the dominance of *taarab* and *maigizo*. As a form associated with overt sexuality and *wahuni* ("rough" urban youth or hoodlums), *soukous* occupied a suspect role in the nationalist gaze.

By 2001, this musical genre had triumphed over drama, *ngoma,* and acrobatics as a new trademark of popular performance. This trend was undoubtedly encouraged by the success of bands such as Twanga Pepeta, which had displaced Muungano as the new *mtani* of TOT. In response to this local enthusiasm, Tanzanian musicians were transforming the form and making it their own; for example, Dar es Salaam bands sang *soukous* in Swahili instead of Lingala and also integrated its sound with local rhythms.[3] Once again, the vigor of popular culture is transforming boundaries of "foreign" and "local."

This vigor was not, however, evident in the performances of Muungano and Mandela. Despite their joint effort to "move with the times," their renditions of *soukous* were characterized by imitation rather than innovation. In May of 2001, Mandela participated for the first time in Mashibotta, a musical competition sponsored by the Ministry of Culture among bands in Dar es Salaam.[4] Although *muziki wa dansi* had long played a primary role in Mandela's performances since every act was punctuated with a musical interlude, its appearance in the competition marked out its attempt to forge a new identity as a band as opposed to a theatre company. Alongside the flashiness of bands such as Kilimanjaro Connection, Mandela appeared tattered, and its musical selections were subdued. In July of that year, Muungano also attempted to jump on the *soukous* bandwagon. I arrived at a performance in Mbagala in mid-July to discover three young men performing a skilled rendition of *soukous* music; the energy in the bar was palpable despite the sparseness of the crowd. These three men, all of whom had immigrated from the Democratic Republic of Congo, were Muungano's latest weapon in the attempt to attract new audiences.[5] Chenga planned to use them as the cornerstone of a band called Kata Kiu (Quench the thirst) that would perform both with the rest of Muungano and independently (2001). Although Chenga's plans did not come to fruition, his actions indicated that he also believed that the days of the sprawling performance had come to an end.

In contrast to the fumbling attempts of Muungano and Mandela, TOT's embrace of *soukous* generated a series of bold new interpretations of long-standing musical forms. Although the company continued to perform *kwaya, achimenengule,* and *taarab,* it became known for its experimental intermingling of these musical forms. *Taarab* had become especially experimental; for example, a bass player launched into a *soukous* riff in the midst of a *taarab* number.[6] When TOT played in Mombasa, the sophisticated Kenyan press was lavish with its praise, characterizing the music as a "refined blend of rumba, rock, benga, and hip hop with a well-choreographed stage show" (*Nation* 2001). In July 2001, TOT held an "inauguration" to celebrate the release of three additional albums with a performance that included a rap by their "latest vocal find," Papii Nguza (*IPP Media* 2001). Nguza provided an indication that TOT was exceeding the dominance of Congolese music to draw upon a thriving local tradition of Swahili rap music (Remes 1999).

Both nationalism and globalization have been theorized as homogenizing forces that seek to stamp out diversity. As a counterpoint to these sweeping explanations that discount local agency, scholars have developed concepts of grassroots nationalism and grassroots globalization in order to call attention to the ways in which these hegemonic discourses are subject to adaptation and transformation. As this book has sought to demonstrate, neither "top-down" nor "bottoms-up" theories of nationalism can do justice to the complexities of Tanzanian popular theatre, which manages to straddle both terms simultaneously in a dynamic process of collaboration and contestation. In a similar vein, the homogenizing sweep of *soukous* music defies theories of globalization, partly because Tanzanian artists are borrowing from a pan-African tradition instead of a Western one, as is usually implied in the term *globalization*. More importantly, however, nationalism and globalization coalesced through the medium of *soukous* to construct a cosmopolitan version of national identity.

Tanzanians have long endured the *mshamba* stereotype, of being perceived as backward and conservative in contrast to the nation's more sophisticated East African counterparts in Uganda and Kenya. As a result of former president Mkapa's fiscal policies, however, Tanzania is increasingly being cast in a more favorable international light. Mkapa has been credited with achieving steady economic growth, keeping a check on inflation, and generally bringing a sense of economic stability to the country. In recognition of these achievements, Tanzania secured a coveted spot on the list of eighteen countries that received debt cancellation by the G-8 countries. Prior to the G-8 summit meeting in 2005 during which the decision was announced, the U.S. and British media called attention to Tanzania as a major success story of sub-Saharan Africa.[7] Previously mocked in international circles for its policies of *ujamaa,* Tanzania now seemed poised on the brink of respectability.

Tanzanian music is also attracting respect. My awareness of the growing international reputation of Tanzanian musicians occurred during a visit to Uganda in 2004. The cable channel East African TV (EATV), which is based in Dar es Salaam, was extremely popular in Kampala. Although the station showed music videos produced throughout East Africa, it was dominated by Tanzanian musicians. Random conversations with Ugandans repeatedly confirmed a sense of admiration for this music; for example, I was told that although Ugandans excel in the creation of drama, Tanzanians are known for their music. As with all dichotomies, this kind of statement was not particularly helpful in terms of an in-depth understanding of local cultural phenomena. What it does clarify, however, is the emergence of a Tanzanian culture that is admired and emulated rather than scorned.

This economic and cultural transition helps to clarify the shift in popular theatre aesthetics. The consolidated performance text is perhaps reflective of an anxiety to shrug off the socialist past and embrace what is perceived as a cosmopolitan version of nationhood. The sprawling, unwieldy performance that pays tribute to the complexities of colonial appropriation, socialist experimentation, and neoliberal politics has been discarded in the wake of a collective rush to participate in a kind of East African musical chic. While Mandela and Muungano languished as reminders of the country's stodgy, old-fashioned past, TOT alone managed to capitalize on this trend toward an East African nationalism.

In July 2001, in one of its few public appearances in Dar es Salaam during my ten-week stay, I was treated to a vivid production of TOT's cosmopolitan nationhood. TOT performed at an official celebration in honor of the twenty-fifth anniversary of the Tazara railway, which was built through Chinese aid to connect Tanzania and Zambia.[8] The celebration itself occurred in front of the railway station and included several official Chinese guests as visual markers of Tanzania's socialist past. *Sarakasi* would have seemed particularly appropriate in this context since both the railway and the National Acrobatics Troupe were manifestations of Nyerere's cordial relations with Mao Zedong and the People's Republic of China.

Not surprisingly, TOT had its own ideas, giving a spirited performance that turned an occasion of state memorialism into a showcase of nation transformation. Instead of *sarakasi,* TOT served up a snazzy new version of *achimenengule* that seemed more suited to appeal to the nation's urban youth than the Chinese representatives. Readers might recall that the previous version of TOT's stage show consisted of women in revealing clothing entering into the audience to perform erotic dances for selected male spectators. In this renovated version, the stage show spotlighted a group of seven teenagers, both boys and girls, who appeared in front of the stage and performed a polished stage show in the *soukous* style. On the one hand, this "new" meaning upheld the company's political agenda. Judging from the enthusiastic response of the youths in the audience, this mix of teenaged boys and girls, dressed in jeans and tank tops, helped to shore up CCM's continued popularity with a generation of youth. On the other hand, these youths were strongly suggestive of another experiment in national culture, one in which a collection of young boys and girls were sent to China to transform an East Asian art form into a Tanzanian tradition. Like their counterparts in the 1960s, this mix of teenaged boys and girls who emphasized their skill rather than their sexuality could be figured as the future of the nation. Not only did they serve as the new ambassadors of CCM, but they were also ambassadors of a fashionable, hip version of Tanzania.

Tanzania's theatrical past continued to haunt the musical present. TOT's very name—Tanzania One Theatre—bore the legacy of popular theatre which relied heavily upon a range of performing arts. Mandela posted advertisements around Gongo la Mboto that promised a feast of *sarakasi, ngoma, vichekesho, maigizo, taarab,* and stage show, even though the actual performance was a sharply reduced repast. Roach writes that "performances so often carry within

Figure 19. The new ambassadors of CCM. TOT's version of *achimenengule,* 2004.

them the memory of otherwise forgotten substitutions—those that were rejected and, even more invisibly, those that have succeeded" (1996, 5). But in the case of TOT and Mandela, I am uncertain what purpose these ghosts served. TOT's famed actors were relegated to singing in the background during *kwaya* and the occasional appearance in *vichekesho*. Though I wonder if these "forgotten but not gone" (Roach 1996, 2) performers might break through this musical exile, I am also reminded of Bahati Jumbe, the female acrobat in the National Acrobatics Troupe whose years of training in the People's Republic of China were summarily dismissed. Once the national troupes were dismantled, she did not perform *sarakasi* again. Moreover, TOT's performers are relatively well-paid—as Komba pointed out with pride (2001), the majority of TOT's members own their own houses—making it highly unlikely that its disgruntled actors would turn to another artistic venue. These developments suggest that the performances might be haunted but in an immaterial way.

Upon returning to Dar es Salaam in 2004, it seemed at first that even the ghosts had been destroyed. Literally. I went to Tukutane Bar only to find a pile of rubble. The bar had been razed, and Mandela, although officially still in existence, no longer put on regular performances. Gazing at the pile of rubble, I was reminded of the students' insistence that westerners preferred happy endings and thought that surely, the hopelessness of the image would effectively block any inclination on my part to write an optimistic conclusion.

But the fixed image of a destroyed building does not do justice to the fluid and contradictory nature of popular performance, nor does it account for the resourcefulness of its agents. After listening to me indulge in nostalgic remembrances about the former vitality of the performances in 1996 and 1997, Mbelemba suggested in an offhand manner that I should come to a bar in Vingunguti for a "special" (*maalum*) performance.[9] I arrived at the designated location with admittedly low expectations. I had mentioned to Mbelemba that I lacked a good photograph of his character Mzee Jangala, and I suspected that he would be making an appearance in order to remedy the situation.[10] Mbelemba knew that I was working on a book, and he was not about to let such an opportunity to have his photograph be published slip by him. Although I looked forward to Jangala's resurrection, I anticipated that the show would include a few half-hearted *ngoma*, perhaps a tame version of *kichekesho*, and that Jangala himself would be subdued.

Mbelemba, Mandela, and the Vingunguti audience collectively pulled the rug from beneath these expectations. They produced a vigorous performance that seemed to draw directly upon my memories of the "glory days" of the mid-1990s, indicating that the ghosts of the performance past were quick to rematerialize. Aside from the lack of *sarakasi*, the lineup was relatively intact. A mixture of coastal and southern *ngoma* intermingled with a *kichekesho* and *igizo*, strung together with bursts of *muziki wa dansi* throughout the performance. The *kichekesho* concluded with a customary brawl in which the ubiquitous *mjumbe* lost his *kikoi;* in the *igizo*, Jangala responded to his AIDS-afflicted son with his usual expressions of rage, berating him for failing to live up to his promise to help the family once he migrated to the city. I watched with the growing awareness that Mandela was providing me with a conclusion to this book, one that not only exceeded the dominance of TOT and *soukous* music but also recalled the academic keywords of transformation and heterogeneity. In the closing funeral scene, the irrepressible Jangala abruptly changed into a quiet, bereaved father. This image of a contrite Jangala would have provided a suitably bittersweet

Figure 20. Mandela's "special performance" (*maonyesho maalum*) in July 2004. This photo was taken at an early point in the performance, when the spectators consisted mostly of children.

ending that would have complicated Western notions of the proverbial happy ending.[11]

The decidedly non-contrite audience, however, had other ideas. Although I was delighted by the parade of images from the past, I was not allowed to enjoy the performance and relax into a nostalgic mood. Because the performance was free, the bar was packed so tightly that I was constantly struggling to maneuver with my camera and to fend off intoxicated local male spectators. Although Mbelemba responded to the crowd's intensity with his fierce admonitions to behave, his warnings that the show would be stopped were ignored. During the funeral scene that concluded the *igizo*, a ruckus at the bar's entrance caused the actor playing the dead son to open his eyes with alarm and the downcast Jangala to direct a quick glare at the audience. The play's bittersweet ending gave way to a forceful reminder of the audience's ability to intervene in narratives of nostalgia. Democracy in the hands of Tanzanian politicians might indeed have become a dull affair, but in the domain of the *walalahoi,* it persisted as a messy and vibrant force that theoretical frameworks and narrative closures could not possibly contain.

GLOSSARY OF SWAHILI TERMS

This glossary includes only those Swahili words that appear more than once in the text. The provided definitions are not all-encompassing but are restricted to their usage in this book.

Baraza (-)	Council; meeting
Igizo (maigizo)	Plays of forty-five minutes to an hour in length that are performed as part of the popular performance; subject matter is often domestic
Khanga (-)	Patterned cloths commonly worn by Tanzanian women, particularly along the coast
Kichekesho (vichekesho)	Comic skits, about ten to fifteen minutes in length, in which a conflict typically escalated into a brawl
Kikoi (vikoi)	Woven cloths commonly worn by coastal men wrapped around their waist, usually signified a Muslim identity
Kukata kiuno	"To cut the waist," a movement in *ngoma* that consists of a sensual rotation of the hips
Kutunza	To present a performer with cash during the show
Kwaya (-)	A derivative of church choir singing, often used to convey educational or political messages as performed by the theatre companies
Mashindano	Competition; refers to a long-standing tradition of competitive musical performance between companies, bands, villages, etc.
Mhuni (wahuni)	"Hoodlum"; a term used to describe tough, usually urban youths
Mlalahoi (walalahoi)	Idiomatic expression for Tanzania's underclass
Mshamba (washamba)	Derogatory term for people from the country; "hicks"
Muziki wa dansi	An umbrella term for "modern" music, such as soukous and rap; usually opposed to *muziki wa kiasili,* "traditional" music
Mzungu (wazungu)	Foreigner, usually with connotations of whiteness
Ngoma (-)	"Traditional" dances, at least in the sense used by the theatre companies
Sarakasi (-)	Acrobatics (from "circus")
Shabiki (mashabiki)	Fans, enthusiastic supporters
Taarab (-)	Extremely popular form of coastal music that intermingles Arabic, indigenous, Indian, and Western traditions; dominated by female Muslim singers performing love songs, although the subject material

	can be quite expansive, and singers also include men and Christians
Ujamaa	Tanzanian socialism; translates literally as "family-hood"
Ushenzi	The state of being "uncivilized"; also **mshenzi**, an "uncivilized" person
Utamaduni	Culture; however, in the context of Tanzanian performance it usually refers to "traditional" culture
Utani	Joking relationship or rivalry between particular ethnic groups, clans, theatre companies, bands, etc.; also **mtani (watani)**, rival

NOTES

Introduction

1. The guest was John Nagenda, the *mshauri mkuu,* or chief advisor, to President Yoweri Museveni.

2. The specific date was July 24, 1997.

3. Although I occasionally refer to these productions as *theatre* since I believe they are comparable to the thriving traditions of popular theatre found throughout sub-Saharan Africa, I prefer the term *performance,* given their sprawling, multimedia nature that encompasses a variety of musical, dramatic, and acrobatic acts. The Swahili term *sanaa za maonyesho* is often translated as "theatre" but is perhaps more accurately translated as the "performing arts."

4. Dar es Salaam's population is about three million. Although the official capital city is Dodoma, Dar serves as the de facto capital since it contains all of the major embassies and government offices. See Remes 1999, 7–8, for a discussion of Dar's uniqueness as the cosmopolitan center of the country.

5. Several studies of Ghanaian and Nigerian popular theatre traditions call attention to their historical links to institutions such as the church and colonial education and thus complicate the notion of autonomy and resistance. Yorùbá popular theatre, for example, emerged from Christian educational theatre (Barber 2000), whereas the origins of Ghanaian concert party traditions can be traced to British imperial propaganda (Cole 2001). Also, in an essay on Yorùbá popular theatre, Biodun Jeyifo makes tantalizing references to the "paradoxes and contradictory manifestations" that the tradition contains (1985, 105); for example, he describes how political factions have co-opted the companies for partisan purposes (111; see also Jeyifo 1984, 117). Aside from such references, however, the popular theatre troupes are consistently theorized as autonomous voices of the disenfranchised African working poor. The field of African popular music provides a useful alternative—Tejumola Olaniyan's *Arrest the Music! Fela and His Rebel Art and Politics.* Olaniyan's emphasis upon the contradictions and paradoxes of the Nigerian musician Fela Anikulapo-Kuti yields an analysis as rich and multilayered as Fela himself.

6. "Baniani Mbaya Kiatu Chake" (a Swahili proverb that translates as "An Evil Indian but His Business Is Good"), Friends Corner, Manzese, 13 July 1997.

7. See Mlama 1991, 23–31, as a representative critique of theatre that serves no obvious social function, which is dismissed as "art for art's sake." Similar sentiments are also expressed in Lihamba 1985 and Mlama 1983.

8. The emcee's statement notwithstanding, the contest *did* judge the contestants on the basis of their skin color, since one reason for Mbelemba's supposed "ugliness" was his unusually dark skin. Also, it was understood that only men would enter the contest, which indicates that the notion of an "ugly" female was less socially acceptable.

9. See also Dominic Thomas's discussion of Congolese literature. Although he does not use the term *grassroots nationalism,* he alludes to a similar kind of reaction against official models of nationalism when he writes that "the nation has been engineered top-down by ideologues and state-sponsored official literature, which has in turn been challenged by orality and non-official and diasporic literature" (2002, 3).

10. I realize that my use of the term *intimacy* is rather unusual in this context. A more conventional term is *neo-patrimonialism,* which refers to the methods of the African "Big Men" (Julius Nyerere, Kwame Nkrumah, Jomo Kenyatta, Idi Amin, Kenneth Kaunda, and Jean-Bédel Bokassa, to name just a few), who consolidated power around their individual leadership. My reading of neo-patrimonialism and clientelism is strongly

influenced by Achille Mbembe, whose theories of conviviality are discussed later in this chapter. For a sampling of readings on neo-patrimonialism or personal rule, see Bayart 1993; Berman 1998; and Kelsall 2002.

11. In an attempt to explain the lack of overt political protest in postcolonial Tanzania, Tim Kelsall and Max Mmuya write: "This may be a result of indigenous norms of respect for elders and leaders, sedimented memories of the brutality of colonial rule, persistent authoritarian policing methods, or simple problems of organization. In the absence of organized protest, dissimulation, foot-dragging, evasion and exit have been the norm" (n.d., n.p.). To this I would add the possibility of a deep-seated *investment* in the existing social order. Although I observed or experienced countless examples of what Aili Tripp (1997) calls "noncompliance" and "foot-dragging" in day-to-day operations in Dar es Salaam, my research indicates that a widespread cultural reluctance to engage in organized political protest is entangled in popular conceptions of Tanzanian identity as fundamentally peaceful in contrast to the internecine tendencies of neighboring countries.

12. For example, confusion reigns over the positions of the *wajumbe,* the leaders of the ten-house cell divisions that developed in the socialist era. It is unclear whether the *wajumbe* remain party positions or if they have shifted to the government. *Wajumbe,* which frequently appear in *vichekesho,* are discussed further in chapter 2.

13. This reading is strongly influenced by John L. and Jean Comaroff's analysis of civil society, in which they suggest that the current mania for the building of civil society in Africa among academics and international creditors alike stems from an abiding faith in the ideals of neoliberalism and the market economy, coupled with a "distrust of sovereign authority [that] . . . borders on paranoia" (1999, 18).

14. Homi K. Bhabha also finds that studies of nationalism usually adhere to a binaristic model insofar as they "read the Nation rather restrictively; either, as the ideological apparatus of state power . . . or, in a more utopian inversion, as the incipient or emergent expression of the 'national-popular sentiment' preserved in a radical memory" (1990, 3).

15. As Fabian points out, the improvisational quality and strategic use of comedy that characterized Zairean popular theatre meant that it was uniquely equipped to convey subversive messages under the most severe forms of cultural and political repression (1990, 58).

16. My understanding of state-society relations in Tanzania could be interpreted as naive; that is, one might say I am whitewashing the coercive apparatuses of the state that seek to maintain its monopoly of power. It should be noted that Nyamnjoh himself did not seem to have the state in mind in his discussion of interdependency and domesticated agency; instead, his examples focus on local communities in Cameroon, many of which must band together in response to the caprices of the state. For the purposes of this study, however, I find that Patrick Chabal and Jean-Pascal Daloz's theories on the fundamental disorder and even "vacuousness" of the African state to be useful. They write that "the argument that the state in Africa has managed to achieve hegemonic domination over society remains unconvincing. However arbitrary, violent or even criminal, state coercion on the continent has rarely been such as to make totalitarianism a realistic political option. We would argue instead that, if anything, the very reverse has occurred: it is the state which has been 'captured' by society" (1999, 26). Although the generalizations of this argument could, of course, be challenged, Chabal and Daloz's ideas do resonate in the context of permeable state-society relations that characterize Tanzania.

17. Askew's *Performing the Nation: Swahili Music and Cultural Politics in Tanzania* is a fascinating account of how musical performance served as a "dominant vehicle" (2002, 292) for the articulation of Tanzanian nationalism. Although she calls attention to the state's appropriation of popular performance, her book emphasizes the ways in which "some of the least privileged citizens of one emergent African nation hijacked and reconfigured the process of nationalism" (12), and therefore she substitutes a grassroots model of nationalism for the more conventional paradigm of "neat, unilineal, top-down transmissions" of nationalist discourse (293). Although I am clearly influenced by her ideas, I found that the networks of *complicity* that surrounded TOT's, Muungano's, and Mandela's performances confound models of either the top-down or "bottoms-up" variety. As a theatre scholar, I also want to acknowledge my intellectual debt to those in

my discipline who have explored the complex intersections between nationalism and the stage. In a statement that helps to capture the unique perspective that theatre studies can offer to contemporary understandings of nationalism, Jeffrey D. Mason writes: "The stage is only an explicit site for performing national identity, one that serves to focus the issues, rhetoric, and images found in the more general forums; its creative freedom and opportunity to take risks encourage attempts to develop, explore, test, and dispute conceptions of national character. In the performative arena, in the interchanges among artists and spectators, we can enact narratives of nation, whether ostensibly actual or openly speculative" (1999, 1). See also Gouniaridou 2005 and Wilmer 2004 as two of the more recent contributions to the field.

18. See Ahluwalia and Zegeye 2002 for a discussion of CCM's strategies in the 1995 and 2000 elections.

19. In addition to *Postcolonial Identities in Africa,* see also Werbner 1998 and 2002 for additional examples of how scholars are integrating anthropology and postcolonial studies to articulate new theoretical models.

20. In the same volume, Paul Stoller also upholds the official/popular, coercive/resistant model when he opposes official art, which he calls "the airbrushed reality" for public consumption, against the "aggressive subjectivity" produced by marginalized groups. He adds that the alternative forms produced by these subjectivities "rose to the surface to stain [read: resist] carefully designed portraits" (2002, 228).

21. See Edmondson 1999b for a more in-depth discussion of how I was regularly "de-hierarchized" in the course of my fieldwork, particularly as a visiting lecturer at the College of Arts.

22. On Wednesdays, Ajwang' and I could usually be found at Tukutane Bar in Buguruni neighborhood for Mandela; Saturdays we attended Muungano's performances at Vijana Social Hall in Kinondoni. On Sundays, we usually went to TOT's performances at Kigongo Bar, which was also located in Buguruni. Thursday and Friday nights varied, depending on the troupes' schedules. During the course of my research I attended performances in the neighborhoods of Buguruni, Gongo la Mboto, Kinondoni, Kunduchi, Magomeni, Mabibo, Manzese, Mbagala, Mwananyamala, Temeke, and Vingunguti.

23. See Fabian 1996 as a particularly striking example of how a series of in-depth interviews with Matulu culminated in a nuanced examination of a popular conception of Zairean history and identity through visual art. See also Barber 2000, 16–17, for an alternative perspective on the value of conducting formal interviews in African contexts. It should be noted that in terms of tracing the historical development of Tanzanian theatre, I found formal interviews to be a valuable resource, and much of my information in chapter 1 is drawn from such interviews. They were less useful, however, when I sought to understand the intentions or meanings of the performances themselves.

24. Some scholars have called attention to the economic tensions exacerbated by structural adjustment policies that are contributing to the fragmentation of Tanzanian society—spates of violence between Christian and Muslim populations, as well as an increase in anti-Asian sentiment, are particularly worrisome trends. See, for example, Kaiser 1996. Despite these tensions, evidence suggests that national identity still trumps religious and ethnic differences. In 1999–2001, a public opinion survey conducted in twelve African countries indicated that Tanzania differs sharply from its neighbors in this regard; for example, only 3 percent of Tanzanians placed their ethnic affiliation first when asked the open-ended question, "Which specific group do you feel you belong to first and foremost?" See Chaligha et al. 2002 for a discussion of these statistics.

25. The exclusion that comes most readily to mind is the Tanzanian Asian population. Although this population is commonly seen as economically privileged, see Joseph 1999 for a nuanced analysis of the anxieties and tensions that this diasporic community endured under Nyerere's rule.

1. Performing, Transforming, and Reforming Tanzania

1. Jean-François Bayart's discussion of hybridity, or what he calls extraversion, also underlines the flexibility and innovative capacity of the state: "The daily processes

of creolisation...suggest...a real ideological interiority which is capable of inspiring institutional or administrative innovation in the pure constitutional and bureaucratic register of power" (1993, 244).

2. See Iliffe 1979 for an account of Tanzania's experience of this epistemic violence. The formal beginning of European colonization in present-day Tanzania began in 1885 when Germany officially claimed the mainland, called Tanganyika, as a protectorate; it then passed to British control as part of the spoils of World War I. The British did not perceive Tanganyika as a significant colony, which meant that they exerted little effort to provide the Tanganyikans with basic social services. John Iliffe writes, "Tanganyika had been Germany's most valued colony. The British wanted only to deny it to others" (1979, 261).

3. On December 9, 1961, Tanganyika became the first country in the East African region to gain independence under the leadership of TANU, the Tanganyika National Union. Nyerere originally took the helm as the prime minister; however, he resigned in January 1962. After elections held in November, he was sworn in as the first president on December 9, 1962. The term *Tanzania* was coined in 1964 when mainland Tanganyika and the island Zanzibar joined to create a republic.

4. See Fanon 1968, 209–212, for a sensitive reading of this nationalist rhetoric.

5. See Ranger 1975 for a thorough and engaging account of *beni,* which swept throughout East Africa in the first half of the twentieth century. Despite the distinctly Western features of the dance, which included brass band accompaniment, the choreography of a military drill, and the hierarchies of officers with European titles within the *beni* membership, Ranger argues for the dance's precolonial roots in order to complicate its "apparently overwhelmingly imitative character" (1975, 6). *Beni* gave rise to several derivative forms, one of which, *ling'oma* of the Nyakyusa, is discussed in chapter 5.

6. Aside from *ngoma,* evidence suggests that all of these performance traditions emerged in the colonial era. See Plastow 1996, 60–71, for a survey of colonial theatre in Tanzania. Additional sources include Askew 2002; Barz 2003; Fair 1994, 2001; Glassman 1995; Hussein 1974; and Ranger 1975.

7. Some scholars have recast the more traditional form of *beni* as a primary influence in the nationalist movement (see Lihamba 1985, 30; and Askew 2002, 95). Given that *beni* had become obsolete in the urban areas by the 1930s, the connection seems rather tenuous, especially when compared to the role of *taarab* and *ngoma* among Muslim women in promoting nationalism.

8. Geiger lists the names of these four groups as Egyptian, Alwatan, Lelemama, and Bombakusema (1997, 67). Geiger does not elaborate on the performance practices of these groups; instead, she classifies all the groups under the name *ngoma.* The names of the groups indicate that Egyptian focused on *taarab* (which was commonly called Egyptian music at the time), whereas at least one performed *lelemama.*

9. Geiger raises similar questions regarding the possibility of "centralized control" (1998, 154).

10. See, for example, Plastow 1996, 129; and Lange 1995, 33.

11. This account was described in a report written by Mrs. Chris Rosenfeld, who was apparently invited to watch the group and provide feedback. This report differs markedly from a more official account located in the Office of Culture's files, "Upanuzi wa National Dance Troupe" (undated, but located with 1970 and 1971 documents), which states that youth of the TANU Youth League were hired from around the country as the troupe's original members. I am inclined to privilege Mrs. Rosenfeld's description since she is writing much more closely after the formation of the group, and because she is a non-ministry official, her account is less likely to be encrusted with official rhetoric.

12. Upon reading a report by the three members who were sent to Guinea, one cultural officer dismissed it as "extremely amateurish" and recommended that they should not be paid more than 110/Tsh (Office of Culture 1964e).

13. After decades of proffering drama and *kwaya* as so-called civilized alternatives to *ngoma,* missionaries in the 1920s and 1930s began worrying that their East African congregations were becoming *too* Europeanized, and they introduced carefully selected *ngoma* into church services and schools (Ranger 1975, 123). Moreover, in 1948, the

British Colonial Office called for the promotion of traditional culture in order to improve the quality of life for their colonial subjects (Plastow 1996, 69). This earnestness complicates attempts to characterize the German and British colonialism as a uniform suppression of indigenous culture, which ignores the more insidious effects of these contradictory policies such as the internalization of colonial attitudes that designated *ngoma* as primitive.

14. Tanzanian theatre scholars Penina Mlama (1983) and Amandina Lihamba (1985) persuasively argue that drama cannot be categorized simply as a European form since dramatic elements are long-standing features in numerous ritual ceremonies. Here, however, I link *maigizo* with the European drama taught in mission schools since the full-length plays (*maigizo*) performed in contemporary popular theatre seldom display the integration of various performance traditions (dancing, music, storytelling, etc.) that is considered a hallmark of indigenous forms of drama.

15. *Ujamaa: The Basis of African Socialism* was originally published as a pamphlet in 1962. Nyerere had been ruminating on his unique theory of socialism for several years prior to the declaration.

16. The policies of the declaration included but were not limited to the nationalization of major means of production, a villagization policy that called for the resettlement of rural populations in planned *ujamaa* cooperative villages, the discouragement of foreign investment and "capitalist practices" of party members, and the adoption of an education for self-reliance policy. Although Nyerere did not mention the arts specifically in his official speeches about the declaration, in an informal discussion with national poets, Nyerere encouraged them "to go and propagate the Arusha Declaration and praise our national culture" (in Lihamba 1985, 81). The eagerness with which artists responded to this single comment is strongly suggestive of the excitement that the declaration generated on a local level.

17. It should be noted that the experiment in acrobatics aside, Nyerere contributed little to these lurching attempts to forge a national culture. Despite the dominance of traditionalist rhetoric in his speeches and writings, he barely mentioned the arts again after his inaugural address, and the frequently re-named Ministry of National Culture and Youth was and continues to be the most ill-funded of the lot (Askew 2002, 184–191).

18. My understanding of this legacy was influenced by a conversation with Rashid Masimbi, a former principal of the College of Arts, who blamed this separation on the colonial legacy of Western education, which treated these forms (acrobatics, dance, and drama) as separate genres that were not to be intermingled (personal conversation, 4 March 1997, Bagamoyo).

19. See Lihamba 1985, 509–510, for a list of the plays performed by the National Drama Troupe and, beginning in 1980, the Bagamoyo College of Arts. Also see pp. 377–396 for a thorough discussion of the formation of the National Drama Troupe and its plays.

20. See Grewal and Kaplan 1994; Kandiyoti 1994; McClintock 1995; Mohanty 1991; Obbo 1989; and Ranchod-Nilsson and Tétreault 2000 as examples of this body of scholarship. Even attempts to complicate this line of argument still adhere to the paradigm of top-down nationalism as a uniformly oppressive force, as illustrated by Sita Ranchod-Nilsson and Mary Ann Tétreault's critique of homogenizing concepts of the gender dimensions of national identities, which refute the "chameleon quality of nationalism" (2000, 7). They proceed, however, to stress the need to go "beyond the 'women are used' argument to evaluate what nationalist movements do *for* women as well as what they might do *to* them" (7). Such statements solidify the dividing line that pits female subjects against nationalism instead of exploring infiltration and interdependence.

21. The file TNA A/5, "Selection of Acrobats" (Office of Culture 1971a), contains numerous documents about this recruitment process.

22. A note of historical context helps to explain the emergence of the one-party system. In 1964, the same year in which the Republic of Tanzania was founded, a five-day mutiny among the armed forces undermined confidence in the state. In an attempt to regain control, the political elite began calling for the legalization of the one-party state

(Yeager 1989, 67). This process culminated in 1965 when the government altered the constitution to reflect TANU's position as the sole legal party. Not surprisingly, as Glassman points out, Nyerere returned to his image of a communal, cooperative African society to justify the creation of a one-party state. Glassman insightfully points out that Nyerere chose the occasion of his speech to the first parliament elected under the 1965 single-party constitution to expound his traditionalist themes of *ujamaa,* justifying the constitution with the argument "that Tanzanians have no differences over social policy but only over the individual leaders who should implement it" (1995, 269). The building of a co-operative, non-argumentative society clearly served TANU's interests.

23. The vulnerability of these troupes sharply differs from the faculty at the theatre department at the University of Dar es Salaam, which began creating plays that were increasingly critical of the state (Lihamba 1985, 295). See Plastow 1996 and Lihamba 1985 for more detailed discussions of the written plays produced by the university theatre department, as well as its pioneering experiments in theatre for social change.

24. In the early 1980s, in response to the crisis, a "culture of noncompliance, including rumors, gossip, and satire, became more prevalent" (Tripp 1997, 179). CCM, for example, became known in popular discourse as *Chukua Chako Mapema* (Take yours as fast as you can) or *Chama Cha Majangili* (The party of crooks). Tanzania earned the nickname of *Bongoland* (*ubongo* is Swahili for "brains"), meaning the country where one requires cleverness to survive (Tripp 1997, 179–180).

25. Instead of using the more complex Protestant tradition of *kwaya,* the cultural troupes demonstrated a widespread preference for the Roman Catholic style of *kwaya* in which the voices adhered to a single melodic line to sing in praise of their president, who, perhaps not coincidentally, was a Roman Catholic himself (Barz 2003, 21–22). It should be noted that postcolonial interpretations of *kwaya* are hardly limited to these patriotic versions; *kwaya* has also become enmeshed in a vibrant network of competitive societies (see Barz 2003 for an in-depth ethnographic exploration of *kwaya* societies in Dar es Salaam).

26. By 1970 *ngonjera* apparently stood "second only to traditional dance in popularity" (Mlama 1991, 103). During the time of my fieldwork, *ngonjera* was seldom performed, although Mandela included poetry recitations in two theatre-for-development productions I saw presented in Dar es Salaam (Mnazi Mmoja, 12 October 1996; Saba Saba Exhibition Grounds, 2 July 1997).

27. As a non-scripted form, the origins of *vichekesho* are especially difficult to excavate. Siti binti Saad was using a form of *vichekesho,* known as *natiki,* as a comic interlude between songs and sometimes in the context of sung performance (Fair 2001, 224). Another potential influence is the silent films of Charlie Chaplin, which were widely seen in the movie theatres in the coastal cities. Students at the College of Arts informed me that the skits developed out of imitations of his films. In his study of colonial drama, Ebrahim Hussein integrates these theories with the argument that Saad was influenced by both film and Indian comedic theatre, which she attended while visiting Bombay for recording in 1928 (1974, 97).

28. I exclude state-sponsored drama competitions from this discussion of *mashindano.* These competitions are linked to the drama competitions sponsored by the British colonial administration instead of the indigenous system of *mashindano.* See Lihamba 1985 for an analysis of state-sponsored competitions.

29. JKT stands for Jeshi la Kujenga Taifa (Army of Nation Building), JWTZ stands for Jeshi la Wanainchi wa Tanzania (Army of Tanzanian Citizens), and Magereza refers to prison guards. The first *ngoma* groups developed spontaneously within the camps as a means of entertainment; it was only after the Arusha Declaration that the army established formal structures for the groups.

30. The artist-soldiers were thoroughly integrated into the workings of the army. Although their main duties revolved around rehearsals and performances, they went through basic training and were expected to serve military duty if the need arose, as Komba did in the Ugandan War of 1979.

31. This brief acknowledgement marks a slight improvement in the National Dance Troupe's reputation. In an editorial on the state of culture published in 1972, the National

Dance Troupe was not even mentioned; instead, the article emphasized JKT (*Uhuru* 1972a).

32. Names of these troupes are drawn from a survey of *Uhuru* advertisements in 1985.

33. *Taarab* bears special mention as one of the most beloved musical forms in Tanzania, particularly along the coast. It emerged in Zanzibar as court music that consisted of Arabic melodies and lyrics sung in praise of Zanzibar's sultans. In an explanation of *taarab*'s elitist links, Fair writes that "[t]he language and performance culture of *taarab* were intended to celebrate and reaffirm the power and exclusivity of Zanzibar's Omani ruling class, as well as their ties to Arabian trading networks and the center of Arab mass culture, Egypt" (2001, 171). In the 1910s, Siti binti Saad (a former slave, according to tradition) and her band initiated a revolution of *taarab* music through singing in Swahili, which popularized the form beyond Zanzibar's elite Arabic-speaking population (174). The revolution extended to content as well as form when Saad co-opted *taarab* as a means of gender and class critique (185–224). Recordings of her music were released in the late 1920s, which catapulted her to stardom throughout the Swahili coast and sparked additional versions of *taarab* in Tanga, Mombasa, and Dar es Salaam, many of which followed a mixed band tradition in which women were usually the lead singers (Fair 1994, 297–300; see also Topp Fargion 2000). It should be noted that Askew thoughtfully deconstructs what she calls the "Zanzibar-centric" historical narrative of *taarab* that describes the form as diffusing outward from the island and spreading across the mainland coast. In her discussion of the differences among the styles of *taarab* in Tanga, Zanzibar, and Dar es Salaam, she points out that *taarab* had a much more organic process of development in these different locations (Askew 2002, 110–116). Despite its inaccuracies, however, *taarab* is still *perceived* as a Zanzibar tradition in the national imagination.

34. In 1964, Zanzibar joined with mainland Tanganyika to create the Republic of Tanzania, shortly after the Afro-Shirazi Party on Zanzibar overthrew the Arab-dominated government through a violent revolution. See Cliff 1969, 248–249, for the events that led up to the union; see Mosare 1969 for background on the Zanzibar revolution. Although Zanzibar and Tanganyika are theoretically "united," Zanzibar has retained a separate government that forges its own policies and occasionally openly defies the mainland's wishes.

35. Although the theatre companies began including *muziki wa dansi* in their repertories around 1984, they largely avoided the risqué style of dancing associated with Zairean *soukous,* preferring the more innocuous *muziki wa ala,* which lacks a distinct definition. It literally refers to instrumental music, i.e., without singing, but Muungano regularly performed vocal music under the *wa ala* rubric. It seemed to refer to "golden oldies" music to distinguish it from more recent renditions of Congolese-influenced music.

36. Bantu Acrobatics, for example, which had incorporated members of the former National Acrobatics Troupe, dismantled in 1986 (*Uhuru* 1986).

37. For special occasions, these institutions would occasionally resurrect these groups. In 1991, for example, numerous banks and parastatals (state-owned enterprises) competed alongside Muungano, Mandela, JKT, JWTZ, and Ujamaa in a state-sponsored regional competition (*Uhuru* 1991a). Also, groups could re-emerge for potentially lucrative performances such as during the Christian holidays of Christmas and Easter and the Islam holidays of Idd el Haj and Idd el Fitr. Such moments of visibility disrupt attempts to determine the specific years when these groups folded.

38. As late as 2001, one of Mandela's performers was still officially a member to DDC Kibisa; despite his ten-year association with Mandela, he is reluctant to resign because it would forfeit his right to the pension that the corporation owes him (Mbelemba 2001).

39. As recently as 2005, at an official occasion to launch the Labour Relations Association of Tanzania, both a cabinet minister and a university official affirmed that their institutions were committed to building socialism, to the incredulity of the audience (*East African* 2005). In a more subtle manner, the memories and histories of socialist-era

cultural troupes continue to circulate in contemporary performance. Countless Tanzanian performers entered the ranks of Muungano, TOT, and Mandela through employment with one of these now-defunct troupes. The collaborative atmosphere of rehearsals encouraged performers to share *ngoma* choreography and *vichekesho* plots picked up during earlier tenures. As an example of this process, I occasionally saw similar plays performed by both TOT and Muungano; indeed, they might even bear the same title, as in the case of "The Shame of Money," which is described in chapter 5. I was assured that the troupes were not stealing the plots from one another, but that it was a story that had existed since *zamani*, "a long time ago."

40. Chenga was born in 1952; Mbelemba and Komba were born in 1954.

41. In 1991, Nyerere publicly announced his support for multipartyism in a statement that sent shock waves through the state and society alike. McHenry believes that Nyerere's official statement of support for multipartyism "indicated his judgment that the party was no longer serving as the democratic link between the people and the government" (1994, 55). He then adds, "Ironically, the multiparty debate seemed to accomplish what Nyerere had been unable to do for five years—it began to awaken the party" (56). (See also Mmuya and Chaligha 1992 for an analysis of Nyerere's change of heart regarding multipartyism.) The following year, the government allowed independent parties to register, provided that they followed certain stipulations meant to preserve the precarious mainland-Zanzibar union and to prevent parties from forming along ethnic lines. It should be noted that the shift to multipartyism was not carried out in response to the will of the general population; in 1992, the Nyalali Commission, which was charged with accumulating the populace's opinions on multipartyism, reported that a considerable majority was opposed to the change.

42. In 1994, after a poorly attended performance, JKT acknowledged that people had forgotten about them in the face of the fierce competition between TOT and Muungano (*Uhuru* 1994).

43. This debate played out in rural areas as well as in urban contexts. See Nyoni 1998 for a fascinating discussion of how multiparty politics and theatre intersected in rural villages in Dodoma and Ruvuma, where cultural troupes were sponsored by both CCM and NCCR-Mageuzi.

2. Alternative Nations

1. A gradual process of economic liberalization began in 1986 once Tanzania agreed to the stipulations of structural adjustment. Political liberalization began in 1992, when the government announced the shift to a multiparty system of government.

2. See also Remes 1999, 2, for a discussion of the shift in Tanzania's "mediascape" in the mid-1990s.

3. It should be noted that the variety-act format is a recurring motif in African popular theatre; for example, similar types of performances that intermingle plays with musical acts are found in South Africa, Ghana, and the former Zaire (Cole 2001; Fabian 1990; Kruger 1999, 14–15). This development is often linked to the influence of European concerts in the colonial era. Tanzanian popular performance is, however, distinctly unique in terms of the staggering diversity of traditions that make up a single show.

4. The pervasiveness of complicity, patronage, and neo-patrimonialism that characterizes state-society relations in Tanzania raises questions concerning the very existence of civil society, loosely defined as social organizations detached from state apparatuses that can represent the population's interests, fill in for its absences, or agitate for social change. Political theorist Tim Kelsall notes that although a variety of prototypical models of civil society existed in Tanzania prior to the nationalist struggle, "the vitality of these civic associations was rapidly co-opted after independence by the state, and it has seldom reasserted itself" (2004, 8). The notion of civil society is perhaps one of the most heated topics in African political theory. For a representative sampling of significant contributions to the discussion, see Bayart 1993, 155–163; Chabal and Daloz 1999, 17–30; Comaroff and Comaroff 1999; Mamdani 1996, 13–16; and Monga 1996. The majority of these authors, save for Monga, challenge the very concept of civil society

in contexts characterized not by "exteriority and antagonism, but plurality and impetus" (Bayart 1993, 163). See Kelsall 2004 and Mercer 1999, 2003, for analyses of how discourses of civil society play out in Tanzanian contexts.

5. See Woods 1999 for an analogous discussion of the ideological overtones of late-nineteenth- and early-twentieth-century American vaudeville.

6. The mutually beneficial relationship between beer halls and theatre troupes begun in the 1980s had cemented over the years. When I began my research in 1996, each of the three troupes owned or rented a bar that served as their rehearsal space and office during the week. Norbert Chenga, for example, owned Snake Garden Bar in Mabibo neighborhood, named in honor of Muungano's prized collection of snakes. The property included a few rooms for housing Muungano's top performers—including the snakes themselves, which were granted the privilege of their own room. Since the bars remained open for business during the rehearsals, an audience was usually present during the process of shaping new plays, practicing new songs, and choreographing new dances.

7. Although the students at the College of Arts often criticize Mandela, they also acknowledge that "*wanajitahidi sana*" (they try very hard). Informal conversations with the performers of the three troupes indicated that Mandela had the most demanding rehearsal and performance schedule, with Muungano a not-too-distant second.

8. My own interest in the troupes could be excused since it was believed that I, like most *wazungu* (foreigners, usually with connotations of being white), was primarily interested in the "traditional arts" that TOT and Muungano performed, especially the *ngoma.*

9. This intersection of class and audience participation was clarified when I saw Muungano perform at the University of Dar es Salaam on 25 October 1996. Although this elite audience, which consisted mainly of male students, clearly enjoyed the show, they remained seated throughout the performance.

10. Although Karin Barber seldom uses the term *hybridity* per se, see Barber 1987 and 1997 for deconstructions of the terms *traditional* and *modern* in the context of the African expressive arts.

11. Another example of hybridization is described in Topp Fargion 1993, which explores the process of "Africanizing" women's *taarab* in Zanzibar. See also Barz 2003, 3–5, for a discussion of the limitations of syncretism (a concept closely related to hybridity) in the context of Tanzanian *kwaya* communities.

12. See Gandhi 1998, 13, for a critique of this celebratory attitude toward hybridization in postcolonial theory.

13. The Chagga have secured this reputation as a result of missionary practices in the nineteenth century. Missionaries were drawn to the Kilimanjaro region, which was populated mostly by Chagga, because of the temperate climate, and they founded numerous schools which gave Chagga children a distinct educational advantage over their fellow Tanganyikan ethnic groups. A similar phenomenon occurred among the Haya in the temperate climate of Bukoba, west of Lake Victoria.

14. Of the performances I saw in 1996 and 1997, Muungano's *ngoma* repertory rotated among seven southern dances, three coastal dances, and two Sukuma ones; Mandela's included seven southern dances, one coastal dance, one Sukuma dance, one Nyakyusa dance, and a dance from Morogoro. The more diverse repertory of TOT included five southern *ngoma;* however, only one of these, *lizombe,* was performed on a regular basis. TOT also alternated among four coastal *ngoma,* a Sukuma dance, as well as dances of the pastoralist Maasai and Kuria people and of the Nyakyusa.

15. I am indebted to Jacqueline Maingard's "Imag(in)ing the South African Nation: Representations of Identity in the Rugby World Cup 1995" (1997) for her thoughtful application of Bhabha's ideas to the staging of ethnic dances as a prelude to the World Cup.

16. "Hali Hii" (These Conditions), performed at T. Garden Bar, Buguruni, 26 July 1997.

17. This incident occurred at Tukutane Bar, Buguruni, 15 September 1997.

18. Title of malaria play unknown. Performed at Saba Saba exhibition grounds, 3 July 1997.

19. The works of Cranford Pratt tend to interpret Nyerere's political theory in a strongly positive, perhaps romanticized, light. See, for example, Pratt 1976.

20. Apparently, the popularity of this form plummeted in the early 1990s, and it disappeared almost entirely from the evening's program (Plane 1995, 54–55; see also Lange 1995, 6–21). By 1996, however, *vichekesho* had staged a comeback, particularly in the performances of Muungano and Mandela.

21. Nyerere instigated a system of the ten-house cell (*shina* or *kijumba*) during his presidency, in which every ten Tanzanian households elected a party representative, or *mjumbe*, who acted as an "ambassador" (*balozi*) between the government and the local neighborhood. This system ensured that the party's presence disseminated throughout all levels of society. The system was in flux during my fieldwork because of multipartyism, for the *wajumbe* were supposed to be affiliated with the state rather than the party, but the policies were unclear since the state and the party were still entangled.

22. "Ameumbuka" ("He Is Deformed"), observed on the following occasions: Kibongwe Bar, Mbagala, 18 July 1997; Police Headquarters, Changombe, 18 July 1997; Vijana Social Hall, 5 July 1997. Mandela's version of this plot could be found in "Tabia" ("Character") performed at T. Garden, Buguruni, 26 July 1997; Vijana Social Hall, 30 August 1997; CCM Hall, Kawe, 13 September 1997.

23. "Sigara" ("Cigarette"), Central Bar, Vingunguti, 27 June 1997; "Kizaizai" ("Chaos"), Tukutane Bar, 16 July 1997.

24. "Je, Huu Ni Ungwana?" ("Is This Civilized?"), Tukutane Bar, Buguruni, 25 June 1997. This *kichekesho* was performed during a cholera epidemic in Dar es Salaam, when people were strictly forbidden to relieve themselves outside of latrines.

25. See Weiss 2002 for a revealing and thoughtful account of how disenfranchised urban male Tanzanians are responding to this exclusion.

26. "Fumanizi Baridi" ("Caught in the Act") observed on the following occasions: Mlandizi, 20 June 1997; Kata ya 15, Temeke, 19 July 1997; Vijana Social Hall, Kinondoni, 20 July 1997; Super Mini, Temeke, 31 July 1997.

27. Plane speculates that *maigizo* developed through a fusion of the improvised *vichekesho* and the written literary plays of the university intellectuals. See Plane 1995 for additional information on the function of written scripts in Muungano's *maigizo*. Although I did not fully investigate this issue during my fieldwork, I noticed that Muungano was unique in that a designated member of the troupe created the scenarios *and* the dialogue for the plays, which were then embellished in performance. For TOT's *maigizo*, the actor Hamza Kassongo ("Mzee Vumbi") created the plots, but the dialogue was supplied by the performers during rehearsals. Mandela's *maigizo* were largely improvised, and all of the performers contributed to the development of the plots. Of the three troupes, Muungano engaged in a relatively authoritarian use of written texts, as opposed to the collaborative nature of Mandela's plays.

28. "Hapendwi Mtu, Inapendwa Pesa" ("He Is Liked Only for His Money"), Vijana Social Hall, Kinondoni, 20 July 1997.

29. Tukutane Bar, Buguruni, 3 September 1997; also observed at Central Bar, Vingunguti, 5 September 1997.

30. Kata ya 15, Temeke, 4 September 1997 (part 1); also observed at Friends Corner Bar, Manzese, 7 September 1997; 14 September 1997 (part 2).

31. Here I am thinking in particular of two plays that used plots of a tyrannical father being challenged by his children and wife in order to offer a critical commentary on multipartyism. Neither of these plays were performed by TOT, Muungano, or Mandela; I am omitting specific information because of the sensitive nature of these critiques. The trope of fatherhood also appeared in plays that were supportive of single-party rule; for example, the now defunct Dar Nyota Theatre created a play called *Vyama Vingi* (Multipartyism) in the early 1990s, in which a peaceful, monogamous household symbolized the single-party state, and multipartyism was represented by a chaotic polygamous household with quarreling wives (Ndomondo 1994, 56).

32. Kata ya 15, Temeke, 19 July 1997. Temeke was filled with graffiti that proclaimed support for NCCR-Mageuzi, which was CCM's main threat on the mainland.

33. See, for example, Askew 2002, 258, for a discussion of TOT's music in which the political form of *kwaya* is placed in opposition to the apolitical form of *taarab.*

34. Vijana Social Hall, Kinondoni, 16 November 1996. The *igizo* was "Shemeji, Shemeji" (a term that refers to sisters-in-law, brothers-in-law, or even a spouse's friends of the opposite sex).

35. This campaign lasted for three days (November 3–5). TOT remained in Muleba district, where the CCM candidate, Wilson Masilingi, was running for parliament. He had won the 1995 election, but the NCCR candidate, Prince Bagenda, had charged that his opponent won through unfair election practices, and a court eventually declared the results invalid. Because of a bureaucratic mishap, Bagenda was not running in the new election.

36. The Swahili phrase was "*Usilitie mdomoni usilolijua / Ukilitia mdomoni utacheua.*"

37. I was temporarily out of the country during the time of this event. The following description is based on newspaper accounts, as well as a videotape and notes made by Robert Ajwang'.

38. These singers alternated among Abdul "Rocks" Misambano, Juma Abdallah, Mhina Panduka, and Gaspar Tumaini. The female dancers alternated among Situmai Rajabu, Margaret Mwiru, Leah Kamaghe, and Mwanaidi Mustafa.

39. Vijana Social Hall, Kinondoni, Dar es Salaam, 30 November 1996.

40. Buganguzi village, Muleba district, Kagera region, 3 November 1997.

41. It is also significant that this chorus of support took place in rural Tanzania, where support for CCM continues unabated. Indeed, it has been argued that the intensive economic and political transition has occurred primarily in urban Tanzania; outside major cities such as Dar, Mwanza, and Arusha, little has changed since the "old days" of the single-party system. See Waters 1997 as a representative example of this body of scholarship.

42. Even the apparent diversity of Tanzania's mediascape is deceptive given that the conglomerate IPP Media, under the leadership of CEO Reginald Mengi, owns several newspaper publications and television stations.

3. National Erotica

1. Vijana Social Hall, Kinondoni, 5 October 1996.

2. See Amadiume 1987 and Mohanty 1991 for further discussion of the imperialist tendencies within Western feminist scholarship.

3. This colonial legacy is perhaps to blame for the oversimplified translation of *ngoma* among the popular theatre companies and at the College of Arts as "tribal dance." This reductive meaning negates the linguistic richness of the term, which encompasses "at once the term for drum, as well as drumming or other musical instrumentation, singing, dancing, and the complexity of constituent behavior and concepts" (Janzen 1992, 290; see also Gunderson 2000, 11; Pels 2000, 102; Topp Fargion 1993, 111). In the performances of Muungano, TOT, and Mandela, the complexity of *ngoma* was regularly reduced to a ten- to fifteen-minute dance categorized as the possession of a single group. Of course, a more basic reason for this oversimplification is simply that the English language has no linguistic equivalent. But I find it interesting that this reductive translation is commensurate with the ways in which these dances were represented in colonial and neocolonial discourse.

4. Lugeye group, Magu, 14 November 1997.

5. What was originally called the Ministry of National Culture and Youth has changed names several times since independence. The most recent change occurred in 2006 when newly elected President Jakaya Kikwete reshuffled his cabinet. The Department of Culture is now located in the Ministry of Information, Culture, and Sports.

6. Like the urban theatre companies in Dar es Salaam, the college also straddles boundaries of official and popular culture, since it serves as a prime source of entertainment for the Bagamoyo community. See Edmondson 1999a, 158–169, and 1999b for more in-depth explorations of the College of Arts as a case study of national culture.

7. These eight *ngoma* include *ukala* of the coastal Zigua, *bugobogobo* of the Sukuma, *mganda wa kikutu* from Morogoro region, *mawindi* of the Nyaturu (Singida region), *lipango* of the Nyakyusa, and three that are of Makonde/Yao origin: *masewe, ngokwa,* and *malivata.*

8. The group from Mbeya performed on 26 September, and the group from Tanga performed on 28 September 1997.

9. The "offending line" is *"mbili mbili kidenyama"* (You have to prepare it). Words and translation provided by Stumai Halili, personal conversation with author, College of Arts, Bagamoyo, 4 April 1997.

10. See the discussion of cultural troupes in chapter 1.

11. Muungano performance at Vijana Social Hall, Kinondoni, 17 August 1997.

12. Friends Corner Hotel, Manzese, 14 September 1997.

13. This performance took place on 20 February 1997.

14. Kigongo Bar, Buguruni, 29 June 1997.

15. As described in Nyoni 2000, 253, this refusal to declare a winner is a common feature in East African competitive performance, perhaps because it would defuse the equilibrium that competitive performance sustains. See chapter 5 for an in-depth discussion of competitive performance.

16. 11 February 1997.

17. I find it telling that I was not solicited to perform in the contest, even though Chenga knew I was in the audience. He also knew that I was taking *ngoma* lessons at the college, and he might have (mistakenly) assumed that I would not fit the stereotype of the awkward *mzungu.*

18. College of Arts, Bagamoyo, 11 April 1997.

19. *Jando* invariably involves male circumcision; however, only certain ethnic groups in Tanzania practice female circumcision, so *unyago* does not necessarily refer to this practice for girls.

20. I saw this version of *masewe* performed for the Workers' Day performance on 1 May 1997 and a few weeks later on 29 May for the final examinations.

21. National Arts Festival, College of Arts, Bagamoyo, 25 September 1996.

22. That year, Moshi traveled to India as part of a cultural exchange program through the support of female administrators in the Ministry of Culture who sought to encourage her efforts in a male-dominated field. Inspired by Indian female dancers performing with snakes and other dangerous animals, she returned to Dar es Salaam resolved to become the first female snake dancer in Tanzania. Although Sukuma/Nyamwezi snake dancing was a relatively common act among the theatre troupes in Dar es Salaam, she knew that the startling novelty of a female snake dancer would give Ujamaa a competitive advantage (Moshi 2001a).

23. At the Saba Saba International Trade Fair in Dar es Salaam in July 2001, Moshi advertised her performance with this phrase.

4. Popular Drama and the Mapping of Home

1. The performance took place at Casanova's Club, Dar es Salaam.

2. Of Tanzania's approximately 130 ethnic groups, the Maasai group is arguably the most internationally famous as indicated in the numerous coffee-table books and Western advertisements depicting male warriors with elaborately braided hair and women adorned with massive beaded neck rings.

3. It should be noted that Williams has plenty of company among African and Africanist scholars. See Monga 1996, 27–29, for a critique of what he calls the "cliché" of the urban-rural dichotomy in the discipline of African political science.

4. See Skurski and Coronil 1993, 233–234, for a more extended critique of Williams. This chapter is indebted to Loren Kruger's analysis of urban and rural dichotomies in South African drama under apartheid (1999, 72–99), which also uses Williams's work as a springboard for her exploration.

5. Mahmood Mamdani (1996) usefully historicizes the rural/urban divide as a colonial legacy of British indirect rule. Although it is not my intent to analyze the state's

investment in this perceived separation between the two spheres, Mamdani's work provides a useful reminder of the political stakes involved in the systematic disenfranchisement of the rural population.

6. Van Dijk's concept of syncretic nostalgia expands upon the ideas of substantive nostalgia as formulated in Strathern 1995 and Battaglia 1995, 93. For more information on the massive population shift that occurred in the rural areas between 1967 (the year of the Arusha Declaration) and 1977 as a result of villagization, see Mascarenhas 1979.

7. *Hatia* (1972), a play by Penina Mlama, explores this potential. The play focuses on a pregnant, unmarried village girl who is told to choose between living in the (modern) city or in a (traditional) rural marriage. She refuses both options and escapes to an *ujamaa* village, where presumably she would not only be accepted but also contribute to the rebuilding of Tanzania.

8. I am thinking of feminist criticisms of Bhabha's work; see, for example, Loomba 1994.

9. See Ivaska 2002 for an alternative perspective on the gendered tropes of post-Arusha national discourse.

10. Vijana Social Hall, Kinondoni, 26 October 1996 (part 1); 2 November 1996 (part 2).

11. The only time a dead male appeared in Muungano's plays was in a play about police corruption: "Ngumu ya Maisha" ("The Difficulties of Life"), Vijana Social Hall, Kinondoni, 11 February 1997.

12. Kigongo Bar, Buguruni, 30 June 1997.

13. "Shoga" ("Girlfriend"), Vijana Social Hall, Kinondoni, 18 October 1996.

14. Kiburugwa Bar, Mbagala, 1 August 1997.

15. Kiburugwa Bar, Mbagala, 1 August 1997.

16. The growing presence of Internet cafes in urban Tanzania has infused this moral panic with fresh energy as public commentators condemn the "degenerating" effects of Internet pornography (Mercer 2006, 16).

17. This play, which was created by third-year drama majors at the College of Arts in Bagamoyo, was performed on 5 March 1997 and 9 May 1997.

18. I saw "Control Yourself" performed on the following dates and locations: Muleba Bar, Mabibo, 12 June 1997; Kigongo Bar, Buguruni, 15 June 1997 and 3 August 1997 (repeated for my benefit so I could tape it); Mlandizi Bar, Mlandizi, 20 June 1997; Vijana Social Hall, Kinondoni, 21 June 1997; CCM Bar, Mwananyamala, 12 July 1997; Kata ya 15, Temeke, 19 July 1997, and at the Mwanza performance described in chapter 5. TOT undoubtedly performed it additional times when I was not in attendance.

19. This tendency is not unique to Tanzanians. In an article about homosexuality in African literature, Chris Dunton (1989) demonstrates that homosexuality is consistently marked as a characteristic of foreigners, or as sign of moral corruption instigated by contact with the West.

20. As countless Western observers of African theatre have noted, African audiences frequently laugh at what would be considered a "serious" moment in Western contexts. While I realize that this tendency is certainly a factor in the audience's response to TOT's play, to simply categorize these bursts of laughter as a manifestation of this cultural difference is, I think, too easy an answer, particularly given the emcee's attempts to coax a more "appropriate" reaction.

21. "Tutafute Muafaka" ("We Must Search for Solutions"), presented by Community Theatre Group at the National Festival on 26 September 1997.

22. The first round occurred in Vijana Social Hall, Kinondoni, October 1997. The second took place in the Morogoro Stadium in Morogoro, 25 October 1997, and the third took place in Kirumba Stadium, Mwanza, 1–2 November 1997. "Such Matters" was performed for the first and second rounds; due to extenuating circumstances (discussed in chapter 5), Muungano substituted another play for the final round.

23. TOT, "Hapendwi Mtu, Inapendwa Pesa" ("He Is Liked Only for His Money"), Vijana Social Hall, Kinondoni, 20 July 1997.

24. Vijana Social Hall, Kinondoni, 23 November 1996.

25. Title of play unknown. Tukutane Bar, Buguruni, 16 June 1997.

26. "Tutapambana" ("We Will Fight Each Other"), Tukutane Bar, Buguruni, 10 September 1997. It should be noted that Makerere's reputation has slipped in recent years, and that the University of Dar es Salaam is now ranked ahead of Makerere. Nevertheless, it is still considered a mark of prestige to have children studying in Uganda.

27. Although former president Benjamin Mkapa hails from Mtwara, the north continues to dominate Tanzanian politics. See Kelsall 2002, 606–607, for a discussion of how the southern regions have attempted to effect political change during the Mkapa era.

28. The barely contained sense of violence that characterized Mbelemba's village also resonates with the destructive path that Nyerere's policy of *ujamaa* ultimately took. Mandela's bitter vision not only thumbed its nose at the nostalgic ideal of traditional African life but also recalled this tumultuous historical moment of state oppression.

29. Title of play unknown. Performed at Vijana Social Hall, Kinondoni, 5 October 1996.

30. T. Garden Bar, Buguruni, 26 July 1997.

31. Central Bar, Vingunguti, 27 June 1997.

32. This comment is based on several informal conversations about the theatre companies that I had with students and faculty at both institutions.

33. "Malezi" ("Upbringing"), CCM Bar, Kawe, 13 September 1997; "Asiyesikia la Mkuu" ("The One Who Doesn't Listen to the Boss"), Tukutane Bar, Buguruni, 3 September 1997.

34. "Tutapambana" ("We Will Fight Each Other"), Tukutane Bar, Buguruni, 10 September 1997.

35. The mooning incident occurred in "Asiyesikia la Mkuu" ("The One Who Doesn't Listen to the Boss"), Tukutane Bar, Buguruni, 3 September 1997. Jangala did not actually drop his pants, but he presented his buttocks to his wayward son and bent over. Even though the spectators were used to Jangala's antics, they were clearly startled.

36. I do not mean to elide TOT's own investment in authoritarianism through placing its interpretation of community alongside Mandela and Muungano; its alliance with the political party complicates, if not refutes, this democratic bent. I believe, however, that "Control Yourself" not only signifies a rupture in the nationalist framework that depends upon urban/rural dichotomies, but also gestures to a transformative moment that exceeds the company's political affiliation.

5. Culture Wars

1. As representative examples of this literature, see Gilman 2000; Kezilahabi 2000; and Nyoni 2000 (all of which are in the *Mashindano* anthology). See also Askew 2002; and Ranger 1975.

2. See Drewal 1991 for a sustained critique of "the dominant notion in scholarly discourse that ritual repetition is rigid, stereotypic, conventional, conservative, invariant, uniform, redundant, predictable, and structurally static" (xiv).

3. Contests were staged in 1994, 1995, 1997, and 1998.

4. In a statement that encapsulates their appropriation of *mashindano* for material gain, Siri Lange quotes a famous television actor, Mzee Small, as saying that "the two troupes were swindlers, as they claimed to be competing but really were just out to perpetuate their business" (2000, 68).

5. See Lange 2000 for a comparison study of the troupes' rivalry as played out in the Swahili press.

6. I am indebted to Kelly Askew's reference to this article (2002, 265).

7. This version of the snake dance can be found throughout marketplaces in Tanzania, as itinerant performers display their handling of snakes in hopes of earning some money through appreciative spectators. In particular, child "snake dancers" are a notorious crowd pleaser. My point is not that Muungano is inventing this particular use of tradition but that it alone of the three troupes uses the snake dance as a trademark. For example, when Muungano regularly advertised alongside other companies in *Uhuru* during the 1980s, it often used a picture of a snake to symbolize the troupe.

8. Friends Corner Hotel, Manzese, 1 December 1996.

9. In a 1994 competition between the two companies, a journalist commented favorably on TOT's performance of *ngoma,* which "was backed beautifully by modern instruments . . . as opposed to Muungano's locally made tools" (*Daily News* 1994). The reporter clearly favored TOT for its sleek, modern look.

10. Kopa, a rising *taarab* star in Zanzibar whom Komba hired in 1993, left TOT for Muungano in 1994. To replace Kopa, Komba hired Nasma Khamis, who, like Kopa, was a member of Zanzibar Culture Club. The feud between Muungano and TOT is believed to have ignited when Chenga "stole" Kopa from TOT. Lange notes that Othman Soud and Kopa were actually dismissed from TOT when they attended a private concert tour without Komba's consent (2000, 76); however, the story described here is the cultural myth that is popularly believed. It also speaks of a time when Muungano and TOT competed on a more equal basis; nowadays, TOT is far more likely to lure performers away from Muungano than vice versa.

11. Rooster (*jogoo*) is also used as a euphemism for male genitalia in a none-too-subtle association of TOT with masculinity.

12. For additional examples of how violence could erupt in *mashindano,* see Cooke and Dokotum 2000; Gearhart 2000; Hill 2000; and Topp Fargion 2000 (all of which are in the *Mashindano* volume).

13. For this first round, I was temporarily out of the country. This description is based on a videotape and detailed notes taken by Robert Ajwang'.

14. Although the choice of this erotic *ngoma* flaunted notions of decorum, Muungano managed to conclude on a relatively low-key note by abruptly curtailing the dance's characteristic sexuality in the final moments. Muungano's rendition of *lizombe* seemed standard until they reached the closing segment, in which two mixed-sex couples simulated intercourse. Typically, the male and female dancers positioned themselves in spoon-fashion so that their hips were aligned; for the contest, however, they kept a distance of about four feet between them. Although the pelvic rotation was still undeniably erotic, the dance was markedly restrained.

15. Vijana Social Hall, Kinondoni, 20 July 1997; Sindbad Bar, Mbagala, 25 July 1997.

16. See Ellison 2000 for more information about this tradition among the Nyakyusa in Mbeya region. The Nyakyusa, like the Chagga and Haya ethnic groups of northern Tanzania, lived in a fairly temperate climate, and therefore the group was targeted by European missionaries, who established several schools in the area. As a result of this greater access to education during the colonial period, the Nyakyusa were once considered one of the more "advanced" ethnic groups.

17. See chapter 1 for a discussion of this process of how the cultural troupes were created.

18. Since green is the color of the CCM flag, Muungano's use of green flags was a direct reversal of what I would have expected. Perhaps this "color switching" was related to TOT's strategies of concealment described in chapter 2.

19. The focal point of the coastal dance *kibati* was the male narrator, Haji Boha, whose long and rambling story of sexual exploits was interspersed with interludes in which the female dancers kneeled on the stage and performed *kukata kiuno.* These interludes consistently drew cheers from the crowd, many of whom crowded onto the stage to tip the dancers. The subdued quality of this dance suited TOT's overall aesthetic of restraint.

20. It should be noted that Muungano also challenged this framework to a lesser extent in the Morogoro competition; for example, the dancers performed a raucous version of *sindimba* in a subtle sign of its resistance to the official constraints of the performance in Dar es Salaam.

21. Lange provides this translation in her discussion of the competition (2000, 77).

22. I am indebted to Charlotte Canning's work on Chautauqua for this notion that the TOT/Muungano contest encouraged the imagining of Tanzania through linking these three disparate communities (1999).

23. Rubya village, Muleba district, Kagera region, 4 November 1997.

24. The extent to which this "full house" translates into a greater number of votes for the party is unclear. Since CCM enjoyed a wide following in Muleba to begin with,

the TOT performances were most likely intended to confirm this support rather than convert CUF voters. In Dar es Salaam, I believe that the especially devoted TOT fans were more likely to be CCM supporters. The majority of the spectators, however, were simply there to enjoy the show—which can be easily done given TOT's muting of its political bent. This belief is based on random observations and comments; I did not attempt formal audience surveys.

6. A Victor Declared

1. Friends Corner Bar; Manzese, June 2, 2001.

2. See Graebner 1997 for a discussion of the political commentary contained in the songs of Remmy Ongala and his band.

3. It should be noted that *soukous* was a form of "Congo Jazz" developed specifically for export throughout Africa and Europe as Congolese musicians became aware of foreigners' preferences for fast-paced dance music. See White 2000 for a thoughtful discussion of the process of commodification of *soukous* music, as well as a nuanced reading of the dominance of lyrics about love.

4. Vijana Social Hall, Kinondoni, 30 May 2001.

5. Their names were not released because they had not yet procured their work permits.

6. This is just one example of the dramatic shift in *taarab* music that TOT had introduced. Instead of a tradition dominated by Muslim women who carried on the legacy of Siti binti Saad from the early twentieth century, the male *taarab* singer Ally Star had become the primary focus. Kopa and Nasma Khamis, the *taarab* stars whose antagonism catapulted the TOT/Muungano rivalry into national fame, had retreated to the background in the wake of Star's popularity. In contrast to these formidable women in glittering evening gowns, who sang passionately but tended to remain stationary, Star, dressed in a modern suit, moved easily around the stage in a manner reminiscent of U.S. pop stars. He leaned forward to caress the faces of female spectators in the audience, causing a stampede of women onto the stage to have their photo taken with him. Star's performance proved especially popular with the teenagers in the audience, several of whom attempted to initiate a "mosh pit" during one of his songs.

7. See, for example, an article in the *International Herald Tribune* (Fitzgerald 2005), and two stories that aired on National Public Radio, "Debt Relief in Tanzania" (2005a) and "Tanzania's Struggle to Become Free of Poverty" (2005b).

8. Tazara station, 18 July 2001.

9. This special performance took place in Central Bar, Vingunguti, 25 July 2004.

10. Unfortunately, Mzee Jangala made his appearance in the *igizo* during nightfall when the stage was poorly lit. As was often the case during these conditions, I failed to take a clear photograph of his performance.

11. In "Hali Hii" ("This Condition"), a play discussed in chapter 4, Jangala also became subdued at his son's death; in that particular play, however, some of his usual antagonistic energy returned when he challenged the audience, wondering who would be in the coffin next.

REFERENCES

Ahluwalia, Pal, and Abebe Zegeye. 2002. "Crisis in the Union and Multi-Party Democracy in Tanzania." In *African Identities: Contemporary Political and Social Challenges,* 88–104. Hants, England: Ashgate.

Akili, Mwangaza. 2001. Interview with author and Robert Ajwang'. Dar es Salaam, 9 July.

Amadiume, Ifi. 1987. *Male Daughters, Female Husbands: Gender and Sex in an African Society.* London: Zed Books.

Amkpa, Awam. 2004. *Theatre and Postcolonial Desires.* London: Routledge.

Anderson, Benedict. 1983. *Imagined Communities: Reflections on the Origin and Spread of Nationalism.* London: Verso.

Askew, Kelly Michelle. 1997. "Performing the Nation: Swahili Musical Performance and the Production of Tanzanian National Culture." Ph.D. diss., Harvard University.

———. 2002. *Performing the Nation: Swahili Music and Cultural Politics in Tanzania.* Chicago: University of Chicago Press.

Bakhtin, Mikhail. 1981. *The Dialogic Imagination: Four Essays by M. M. Bakhtin.* Ed. Michael Holquist. Austin: University of Texas Press.

Balme, Christopher B. 1998. "Staging the Pacific: Framing Authenticity in Performances for Tourists at the Polynesian Cultural Center." *Theatre Journal* 50 (1): 53–70.

Barber, Karin. 1987. "Popular Arts in Africa." *African Studies Review* 30 (3): 1–78.

———. 1997. "Views of the Field: Introduction." In *Readings in African Popular Culture,* ed. Barber, 1–12. Bloomington: Indiana University Press.

———. 2000. *The Generation of Plays: Yoruba Popular Life in the Theatre.* Bloomington: Indiana University Press.

Barber, Karin, Alain Ricard, and John Collins. 1997. *West African Popular Theatre.* Bloomington: Indiana University Press.

Barz, Gregory F. 2003. *Performing Religion: Negotiating Past and Present in Kwaya Music of Tanzania.* Amsterdam: Rodopi.

Battaglia, Debbora. 1995. "On Practical Nostalgia: Self-Prospecting among Urban Trobrianders." In *Rhetorics of Self-Making,* ed. Battaglia, 77–96. Berkeley: University of California Press.

Bayart, Jean-François. 1993. *The State in Africa: The Politics of the Belly.* Trans. Mary Harper, Christopher Harrison, and Elizabeth Harrison. London: Longman.

Berman, Bruce J. 1998. "Ethnicity, Patronage and the African State: The Politics of Uncivil Nationalism." *African Affairs* 97 (388): 305–341.

Bernard, Kise. 2001. Interview with author and Robert Ajwang'. Bagamoyo, 4 July.

Bhabha, Homi K. 1984. "Representation and the Colonial Text." In *The Theory of Reading,* ed. Frank Gloversmith, 93–122. Sussex: Harvester.

———. 1990. "Introduction: Narrating the Nation." In *Nation and Narration,* ed. Bhabha, 1–7. London: New York.

———. 1994. *The Location of Culture.* London: Routledge.

Campbell, John, Joachim Mwami, and Mary Ntukula. 1995. "Urban Social Organization: An Exploration of Kinship, Social Networks, Gender Relations and Household and Community in Dar es Salaam." In *Gender, Family, and Household in Tanzania,* ed. Colin Creighton and C. K. Omari, 221–252. Aldershot, England: Avebury.

Canning, Charlotte. 1999. "The Most American Thing in America: Producing National Identities in Chautauqua." In *Performing America: Cultural Nationalism in American*

Theater, ed. J. Ellen Gainor and Jeffery D. Mason, 91–105. Ann Arbor: University of Michigan Press.

Chabal, Patrick, and Jean-Pascal Daloz. 1999. *Africa Works: Disorder as Political Instrument.* Oxford: James Currey.

Chaligha, Amon, Robert Mattes, Michael Bratton, and Yul Derek Davids. 2002. "Uncritical Citizens or Patient Trustees? Tanzanians' Views of Political and Economic Reform." Afrobarometer Paper no. 18, http://www.afrobarometer.org.

Chatterjee, Partha. 1993. *The Nation and Its Fragments: Colonial and Postcolonial Histories.* Princeton, N.J.: Princeton University Press.

Chenga, Norbert Joseph. 2001. Interview with author and Robert Ajwang'. Dar es Salaam, 10 July.

Chibwana, Mary. 2001. Interview with author and Robert Ajwang'. Dar es Salaam, 3 July.

Cliff, Lionel. 1969. "From Independence to Self-Reliance." In *A History of Tanzania,* ed. I. N. Kimambo and A. J. Temu, 239–257. Evanston: Northwestern University Press.

Cole, Catherine. 2001. *Ghana's Concert Party Theatre.* Bloomington: Indiana University Press.

Comaroff, John L., and Jean Comaroff. 1999. Introduction to *Civil Society and the Political Imagination in Africa,* ed. the Comaroffs, 1–43. Chicago: University of Chicago Press.

Conquergood, Dwight. 1991. "Rethinking Ethnography: Towards a Critical Cultural Politics." *Communication Monographs* 58 (2): 179–194.

———. 1992. "Ethnography, Rhetoric, and Performance." *Quarterly Journal of Speech* 78: 80–123.

Cooke, Peter, and Okaka Opio Dokotum. 2000. "*Ngoma* Competitions in Northern Uganda." In *Mashindano! Competitive Music Performance in East Africa,* ed. Frank Gunderson and Gregory F. Barz, 271–278. Dar es Salaam: Mkuki na Nyota.

Coulson, Andrew. 1982. *Tanzania: A Political Economy.* Oxford: Clarendon.

Daily News. 1994. "Singers Thrill Fans in Dar." 28 March.

Dar Leo. 1997a. "TOT Imeshindwa Sanaa ya Maonyesho." 14 October.

———. 1997b. "Komba Amshuku Kunyoa Upara." 16 October.

———. 1997c. "Komba, Chenga Watambiana." 17 October.

Davidson, Basil. 1992. *The Black Man's Burden: Africa and the Curse of the Nation-State.* New York: Times Books (Random House).

De Boeck, Filip. 1996. "Postcolonialism, Power and Identity: Local and Global Perspectives from Zaire." In *Postcolonial Identities in Africa,* ed. Richard Werbner, 75–106. London: Zed Books.

———. 1998. "Beyond the Grave: History, Memory and Death in Postcolonial Congo/Zaire." *Memory and the Postcolony: African Anthropology and the Critique of Power,* ed. Richard Werbner, 21–57. London: Zed Books.

Denning, Michael. 1990. "The End of Mass Culture." *International Labor and Working-Class History* 37: 4–18.

Desai, Gaurav. 1990. "Theater as Praxis: Discursive Strategies in African Popular Theater." *African Studies Review* 33 (1): 65–92.

Desmond, Jane. 1997. "Invoking 'The Native': Body Politics in Contemporary Hawaiian Tourist Shows." *TDR* 41 (4): 83–109.

Dolan, Jill. 1993. "Geographies of Learning: Theatre Studies, Performance, and the 'Performative.'" *Theatre Journal* 45 (4): 417–441.

Drewal, Margaret. 1991. "The State of Research on Performance in Africa." *African Studies Review* 34 (3): 1–64.

Dunton, Chris. 1989. "'Wheyting Be Dat?' The Treatment of Homosexuality in African Literature." *Research in African Literatures* 20 (3): 422–448.

East African. 1999. "As 'Kingmaker' Dies: Whither Tanzania Politics and Society." 26 October. Lexis Nexis, http://web.lexis-nexis.com.

———. 2005. "How CCM Lost Socialism on the Capitalist Road." April 25. Lexis Nexis, http://web.lexis-nexis.com.

Edmondson, Laura. 1999a. "Popular Theatre in Tanzania: Locating Tradition, Woman, Nation." Ph.D. diss., University of Texas at Austin.

————. 1999b. "'Saving Whiteface' in Tanzania: Intercultural Discomforts." *Theatre Topics* 9 (1): 31–50.

Ellison, James G. 2000. "Competitive Dance and Social Identity: Converging Histories in Southwest Tanzania." In *Mashindano! Competitive Music Performance in East Africa,* ed. Frank Gunderson and Gregory F. Barz, 199–231. Dar es Salaam: Mkuki na Nyota.

Fabian, Johannes. 1990. *Power and Performance: Ethnographic Explorations through Proverbial Wisdom and Theater in Shaba, Zaire.* Madison: University of Wisconsin Press.

————. 1996. *Remembering the Present: Painting and Popular History in Zaire.* Berkeley: University of California Press.

Fair, Laura. 1994. "Pastimes and Politics: A Social History of Zanzibar's *Ng'ambo* Community, 1890–1950." Ph.D. diss., University of Minnesota.

————. 2001. *Pastimes and Politics: Culture, Community, and Identity in Post-Abolition Urban Zanzibar, 1890–1945.* Athens: Ohio University Press.

Fanon, Frantz. 1968. *The Wretched of the Earth.* Trans. Constance Farrington. New York: Grove.

Fitzgerald, Niall. 2005. "A Continent's Success Stories Go Unreported: Quiet Progress in Africa." *International Herald Tribute:* 30 June, p. 6. Lexis-Nexis, http://web.lexisnexis.com.

Gandhi, Leela. 1998. *Postcolonial Theory: A Critical Introduction.* New York: Columbia University Press.

Gearhart, Rebecca. 2000. "*Rama Maulidi:* A Competitive Ritual *Ngoma* in Lamu." In *Mashindano! Competitive Music Performance in East Africa,* ed. Frank Gunderson and Gregory F. Barz, 347–366. Dar es Salaam: Mkuki na Nyota.

Geiger, Susan. 1987. "Women in Nationalist Struggle: TANU Activists in Dar es Salaam." *International Journal of African Historical Studies* 20 (1): 1–26.

————. 1997. *TANU Women: Gender and Culture in the Making of Tanganyikan Nationalism, 1955–1965.* Portsmouth, N.H.: Heinemann.

————. 1998. "Sightings, Sites, and Speech in Women's Construction of a Nationalist Voice in Tanzania." In *Making Worlds: Gender, Metaphor, Materiality,* ed. Susan Hardy Aiken, Ann E. Brigham, Sallie A. Marston, and Penny M. Waterstone, 141–159. Tucson: University of Arizona Press.

Gellner, Ernest. 1983. *Nations and Nationalism.* Oxford: Basil Blackwell.

Gilman, Lisa. 2000. "Putting Colonialism into Perspective: Cultural History and the Case of *Malipenga Ngoma* in Malawi." In *Mashindano! Competitive Music Performance in East Africa,* ed. Frank Gunderson and Gregory F. Barz, 319–346. Dar es Salaam: Mkuki na Nyota.

Glassman, Jonathon. 1995. *Feasts and Riot: Revelry, Rebellion, and Popular Consciousness on the Swahili Coast, 1856–1888.* Portsmouth, N.H.: Heinemann.

Gounaridou, Kiki, ed. 2005. *Staging Nationalism: Essays on Theatre and National Identity.* Jefferson, N.C.: McFarland.

Graebner, Werner. 1997. "Whose Music? The Songs of Remmy Ongala and the Orchestra Super Matimila." In *Readings in African Popular Culture,* ed. Karin Barber, 110–117. Bloomington: Indiana University Press.

Grewal, Inderpal, and Caren Kaplan. 1994. "Introduction: Transnational Feminist Practices and Questions of Modernity." In *Scattered Hegemonies: Postmodernity and Transnational Feminist Practices,* ed. Grewal and Kaplan, 1–36. Minneapolis: University of Minnesota Press.

Guardian. 1996. "Music, Art, and Govt Support." 23 November: p. 5.

————. 1997a. "Life for Rape Idea Not Convincing." 25 July: p. 1.

————. 1997b. "The Unique Wedding of Song, Entertainment and Politics." 6 September: p. 6.

————. 1997c. "Religious Leaders Can Fight Vices." 17 September 1997: p. 1.

————. 1997d. "Paramount Chiefs Differ over Mwalimu's Remarks." 26 September: p. 1.

————. 1997e. "National Dancing Style and Obscenities." 15 November: p. 6.

————. 2005. "Tanzania: Editorial Says Electorate Yearning for Vibrant Opposition." 11 May. Lexis-Nexis, http://web.lexis-nexis.com.

Gunderson, Frank. 2000. *"Kifungua Kinywa,* or Opening the Contest with *Chai."* In *Mashindano! Competitive Music Performance in East Africa,* ed. Gunderson and Gregory F. Barz, 7–17. Dar es Salaam: Mkuki na Nyota.

Hannerz, Ulf. 1987. "The World in Creolization." *Africa* 57 (4): 546–559.

Herzfeld, Michael. 1997. *Cultural Intimacy: Social Poetics in the Nation-State.* New York: Routledge.

Hill, Stephen. 2000. *"Mchezo Umelala* ["The Dance Has Slept"]: Competition, Modernity, and Economics in Umatengo, Tanzania." In *Mashindano! Competitive Music Performance in East Africa,* ed. Frank Gunderson and Gregory F. Barz, 367–378. Dar es Salaam: Mkuki na Nyota.

Hobsbawm, Eric. 1983. "Introduction: Inventing Traditions." In *The Invention of Tradition,* ed. Hobsbawm and Terence Ranger, 1–14. Cambridge: Cambridge University Press.

Hussein, Ebrahim. 1970. *Kinjeketile.* Dar es Salaam: Oxford University Press.

———. 1974. "On the Development of Theatre in East Africa." Ph.D. diss., Humboldt University.

Hyden, Goran. 1980. *Beyond Ujamaa in Tanzania: Underdevelopment and an Uncaptured Peasantry.* Berkeley: University of California Press.

Iliffe, John. 1979. *A Modern History of Tanganyika.* Cambridge: Cambridge University Press.

IPP Media. 2001. "VP Offers to Be Patron of Artistes." 31 July. http://www.ippmedia .com/.

Ivaska, Andrew M. 2002. "'Anti-Mini Militants Meet Modern Misses': Urban Style, Gender and the Politics of 'National Culture' in 1960s Dar es Salaam, Tanzania." *Gender and History* 14 (3): 584–607.

Janzen, John M. 1992. *Ngoma: Discourses of Healing in Central and Southern Africa.* Berkeley: University of California Press.

Jewsiewicki, Bogumil. 1997. "Painting in Zaire: From the Invention of the West to the Representation of Social Self." In *Readings in African Popular Culture,* ed. Karin Barber, 99–110. Bloomington: Indiana University Press.

Jeyifo, Biodun. 1984. *The Yoruba Popular Travelling Theatre of Nigeria.* Lagos: Nigeria Magazine.

———. 1985. *The Truthful Lie: Essays in a Sociology of African Drama.* London: New Beacon Books.

Joseph, May. 1999. *Nomadic Identities: The Performance of Citizenship.* Minneapolis: University of Minnesota Press.

Jumbe, Bahati Shabani. 2001. Interview with author and Robert Ajwang'. Dar es Salaam, 28 June.

Kaiser, Paul J. 1996. "Structural Adjustment and the Fragile Nation: The Demise of Social Unity in Tanzania." *Journal of Modern African Studies* 34 (2): 227–237. JSTOR, http://www.jstor.org/.

Kandiyoti, Deniz. 1994. "Identity and Its Discontents: Women and the Nation." In *Colonial Discourse and Post-Colonial Theory: A Reader,* ed. Patrick Williams and Laura Chrisman, 376–391. New York: Columbia University Press.

Kelsall, Tim. 2002. "Shop Windows and Smoke-Filled Rooms: Governance and the Re-Politicisation of Tanzania." *Journal of Modern African Studies* 40 (4): 597–619. JSTOR, http://www.jstor.org/.

———. 2004. *Contentious Politics, Local Governance and the Self: A Tanzanian Case Study.* Uppsala, Sweden: Nordiska Afrikainstitutet.

Kelsall, Tim, and Max Mmuya. N.d. "Accountability in Tanzania: Historical, Political, Economic and Sociological Dimensions." Unpublished manuscript.

Kezilahabi, E. 2000. *"Ngoma* Competitions in Traditional Bakerebe Society." In *Mashindano! Competitive Music Performance in East Africa,* ed. Frank Gunderson and Gregory F. Barz, 175–198. Dar es Salaam: Mkuki na Nyota.

Komba, John Damian. 2001. Interview with author and Robert Ajwang'. Dar es Salaam, 8 July.

Kopa, Khadija. 2001. Interview with author and Robert Ajwang'. Dar es Salaam, 18 July.

Kruger, Loren. 1992. *The National Stage: Theatre and Cultural Legitimation in England, France, and America.* Chicago: University of Chicago Press.

————. 1999. *The Drama of South Africa: Plays, Pageants and Publics since 1910.* London: Routledge.

Lange, Siri. 1995. *From Nation-Building to Popular Culture: The Modernization of Performance in Tanzania.* Bergen, Norway: Christian Michelsen Institute.

————. 2000. "Muungano and TOT: Rivals on the Urban Cultural Scene." In *Mashindano! Competitive Music Performance in East Africa,* ed. Frank Gunderson and Gregory F. Barz, 67–85. Dar es Salaam: Mkuki na Nyota.

Layoun, Mary. 1994. "The Female Body and 'Transnational' Reproduction; or, Rape by Any Other Name?" In *Scattered Hegemonies: Postmodernity and Transnational Feminist Practices,* ed. Inderpal Grewal and Caren Kaplan, 63–75. Minneapolis: University of Minnesota Press.

Lete Raha. 1997a. "Uzinduzi wa Awamu ya Tatu ya TOT." 5–11 October.

————. 1997b. "TOT na 'Achimenengule': Uzi Huo Huo." 12–18 October: 10.

Lienhardt, Peter. 1968. Introduction to *The Medicine Man: Swifa ya Nguvumali,* by Hasani bin Ismali, 1–83. Ed. and trans. Lienhardt. Oxford: Clarendon.

Lihamba, Amandina. 1985. "Politics and Theatre in Tanzania after the Arusha Declaration, 1967–1984." Ph.D. diss., University of Leeds.

Lofchie, Michael F. 1976. "Agrarian Socialism in the Third World: The Tanzanian Case." *Comparative Politics* 8 (3): 488–489. JSTOR, http://www.jstor.org.

Loomba, Ania. 1994. "Overworlding the Third World." In *Colonial Discourse and Post-Colonial Theory: A Reader,* ed. Patrick Williams and Laura Chrisman, 305–323. New York: Columbia University Press.

————. 1998. *Colonialism/Postcolonialism.* London: Routledge.

MacCannell, Dean. 1992. *Empty Meeting Grounds: The Tourist Papers.* New York: Routledge.

Maingard, Jacqueline. 1997. "Imag(in)ing the South African Nation: Representations of Identity in the Rugby World Cup 1995." *Theatre Journal* 49 (1): 15–28.

Majira. 1997a. "Muungano na TOT Kuoneshana Ustadi Leo." 18 October.

————. 1997b. "Muungano Wajigamba." 18 October.

Maliyamkono, T. L. 1995. *The Race for the Presidency: The First Multiparty Democracy in Tanzania.* Dar es Salaam: Tanzania Publishing House.

Mamdani, Mahmood. 1996. *Citizen and Subject: Contemporary Africa and the Legacy of Late Colonialism.* Princeton, N.J.: Princeton University Press.

Marcus, George E. 1998. *Ethnography through Thick and Thin.* Princeton, N.J.: Princeton University Press.

Martin, David. 2000. "Chama Cha Mapinduzi and Mkapa Win Easily." *Southern African Research and Documentation Center.* 3 November. Lexis-Nexis, http://web.lexis-nexis.com.

Mascarenhas, Adolpho. 1979. "After Villagization—What?" In *Towards Socialism in Tanzania,* ed. Bismarck U. Mwansasu and Cranford Pratt, 145–165. Toronto: University of Toronto Press.

Masiaga, Werema. 2001. Interview with author and Robert Ajwang'. Bagamoyo, 3 July.

Mason, Jeffrey D. 1999. "American Stages (Curtain Raiser)." In *Performing America: Cultural Nationalism in American Theatre,* ed. Mason and J. Ellen Gainor, 1–6. Ann Arbor: University of Michigan Press.

Maybury-Lewis, David. 1989. "Introduction: The Quest for Harmony." In *The Attraction of Opposites: Thought and Society in the Dualistic Mode,* ed. Uri Almagor and Maybury-Lewis, 1–17. Ann Arbor: University of Michigan Press.

Mazrui, Ali. 1967. "Tanzaphilia." *Transition* 31 (6): 20–26.

Mbatta, Basil. 1997. Interview with author and Robert Ajwang'. Bagamoyo, 19 September.

Mbelemba, Bakari Kassim Mohamed. 2001. Interview with author and Robert Ajwang'. Dar es Salaam, 12 July.

Mbembe, Achille. 2001. *On the Postcolony.* London: University of California Press.

Mbughuni, Louis A. 1974. *The Cultural Policy of the United Republic of Tanzania.* Paris: UNESCO Press.

Mbughuni, Louis A., and Gabriel Ruhumbika. 1974. "TANU and National Culture." In *Towards Ujamaa: Twenty Years of TANU Leadership,* ed. Ruhumbika, 275–287. Nairobi: East African Literature Bureau.

McClintock, Anne. 1995. *Imperial Leather: Race, Gender and Sexuality in the Colonial Contest.* New York: Routledge.

McHenry, Dean E., Jr. 1994. *Limited Choices: The Political Struggle for Socialism in Tanzania.* Boulder, Colo.: Lynne Rienner.

Mercer, Claire. 1999. "Reconceptualizing State-Society Relations in Tanzania: Are NGOs Making a Difference?" *Area* 33 (3): 247–258.

———. 2003. "Performing Partnership: Civil Society and the Illusions of Good Governance in Tanzania." *Political Geography* 22: 741–763.

———. 2006. "Telecentres and Transformations: Modernizing Tanzania through the Internet." *African Affairs* 105 (419): 243–264.

Metz, Steven. 1982. "In Lieu of Orthodoxy: The Socialist Theories of Nkrumah and Nyerere." *Journal of Modern African Studies* 20 (3): 377–392. JSTOR, http://www.jstor.org.

Mfanyakazi. 1997. "TOT, Muungano Nani Zaidi Leo?" 8 October.

Miguel, Edward. 2004. "Tribe or Nation? Nation Building and Public Goods in Kenya versus Tanzania." *World Politics* 56 (3): 327–362. JSTOR, http://www.jstor.org.

Mkoloma, Saidi. 2001. Interview with author and Robert Ajwang'. Dar es Salaam, 13 July.

Mlama, Penina Muhando. 1972. *Hatia.* Nairobi: East African Publishing House.

———. 1983. "Tanzanian Traditional Theatre as a Pedagogical Institution: The Kaguru Theatre as a Case Study." Ph.D. diss., University of Dar es Salaam.

———. 1991. *Culture and Development in Africa: The Popular Theatre Approach.* Uppsala, Sweden: Nordiska Afrikaininstitutet.

Mmuya, Max. 1998. *Tanzania: Political Reform in Eclipse: Crises and Cleavage in Political Parties.* Dar es Salaam: Friedrich Ebert Stiftung.

Mmuya, Max, and Chaligha, Amon. 1992. *Towards Multiparty Politics in Tanzania.* Dar es Salaam: Dar es Salaam University Press.

Mohanty, Chandra Talpade. 1991. "Under Western Eyes: Feminist Scholarship and Colonial Discourses." In *Third World Women and the Politics of Feminism,* ed. Mohanty, Ann Russo, and Lourdes Torres, 51–80. Bloomington: Indiana University Press.

Mollel, Tololwa Marti. 1985. "African Theatre and the Colonial Legacy: Review of the East African Scene." *Utafiti* 12 (1): 20–29.

Monga, Célestin. 1996. *The Anthropology of Anger: Civil Society and Democracy in Africa.* Trans. Linda L. Fleck and Monga. Boulder, Colo.: Lynne Rienner.

Moore, Sally Falk. 1996. "Post-socialist Micro-politics: Kilimanjaro 1993." *Africa: Journal of the International African Institute* 66 (4): 587–606. JSTOR, http://www.jstor.org.

Mosare, Johannes. 1969. "Background to the Revolution in Zanzibar." In *A History of Tanzania,* ed. I. N. Kimambo and A. J. Temu, 214–238. Evanston, Ill.: Northwestern University Press.

Moshi, Salma Selemani. 2001a. Interview with author and Robert Ajwang'. Dar es Salaam, 17 June.

———. 2001b. Press clippings compiled by Moshi in author's possession.

Mulligan-Hansel, Kathleen Marie. 1999. "The Political Economy of Contemporary Women's Organizations in Tanzania: Socialism, Liberalization and Gendered Fields of Power." Ph.D. diss., University of Wisconsin–Madison.

Mwakalinga, Mona N. 1994. "How Women Use Dance as a Means of Conscientization: Nsimba Dance as a Case Study." B.A. thesis, University of Dar es Salaam.

Mwananchi. 1995. "Pambano la Muungano na TOT." 13–16 March.

Mzalendo. 1997. "Waatalamu wa Saikolojia Watafiti Kuhusu Wabakaji." 3 August.

Nairn, Tom. 1977. *The Break-up of Britain: Crisis and Neo-nationalism.* London: New Left Books.

Nation. 2001. "Taarab Group Pulls in Crowds." 18 July.

————. 2005. "Kikwete Wins Election by the Biggest Margin Ever." 19 December. Lexis-Nexis, http://web.lexis-nexis.com.

National Public Radio. 2005a. "Debt Relief in Tanzania." *Talk of the Nation:* June 14. Lexis-Nexis, http://web.lexis-nexis.com.

————. 2005b. "Tanzania's Struggle to Become Free of Poverty." *All Things Considered:* July 5. Lexis-Nexis, http://web.lexis-nexis.com.

Ndomondo, Mathayo Bernard. 1994. "The Significance of *Vichekesho* in Contemporary Tanzanian Society, 1985–1994." B.A. thesis, University of Dar es Salaam.

Nipashe. 1997a. "Serengeti Yabeza Mipasho ya TOT na Muungano." 25 July: 9.

————. 1997b. "Komba 'Amrushia Dongo' Chenga." 16 October.

————. 1997c. "Mpambano wa TOT, Muungano Leo." 18 October.

Nyamnjoh, Francis B. 2002. "'A Child Is One Person's Only in the Womb': Domestication, Agency and Subjectivity in the Cameroonian Grassfields." In *Postcolonial Subjectivities in Africa,* ed. Richard Werbner, 111–137. London: Zed Books.

Nyerere, Julius Kambarage. 1967. *Freedom and Unity: A Selection from Writings and Speeches, 1952–1965.* Dar es Salaam: Oxford University Press.

————. 1968a. *Freedom and Socialism: A Selection from Writings and Speeches, 1965–1967.* Dar es Salaam: Oxford University Press.

————. 1968b. *Ujamaa: Essays on Socialism.* Dar es Salaam: Oxford University Press.

Nyoni, Frowin Paul. 1998. "Conformity and Change: Tanzanian Rural Theatre and Socio-Political Changes." Ph.D. diss., University of Leeds.

————. 2000. "The Social Significance of *Mganda-wa-Kinkachi* Dance Contests among the Matengo." In *Mashindano! Competitive Music Performance in East Africa,* ed. Frank Gunderson and Gregory F. Barz, 233–254. Dar es Salaam: Mkuki na Nyota.

Obbo, Christine. 1989. "Sexuality and Economic Domination in Uganda." In *Woman-Nation-State,* ed. Nira Yuval-Davis and Floya Anthias, 79–91. London: Macmillan.

Office of Culture. 1963. Memo, TNA (Tanzania National Archives) F2/5, #34. 8 October.

————. 1964a. Memo, TNA F2/5, #41. 19 March.

————. 1964b. Memo, TNA D1/5, np. 24 March.

————. 1964c. Memo, TNA F2/5, #45. 15 July.

————. 1964d. Memo, TNA D1/5, #20. 20 October.

————. 1964e. Memo, TNA D1/5, #22. 19 December.

————. 1965. Memo, TNA S 6/3, #66. 9 Aug.

————. 1966. Memo, TNA S 6/3, np. 6 May.

————. 1967. Memo, TNA S 6/3, #111, #114, #115. 10 March.

————. 1968. Memo, TNA S 6/3, #174. 11 Nov.

————. 1969a. Letter, TNA S 6/3, #201. 22 February.

————. 1969b. Memo, TNA D1/1, vol. 1, np. 9 June.

————. 1969c. Memo, TNA S 6/3, #217. 5 August.

————. 1970. Memo, TNA S 6/3, #231. 15 May.

————. 1971a. Assorted memos. TNA A/5, #1 to #14.

————. 1971b. Memo, TNA D1/1, vol. 2, np. 2 August.

————. 1972. Minutes of meeting, TNA D1/1, vol. 2, #128. June 19.

————. 1974. Letter, TNA D1/4, #63. 17 June.

————. 1976a. Letter, TNA SL/D1/16, #3. 7 February.

————. 1976b. Letter, TNA SL/D1/16, #14. 10 September.

————. Undated. "Upanuzi wa Kikundi cha Ngoma cha Taifa." TNA D1/1, vol. 2, #41.

Olaniyan, Tejumola. 2004. *Arrest the Music! Fela and His Rebel Art and Politics.* Bloomington: Indiana University Press.

Patton, Cindy. 1992. "From Nation to Family: Containing 'African AIDS.'" In *Nationalisms and Sexualities,* ed. Andrew Parker, Mary Russo, Doris Sommer, and Patricia Yaeger. New York: Routledge.

Pels, Peter. 2000. "*Kizungu* Rhythms: Luguru Christianity as *Ngoma.*" In *Mashindano! Competitive Music Performance in East Africa,* ed. Frank Gunderson and Gregory F. Barz, 101–142. Dar es Salaam: Mkuki na Nyota.

Piot, Charles. 1999. *Remotely Global: Village Modernity in West Africa.* Chicago: University of Chicago Press.

Plane, Mark. 1995. "Orality, Literacy, and Popular Theatre Practice in Tanzania." Ph.D. diss., University of Wisconsin–Madison.

Plastow, Jane. 1996. *African Theatre and Politics: The Evolution of Theatre in Ethiopia, Tanzania and Zimbabwe.* Amsterdam: Rodopi.

Pratt, Cranford. 1976. *The Critical Phase in Tanzania, 1945–1968: Nyerere and the Emergence of a Socialist Strategy.* Cambridge: Cambridge University Press.

Radcliffe-Brown, A. R. 1940. "On Joking Relationships." *Africa* 13 (1): 195–210.

Ranchod-Nilsson, Sita, and Mary Ann Tétreault. 2000. "Gender and Nationalism: Moving beyond Fragmented Conversations." In *Women, States and Nationalism,* ed. Ranchod-Nilsson and Tétreault, 1–17. New York: Routledge.

Ranger, Terence O. 1975. *Dance and Society in Eastern Africa, 1890–1970: The Beni Ngoma.* Berkeley: University of California Press.

Remes, Pieter. 1999. "Global Popular Musics and Changing Awareness of Urban Tanzanian Youth." *Yearbook for Traditional Music* 31: 1–26. JSTOR, http://www .jstor.org.

Roach, Joseph. 1996. *Cities of the Dead: Circum-Atlantic Performance.* New York: Columbia University Press.

Said, Edward. 1993. *Culture and Imperialism.* New York: Alfred A. Knopf.

Semzaba, Edwin. 1980. *Tendehogo.* Dar es Salaam: Tanzania Publishing House.

Sharpe, Jenny. 1994. "The Unspeakable Limits of Rape: Colonial Violence and Counter Insurgency." In *Colonial Discourse and Post-Colonial Theory: A Reader,* ed. Patrick Williams and Laura Chrisman, 221–243. New York: Columbia University Press.

Shivji, Issa G. 1992. "The Politics of Liberalization in Tanzania: The Crisis of Ideological Hegemony." In *Tanzania and the IMF: The Dynamics of Liberalization,* ed. Horace Campbell and Howard Stein, 43–58. Boulder, Colo.: Westview.

Skurski, Julie, and Fernando Coronil. 1993. "Country and City in a Postcolonial Landscape: Double Discourse and the Geo-Politics of Truth in Latin America." In *Views beyond the Border Country: Raymond Williams and Cultural Politics,* ed. Dennis L. Dworkin and Leslie G. Roman, 231–259. New York: Routledge.

Sommer, Doris. 1990. "Irresistible Romance: The Foundational Fictions of Latin America." In *Nation and Narration,* ed. Homi K. Bhabha, 71–98. London: New York.

Songoyi, Elias M. 1983. "Commercialization and Its Impact on Traditional Dances." B.A. thesis, University of Dar es Salaam.

———. 1990. "The Artist and the State in Tanzania." M.A. thesis, University of Dar es Salaam.

Spivak, Gayatri Chakravorty. 1985. "The Rani of Sirmur." In *Europe and Its Others,* vol. 1, ed. Francis Barker, Peter Hulme, Margaret Iversen, and Diana Loxley, 128–151. Colchester: University of Essex Press.

———. 1988. *In Other Worlds: Essays in Cultural Politics.* New York: Routledge.

———. 1990. *The Post-Colonial Critic: Interviews, Strategies, Dialogues,* ed. Sarah Harasym. New York: Routledge.

———. 1992. "Woman in Difference: Mahasweta Devi's 'Doulouti the Bountiful.'" In *Nationalisms and Sexualities,* ed. Andrew Parker, Mary Russo, Doris Sommer, and Patricia Yaeger, 96–117. New York: Routledge.

Spoti. 1997. "Wazo la TOT Lisipigwe Teke." 5 October.

Stambach, Amy. 1999. "Curl Up and Dye: Civil Society and the Fashion-Minded Citizen." In *Civil Society and the Political Imagination in Africa,* ed. John L. and Jean Comaroff, 251–266. Chicago: University of Chicago Press.

Stoller, Paul. 2002. "Afterword: The Personal, the Political and the Moral: Provoking Postcolonial Subjectivities in Africa." In *Postcolonial Subjectivities in Africa,* ed. Richard Werbner, 225–230. London: Zed Books.

Strathern, Marilyn. 1995. "Nostalgia and the New Genetics." In *Rhetorics of Self-Making,* ed. Debbora Battaglia, 97–120. Berkeley: University of California Press.

Stren, Richard E. 1981. "Review: Ujamaa Vijijini and Bureaucracy in Tanzania." *Canadian Journal of African Studies* 15 (3): 591–598. JSTOR, http://www.jstor.org.

Sunday Observer. 1997. "The Rape Scandal," 3 August: p. 6.

Swantz, Marja-Liisa. 1995. *Blood, Milk, and Death: Body Symbols and the Power of Regeneration among the Zaramo of Tanzania.* Westport, Conn.: Bergin and Garvey.

Tanzania Media Women's Association (TAMWA). 1997. "Report: Lobbying Policy Makers for the Establishment of a Commission on Human Rights." Unpublished manuscript in author's possession.

Thomas, Dominic. 2002. *Nation-Building, Propaganda, and Literature in Francophone Africa.* Bloomington: Indiana University Press.

Topp Fargion, Janet. 1993. "The Role of Women in *Taarab* in Zanzibar: An Historical Examination of a Process of 'Africanisation.'" *World of Music* 35 (2): 109–125.

———. 2000. "'Hot Kabisa!' The *Mpasho* Phenomenon and Taarab in Zanzibar." In *Mashindano! Competitive Music Performance in East Africa,* ed. Frank Gunderson and Gregory F. Barz, 39–54. Dar es Salaam: Mkuki na Nyota.

Tripp, Aili Mari. 1996. "East African Urban Women's Movements and Liberalization." In *Courtyards, Markets, City Streets: Urban Women in Africa,* ed. Kathleen Sheldon, 285–308. Boulder, Colo.: Westview.

———. 1997. *Changing the Rules: The Politics of Liberalization and the Urban Informal Economy in Tanzania.* Berkeley: University of California Press.

Turner, Victor. 1975. *Revelation and Divination in Ndembu Ritual.* Ithaca: Cornell University Press.

Uhuru. 1969a. "Ngoma za kila siku hazitujengei nchi." 9 January, p. 3.

———. 1969b. "Ngoma kutwa!" 10 January, p. 4.

———. 1970. Photograph of sarakasi troupe. 10 June, p. 6.

———. 1972a. "Utamaduni wetu ndiyo hadhi yetu." 19 September, p. 8.

———. 1972b. Photograph of sarakasi troupe. 8 December, p. 1.

———. 1978a. "Sarakasi." 7 November, p. 11.

———. 1978b. "Tumepiga hatua kukuza utamaduni wetu." 10 December, 5–6.

———. 1985. Advertisement of competition between JWTZ, DDC Kibisa, Muungano, and JKT. 28 February, p. 7.

———. 1986. "Wasanii wetu hawajahamia Muungano." 25 April, p. 12.

———. 1989. "Wasanii waanzisha kikundi." 8 May, p. 12.

———. 1990. "Wachezaji wa Jukwaani wasiwe wabbaishafji." 19 May, p. 15.

———. 1991a. "Mashindano ya sanaa Dar kujfanyika Septemba." 14 June, p. 16.

———. 1991b. "Khadija 'Kopa" mwimbaji mcheshi." August 28, p. 10.

———. 1991c. Photograph of army troupes performing in competition. 4 September, p. 16.

———. 1992a. "Kitakapoanza maonyesho itakuwa 'kivumbi na jasho'" June 24, p. 10.

———. 1992b. "Tanzania One Theatre: Kikundi kipya tishio katika usanii." 11 July, p. 15.

———. 1994. "JKT Sanaa warejea ulingoni na 'vitu' vipya." 26 January, p. 10.

———. 1995. "Kushamiri kwa 'mipasho' katika muziki wa taarab." October 13, p. 10.

———. 1997. "John Komba Atamba Muungano Haiiwezi TOT." 15 October.

van Dijk, Rijk. 1998. "Pentecostalism, Cultural Memory and the State: Contested Representations of Time in Postcolonial Malawi." In *Memory and the Postcolony: African Anthropology and the Critique of Power,* ed. Richard Werbner, 155–181. London: Zed Books.

Vestin, Martha. 1993. "Report: Bagamoyo College of Arts." Unpublished.

Von Fremd, Sarah Elizabeth. 1995. "Political Power and Urban Popular Theater in Uganda." Ph.D. diss., Northwestern University.

Waters, Tony. 1997. "Beyond Structural Adjustment: State and Market in a Rural Tanzanian Village." *African Studies Review* 40 (2) (September 1997): 59–89.

Weiss, Brad. 2002. "Thug Realism: Inhabiting Fantasy in Urban Tanzania." *Cultural Anthropology* 17 (1): 93–124.

Werbner, Richard. 1996. "Multiple Identities, Plural Arenas." In *Postcolonial Identities in Africa,* ed. Werbner, 1–25. London: Zed Books.

———, ed. 1998. *Memory and the Postcolony: African Anthropology and the Critique of Power.* London: Zed Books.

———. 2002. "Introduction: Beyond Oblivion: Confronting Memory Crisis." In *Post-colonial Subjectivities in Africa,* ed. Werbner, 1–17. London: Zed Books.

White, Bob. 2000. *"Soukouss* or Sell-Out? Congolese Popular Dance Music as Cultural Commodity." In *Commodities and Globalization: Anthropological Perspectives,* ed. Angelique Haugerud, M. Priscilla Stone, and Peter D. Little, 33–58. Lanham: Rowman and Littlefield.

Williams, Raymond. 1973. *The Country and the City.* New York: Oxford.

Wilmer, S. E. 2004. *Writing and Rewriting National Theatre Histories.* Iowa City: University of Iowa Press.

Woods, Leigh. 1999. "American Vaudeville, American Empire." In *Performing America: Cultural Nationalism in American Theater,* ed. Jeffrey D. Mason and J. Ellen Gainor. Ann Arbor: University of Michigan Press.

Yeager, Rodger. 1989. *Tanzania: An African Experiment.* 2nd ed. Boulder, Colo.: Westview.

INDEX

Italicized page numbers indicate illustrations.

Laura Edmondson is an assistant professor of theatre studies
at Dartmouth College.